Making Reputations

Making Reputations

Power, Persuasion and the Individual in Modern British Politics

Edited by

Richard Toye and Julie Gottlieb

I.B.TAURIS
LONDON · NEW YORK

Published in 2005 by I.B.Tauris & Co Ltd
6 Salem Road, London W2 4BU
175 Fifth Avenue, New York NY 10010
www.ibtauris.com

In the United States of America and Canada distributed by
Palgrave Macmillan a division of St. Martin's Press
175 Fifth Avenue, New York NY 10010

International Library of Political Studies 5

ISBN 1 85043 841 2
EAN 978 1 85043 841 0

A full CIP record for this book is available from the British Library
A full CIP record for this book is available from the Library of Congress

Library of Congress catalog card: available

Printed and bound in Great Britain by TJ International Ltd, Padstow,
Cornwall
Camera-ready copy edited and supplied by the authors

WITHDRAWN

Books are to be returned on or before
the last date below.

LIBREX–

Contents

List of Illustrations

Contributors

Paul Corthorn is currently Lecturer in Twentieth Century British Political History in the School of History at the University of Liverpool. He has written several articles on the British Labour party, and his first book – on the wider British Left in the 1930s – will be published by IB Tauris in 2005.

Martin Farr was born in London in 1971, and since 2000 has been a lecturer in modern British history at the School of Historical Studies, the University of Newcastle. He has just written the first biography of Reginald McKenna, and will shortly complete his research into Liberals and war with 'The Personnel of Armageddon'.

Jo Fox is a Lecturer in Modern History at the University of Durham. Author of *Filming Women in the Third Reich* (2000), her current research focuses on a comparative history of film propaganda in Britain and Germany during the Second World War.

Sam Gallagher read history at Trinity Hall, Cambridge from 2000 to 2003. Since then, he has pursued a career in publishing,working first for Varsity Publications and now Bladonmore Media.

Julie Gottlieb is a lecturer in Modern British History at the University of Sheffield. She is the author of *Feminine Fascism: Women in Britain's Fascist Movement, 1923-1945* (I.B. Tauris, 2000), and co-editor with Thomas Linehan of *The Culture of Fascism: Visions of the Far Right in Britain* (I.B. Tauris, 2004), and she is currently researching British women's resistance to fascism at home and abroad.

Helen Jones is a Senior lecturer in History at Goldsmiths College, University of London. She has published in the field of modern British history. Her books include *Health and Society in Twentieth-Century Britain* (1994), *Women in British Public Life, 1914-50* (2000), and *British Civilians in the Front Line, 1939-45* (2005).

Peter Marsh is Honorary Professor of History at the University of Birmingham and author of a number of books referred to in his chapter including, most notably, a biography of Joseph Chamberlain.

Kevin Morgan teaches politics at the University of Manchester. His most recent publications are *Communists in British Society* (Rivers Oram, 2005, with Gidon Cohen and Andrew Flinn), and two related volumes *The Webbs and Soviet Communism* and *Parties, Patrons and Roubles* (both 2005).

Ánneke Ribberink is a university lecturer in contemporary history at the Free University (Vrije Universiteit) Amsterdam. She obtained her doctorate with a thesis on the origins of the second feminist wave in the Netherlands. Her current research concentrates on famous political women at an international level.

Penny Summerfield is Professor of Modern History at University of Manchester. She has published extensively on British women and the Second World War as well as on oral history theory and method. Her recently completed book, *Contesting Home Defence: Men, Women and the Home Guard in Britain in the Second World War*, is to be published soon.

Henk te Velde is professor of Political Culture in the Modern Age at the University of Groningen. His most recent book is *Stijlen van leiderschap. Persoon en politiek van Thorbecke tot Den Uyl* (2002, Styles of leadership. Personality and politics from Thorbecke to Den Uyl, a comparative study of political leadership in the Netherlands).

Richard Toye is a Fellow of Homerton College, Cambridge. He is the author of *The Labour Party and the Planned Economy, 1931-1951* (2003). He is currently researching the political relationship between David Lloyd George and Winston Churchill.

Kristin Zimmerman received her BA in history from Harvard University and her Ph.D. in history from Stanford University. Her doctoral dissertation was entitled 'Speaking to the people: Liberal crisis and extra-parliamentary speech, 1850-1870', and her work concerns the relationship between MPs, public political speech and changes in the press in Victorian Britain.

Introduction

Richard Toye and Julie Gottlieb

Upon the death of Lloyd George in March 1945, Aneurin Bevan paid tribute to him in the House of Commons. Inescapably, he compared him to Churchill, the other outstanding political personality of the age. He reminded his listeners of the period after 1922 when Lloyd George was out of power: 'He (Mr. Bevan) thought as he watched him during that period and also watched the present Prime Minister, who also for some time was out of office, that it must cause some members to feel extremely humble. Here were two of the most eminent and brilliant Parliamentarians of this era denied employment by the State. It showed that even the most superabundant personal qualities were irrelevant if not associated with the great mass machines.'[1] This was an important lesson. The fact that even the most impressive individuals operate within systemic constraints does not, however, absolve historians from studying their impact within such boundaries. Indeed, the examination of the careers of particular politicians forms an important means to explore the nature of those boundaries, and to discover where they lie. This book – with its themes of power, personality and persuasion – does not, therefore, seek to invoke the individual character of politicians as a mono-causal explanation for all that has happened in British politics since the late nineteenth century. Rather, it is based on the belief that, if one is to understand mass machines, it is necessary to engage in a quest for the frequently elusive ghosts within them.

This requires reflection on precisely why personality in politics is important. A highly significant recent book edited by Anthony King has cast doubt on the common assumption that leaders' and candidates' personalities are a major determinant of the outcomes of elections. Of the eleven British general elections in and after 1964, King argues, only three stand out as occasions where the electorate's preferences regarding party leaders may on their own have tipped the balance.[2] Thus *direct* personality effects – 'the influence that a leader or candidate exerts on the voters by virtue of who he or she is, how he or she appears, and how he or she publicly comports him or herself – appear to be limited.'[3] By contrast, he argues, *indirect* personality effects are hugely important: 'Influence of this type is exerted … via the leader's influence on, typically, either his political party or his government or administration.'[4] Furthermore, King argues, 'although a person's underlying personality or character may not be open to manipulation, his or her "presentation of self' – his or her persona – certainly is. The leader or candidate's political style – the way in which he or she operates in the political world – is also to a considerable extent a matter of choice.'[5] It is with indirect personality effects, then, together with the processes by which politicians' public personae are constructed (by historians as well as by contemporaries), which our book is chiefly concerned.

Underpinning our consideration of these issues are two further matters: rhetoric and reputation. That is to say, we are interested in the ways in which politicians – and contemporary commentators and also historians – use language to shape the ways in which they and their opponents are viewed. This approach is now being explored by increasing numbers of historians – an excellent example being Philip Williamson's work on Stanley Baldwin[6] - and the contributions to this volume demonstrate its continuing salience. They explore the interrelationship between power (the state's reserve power of coercion that lies behind all political acts), personality (the real or supposed traits of individuals that affect political outcomes), and persuasion (the role of politicians as would-be public educators and political preachers).

The contributors to the volume address these questions and problems from a variety of directions, and in some cases reach radically different conclusions. Some address the methodological problems involved in – and the validity of – writing political biography. Some explore the impact of hitherto overlooked individuals in key political crises. Others, applying cultural history methodologies to high politics, focus on the ways in which politicians have constructed their own personae (or had them constructed for them) on the platform, in the media, or through the processes of political action. Collectively, the contributors hope to provide an account of the role of personality that explores the questions of not only the individual and historical agency – the success or failure of particular politicians' attempts to shape events – but that of how politicians' public and reputations are constructed and revised.

There are many thematic and methodological overlaps among the contributions to this book. We have chosen to order the chapters chronologically, in order to highlight the continuities and changes in the ways that the politics of personality has been managed by British politicians. In his introductory chapter, 'Constructing Life Stories' Peter Marsh explores some of the key themes of the volume in the light of his own experience as a biographer. In Chapter 2, Kristin Zimmerman explores the process by which Robert Lowe, just two and a half years after he was widely labelled 'the maligner of the working classes' after his blistering attack on the Liberal government's Reform Bill, experienced a revival of reputation such that he became Chancellor of the Exchequer in Gladstone's first administration. Martin Farr, in Chapter 3, uses a high-political approach to examine the impact of a neglected individual, Reginald McKenna, on the political crises of the First World War, exploiting important new sources in order to do so. In Chapter 4, Henk Te Velde uses the Weberian concept of charismatic leadership to examine the late-nineteenth and early-twentieth century British case in comparative European perspective. He observes how 'Even the type of political leadership that seemed to exclusively concentrate on the extraordinary qualities of an individual appeared in reality to have quite strong social aspects.' In Chapter 5, Kevin Morgan looks at the master narrative for communist leaders' lives represented by 1930s memoirs and shows the possible political significance of the fact that the autobiography of Harry Pollitt (the British Communist leader) provided a very different type of account from that produced by French and American leaders. At the opposite end of the political spectrum, in Chapter 6 Julie Gottlieb offers a narrative and a reading of one British fascist life, that of Olive Hawks, a young woman who rose to the position of Chief Women's Organiser in Sir Oswald Mosley's British Union of Fascists and who, after the Second World War, transformed herself into a moderately prolific novelist relatively uninterested in politics. Gottlieb asks how the political biographer can seek to gain access to such a figure, a woman more obscure than most of the figures in this volume due to the marginality of her political affiliation, her sex, and her own mystery and obfuscation. In Chapter 7, Jo Fox reflects on representations of leadership past and present in Second World War feature films. She shows how images of past conflict were intended to boost morale and also Churchill's own authority. In Chapter 8, developing this theme, Helen Jones demonstrates the very careful way in which the personality of Churchill's wife Clementine was presented to the public during these same years. She also points to the importance that visual imagery has for the historian. In Chapter 9, Richard Toye provides a detailed examination of the origins of Roy Harrod's much-maligned *Life of John Maynard Keynes*. Toye offers a qualified defence of Harrod's work, suggesting that Harrod's own reputation as a biographer fell victim to the changed biographical conventions of the latter part of the twentieth century. Penny Summerfield, in Chapter 10, rescues Edith Summerskill, a neglected but significant political figure, from the condescension not only of posterity but also of many of Summerskill's contemporaries. In Chapter 11, Paul Corthorn shows how Michael Foot, as Labour leader in the 1980s, made frequent references to the events of the 1930s, using them as rhetorical weapons against opponents both within and without his own party. This, for the most part, was an unsuccessful strategy, but one which, however, teaches important lessons about the way politicians manipulate the past for their own purposes. In Chapter 12, Anneke Ribberink considers the legacy of Foot's nemesis, Margaret Thatcher. Adopting a gender perspective, she examines the ramifications of Thatcher's observation 'I don't think of myself as the first woman Prime Minister'. Finally, Sam Gallagher looks at the highly significant relationship between New Labour and *The Sun* newspaper. He shows not only how Tony Blair and his advisers overrated the paper's political importance, but also how *The Sun* exploited Blair's image, associating itself with him alone whilst continuing to show disdain for the Labour Party of which he was leader.

Most of the contributors to this volume took part in an international conference, organised by Julie Gottlieb and Richard Toye, that was held at the University of Manchester in June 2002. Therefore the editors would like to take this opportunity to thank all those persons and institutions that made the current volume possible: the University of Manchester for a small conference grant; the School of History and Classics, University of Manchester, for providing facilities and administrative support; all those colleagues who gave papers and who contributed to lively discussions; students and friends who helped with every aspects of the publicity and organisation of the conference; and Dr Lester Crook, our editor at I. B. Tauris, for his advice and his support for this project. While as mere historians few of the contributors have the 'power' that the subjects of their studies enjoyed or exploited, this volume will, it is hoped, provide a showcase for their personalities and persuasive abilities.

1

Constructing Life Stories

Peter Marsh

A.S. Byatt has entitled one of her novels *The Biographer's Tale.*[1] It tells the story of a young graduate student, Phineas Nanson, in the English department of a university college in London who is on the run from post-structuralism. He takes counsel with an old philologist, Ormerod Goode, an Anglo-Saxon and Ancient Norse expert who specialises in place-names.

'I have decided to give it all up,' Nanson begins; 'I've decided I don't want to be a postmodern literary theorist.'

'We should drink to that,' says Ormerod Goode. 'Come into my office.'

Once inside, Nanson unburdens himself. 'I feel,' he says, 'an urgent need for a life full of *things.* Full of facts'—an assertion to warm the hearts of most historians.

'*Verbum caro factum est,*' says Ormerod Goode opaquely; and he draws Nanson on toward biography. 'The art of biography is a despised art,' Goode instructs the neophyte, 'because it is an art of things, of facts, or arranged facts. Consider the fact that no human individual resembles another. We are not clones. From egg to eventual decay, each of us is unique. What can be nobler or more exacting than to explore, to constitute, to open, a whole man, a whole opus, to us? What resources - scientific, intellectual, psychological, historical, linguistic and geographic - does a man - or a woman - not need, who would hope to do justice to such a task?'

Doubling the challenge, Goode suggests that Nanson tackle a biography of a biographer. The double challenge allows Byatt to carry her *Biographer's Tale* into the ever more subjective terrain beloved by novelists. She draws Nanson still farther on to what he calls 'that most evasive and self-indulgent' of literary forms, autobiography.

And so will I. But the tale I will tell is much more restricted than the one Byatt allows Nanson to indulge in. The characters in a novel must go public with their love lives, something that historians, mercifully, are not obliged to do. I want to reflect here on my experience as a biographer of Joseph Chamberlain in order to explore the advantages and pitfalls of the biographical form; and I want to relate these explicitly to some of the themes raised in other chapters in this book. To supplement that experience, I will examine the varying approaches to biography in three more recent studies of the life of another key late-nineteenth century politician, Lord Salisbury.

As is to be expected, the way in which life stories are constructed is affected profoundly by the kind of evidence that is available. Although there is a haphazard element in what survives, and in what particular historians get to see, there is also a political element. Not only do politicians, during their lifetimes, sometimes make efforts to conserve or to destroy materials that may have an impact on their posthumous reputations. After they are dead, their descendants and executors often try to control who sees what. This may require less privileged biographers to approach their subjects in an oblique fashion - though this can be a spur to intellectual creativity. In Byatt's novel, Nanson discovers his biographical subject's own lecture notes on biography: 'First find your facts. Select your facts. Arrange your facts. Consider missing facts. Explain your facts.' The advice is excellent but deceptive in its simplicity. The process of finding one's facts is mediated by constraints of time, budget and availability of information; the 'missing facts' are by definition unknowable; and the selection, arrangement and explanation of the facts that one does find are subject to the preoccupations and even the whims of the biographer. Accordingly life stories and the reputations that in part derive from them are indeed constructed, and not by one actor alone. If biography is the art of 'arranged facts', then it is a subjective process; and this, as much as its being 'full of things', is actually one of its major attractions.

When asked, after the publication of my biography of Joseph Chamberlain[2], whether I would write another, my recurrent reaction has been to say, Never again! Biography is an enslaving form of historical writing. In the other fields of history in which I have worked, ecclesiastical, political, and economic, the historian is free to select both the particular subject and the manner of tackling it that seem most likely to illuminate the question that he or she is asking. But the subject of a biography is to a great extent given from the outset. It is a subject, not a question. The subject dictates what the biographer must regard as important.

In death as in life, Joseph Chamberlain proved to be an especially autocratic subject. There was no chapter of his life that I could skip over as of little importance not just to his personal story but beyond that to the history of Britain and its empire. The social and political background of Joseph Chamberlain, his apprenticeship in business, was of signal importance because he was the first manufacturing industrialist to rise to the front rank in British politics.

Nor could I not escape from the bondage of a biographer by confessing that there were chapters in his life story from which I recoiled. I had no sympathy with his aggressive secularism and almost complete lack of religious sensibilities. That characteristic of him struck me as a profound defect, particularly in an age so taken with religion. I knew that many of his contemporaries would have agreed with me on that score. But I was also repelled by what many of his contemporaries found attractive, his imperialism - and how could anyone do justice to the life of Joseph Chamberlain who found imperialism repulsive? As a Canadian, I lay the blame for the blandness of my country upon its reluctance to rebel against the tutelage of Britain. Domineering British imperialists like Chamberlain had deprived my country of character.

But then the contradictory questions started to intrigue me. I began negatively. Why were the ablest leaders from the established elite in both of the major parties, men born into the aristocracy or schooled at Oxford and Cambridge, Gladstone among the Liberals and Salisbury among the Conservatives—why were they able to outmanoeuvre, in Chamberlain, the ablest leader that the new elite of manufacturing industry contributed to British public life? I knew how through the Home Rule crisis Gladstone contrived to drive Chamberlain as a looming rival out of the Liberal party. I knew too how Salisbury, leader of the Tory right, contrived to bind Chamberlain from the Liberal left into an alliance of forces that held power for the next twenty years while keeping Chamberlain out of the premiership.

Yet there was something sterile about that particular achievement of Gladstone and more generally about Salisbury's accomplishment. Gladstone's crusade for Home Rule deprived the Liberal party of real power for twenty years without accomplishing anything for Ireland. Salisbury's strategy of keeping the evolution of Conservative domestic policy down to a minimum for fear of alienating support on which the party relied was successful throughout his term as leader, but no longer. After his retirement and the rejection by the electorate of Chamberlain's proposals for imperial preference and tariff reform, the Conservative and Unionist party faced a much bleaker future than the Liberals, until it was rescued by the First World War. Like the House of Lords as described by Gilbert and Sullivan, in domestic as distinct from foreign affairs Lord Salisbury did nothing in particular and did it very well.

Approached along this line of thinking, Joe Chamberlain began to look more impressive. He was that rare phenomenon in politics, an original force, and in so many ways: in urban affairs, in party organisation, in rhetoric both on the platform and in parliament, in social policy, management of the empire, and prescription for the British and imperial economy. Original but dangerous: he shattered both of the parties to which he affiliated himself. Both of the causes to which he attached himself in national politics turned out to be failures: Home Rule in the long run, and tariff reform in the short.

Dangerous but formative: Joseph Chamberlain was one of those rare individuals who do not merely reflect but shape the undercurrents of political history. The most serious criticism levelled at biography is that it focuses on flecks of froth on the great sea of history. But Joseph Chamberlain affected the tides: as the young Winston Churchill put it, '"Joe" was the one who made the weather.'³ In British political history nearly all the people of whom that could be said became prime ministers. Joseph Chamberlain is the outstanding exception. He initiated practices and policies that shaped the course of British politics and of both major parties for the next generation or two.

Another dividend in writing the biography of a major figure in political life is methodological. These men and women have secretaries who collect and preserve their correspondence, while their influence and fame also induces recipients of their letters to save them. This is a particularly valuable source for the great age of letter writing between the introduction of the penny post and the invention of the telephone. That was also the great era for elite newspapers; and Chamberlain was one of the three or four Englishmen of that age whose every word in public was taken down and published.

This advantage applies only to major, not to minor figures, and to politics, not to other walks of life where less is committed to paper or published. Julie Gottlieb shows in her essay on Olive Hawks later in this volume how much be done with a figure on the margins of political life as she teases the significance out of the stray pieces of surviving information. There are rare benefits to be had from these biographical byways.

Paradoxically the tyranny of biography, the twists and turns in a person's life that a would-be biographer must follow, is one of its greatest benefits. It sends the biographer along paths that he or she could not foresee. The unfamiliar terrain is often rocky and can lead to a dead end. But more often it is the road to discovery.

I encountered all of those experiences over Joseph Crowe. I came upon him when looking into the episode that prompted Joseph Chamberlain to question the wisdom of free trade. Chamberlain was delegated, as President of the Board of Trade in the early 1880s, to defend the Gladstone government's conduct of negotiations to renew the Anglo-French commercial treaty of 1860 against charges by Conservative fair traders that too much was being conceded to the French. Chamberlain upheld the government successfully. But the debate led him to reflect on the way in which Britain's comparative lack of tariffs weakened its bargaining position in international trade talks. Looking into the volumes of correspondence at the Public Record Office on the renewal of the Anglo-French treaty, I came across Crowe. He was brought into the talks from the British embassy in Paris and was eventually rewarded with the unprecedented title of Commercial Attaché for Europe. Intrigued by the implications that such a title would have nowadays, I pushed on—and reached, to begin with, a dead end.

I learned from the Dictionary of National Biography that though Crowe was eventually knighted for his diplomatic service, he was best known as a writer on Renaissance art. I discovered too from a volume of autobiography he had written that his first love was art. When he found that he was not sufficiently good as a painter to make his living that way, he abandoned art for journalism and then combined the two skills by covering the Crimean War for the *Illustrated London News*, drawing as well as writing about what he saw. His fluency as a linguist in both French and German extended his competency in journalism. Covering the opening wars of Italian unification for *The Times*, he attracted the attention of Lord John Russell, who sent him on a mission of enquiry through disunited Germany and then appointed him to look after Britain's commercial interests in the central market town of Leipzig as consul general.

Crowe used his steady income from this position to fund the explorations into Flemish and Italian Renaissance art that he continued to conduct together with his Italian collaborator, Cavalcaselle. I was intrigued by the use that Crowe made of his diplomatic position in his art historical researches. He asked colleagues in the diplomatic service to make notes on works of art too far away for him to reach by himself. The fame that Crowe acquired from the books that he and Cavalcaselle wrote gave him ready access to the stately homes and palaces of the aristocratic ambassadors of Europe who wanted to know more about the paintings on their walls. I pursued this line of art historical enquiry into the library of the Victoria and Albert Museum, on to the Marcelliana library in Venice, and finally to Hatfield House, the home of Lord Salisbury who had elevated Crowe to a position as commercial attaché for Germany and Austria. It was at Hatfield that my pursuit of Crowe's work on Renaissance art reached its dead end. I came upon a letter to Salisbury from Crowe in which he claimed to have written all the many volumes of art criticism that bore the name of his Italian collaborator, Cavalcaselle, as well as his own; but he went on to confess that all the ideas came from Cavalcaselle. Further exploration of Crowe's career as an art historian was surely now pointless. Fortunately I was not under the biographer's imperative to complete my study of that chapter of Crowe's life as an end in itself.

After all, I had first come upon him in the reports and correspondence on the ultimately unsuccessful attempt in the 1880s to renew the tariff-reducing treaty that Richard Cobden had negotiated with France twenty years earlier. That treaty had become the centrepiece of a whole cluster of commercial treaties through which the states of western and central Europe had lowered the barriers to trade among themselves, creating something approaching a common market. I returned to the diplomatic archives to examine the negotiating process that resulted in the formation of what has been called Europe's first free trade area.

And who should I run into again but Joseph Crowe, reporting this time from Leipzig on how Cobden's treaty with France affected Britain's market in central Germany. With a ready pen, an eye for the significant detail, and access to the German princely elite, Crowe sent the Foreign Office increasingly perceptive reports. They earned him promotion to Düsseldorf and the heartland of German industry after the Franco-Prussian War, and then to Berlin when Bismarck threatened to dismantle the network of tariff-reducing treaties that France and Britain had spread across Europe in the 1860s. As I followed Crowe's reports into the 1890s, I came upon the full story of the creation, weakening and reconstruction of the first European free trade area. This time Crowe led me on a road of discovery.

Though I do not intend to revert to full fledged biography, it continues to form an essential part of my approach to the study of history. It has always done so. My study, for example, of the resilience of Conservatism in face of the widening of the electorate[4] focussed on that most right wing of Conservative leaders, the third Marquess of Salisbury. The advantage of using biography as a tool in a thematic study rather than as the subject of study in itself is the freedom it gives you to ignore what is not pertinent to your thematic purposes. Biography is a terrible taskmaster on its own but can be enormously helpful as a tool.

Three biographical studies of Lord Salisbury that have come out in recent years illustrate several traditional ways of approaching biography, namely as a Life, as a Life and Times, and thematically. As is so often true, there were particular problems here having to do with the archives. Access to the papers of Lord Salisbury controlled by his heirs; and they wanted to place the writing of the biography in appropriately Conservative hands. Once Andrew Roberts was secured for the assignment, other scholars were allowed only restricted access to these papers. Massive, however, though the Salisbury papers are, they do not begin to exhaust even the most important archival material on him: for Salisbury was among the longest serving and most skilful of Foreign Secretaries, and the red-penned commentary through which he controlled the Foreign Office is strewn throughout its papers.

Roberts handled the job well, as the shower of favourable reviews that greeted his book[5] attest. It is reflective of the best in 20th-century political biography: well informed, well argued, and well written, kept to one volume, with some fast-paced narrative, engaging character-sketches, and glimpses into the recesses of that most remote of families and reclusive of prime ministers. But he took only about four years for the task, a long time for a busy journalist but breathtaking speed for most of us plodding historians. In that time he could not begin to exhaust even the family archive, let alone the Foreign Office papers. David Steele, whose biography of Salisbury[6] came out at the same time as Roberts's, found fascinating material in the Salisbury papers that Roberts hurried by.

David Steele's biography is a Life & Times rather than a straightforward Life, and he displays the interest of the historian in policy more than in personality. He is not distracted by the narrative needs of biography to which Roberts pays greater heed. There are dividends as well as drawbacks to the fragmenting impact of narrative on policy analysis. It helps Roberts to bring out, for example, the unusual amount of secrecy and lack of consultation in Salisbury's conduct of foreign policy. And sometimes it is Roberts who provides the most coherent account of an initiative in policy, for example of the achievement of Salisbury along with Bismarck in carving up Africa without precipitating war in Europe.

Steele, on the other hand, is more persuasive than Roberts on the pivotal controversy over Home Rule. Steele argues that, in what was 'perhaps his boldest initiative', Salisbury in 1885 explored the possibility of granting Ireland Home Rule before concluding that, for the moment, it was out of the question. Salisbury later denied doing so after Parnell and Gladstone joined forces in support of an extensive form of Home Rule. Roberts is anxious to support Salisbury's denial. But Steele's examination of Salisbury's dealings with the Home Rule sympathiser whom he made Irish Viceroy, Lord Carnarvon, and with Canon McColl as an intermediary with Gladstone, leaves Salisbury looking not just disreputable, as even Roberts would concede, but deceitful.

The latest biographical study of Lord Salisbury[7] is by Michael Bentley. Bentley's approach is thematic. With chapter headings such as Time, Space, Society, the State, and the Party, it makes no attempt to encompass all of Salisbury's concerns. There are nevertheless biographically interesting insights in this study, for example on the young Salisbury's very limited impact on parliamentary debate until he was forced to take up journalism. One cannot but sense Bentley's disappointment at being denied full access to the Salisbury papers. He is often obliged to base his commentary on stray bits of evidence gleaned from his wide reading and research in other archives. And he so loves his subject. This is a book by a genuine Tory revelling in his encounter with the greatest exemplar of Toryism. Bentley succeeds nonetheless in bringing out the remarkably calm rationality of Salisbury's response to some of the new movements such as socialism from which he recoiled.

Bentley's engagement with Salisbury is delightfully personal and subjective. There is no pretence at the austere objectivity that commonly characterises biographical writing. That pretence is of course an epistemological impossibility. The subject of a biography is a given, but not the way that the biographer perceives and interprets the subject. This has always been obvious with that most self-serving form of life-story writing, the autobiography.

The predominant theme that ties the ensuing chapters of this book together is how life stories of political leaders have been constructed or manipulated, whether by biographers or by the politicians themselves or by the media. This book thus bears a fitting title. It is mainly about *Personality* and *Persuasion*. Indirectly it also suggests that, despite all the attention political leaders have received in their own day and from historians, they have much less *Power* than is commonly supposed.

This point is evident even in Martin Farr's chapter which concentrates on the politics of personality, in this case within the Asquith coalition. The central clash in personality there between Lloyd George and McKenna contributed to but was far from decisive in the coalition's collapse. A related point is made, again obliquely, in the chapters by J. Fox and Anneke Ribberink. They deal with political leaders of undoubted power, leaders who 'made the weather', Churchill and Thatcher. Both Churchill and Thatcher nevertheless paid close attention to the image they conveyed, to how they were perceived, thus testifying that their power over the political winds and tides depended ultimately on their ability to persuade.

These efforts by Churchill and Thatcher may be interpreted as forms of self-representation, autobiography. This is eminently true of Churchill, an inveterate writer of his own Life and Times. Kevin Morgan introduces a more orthodox and yet paradoxically deviant form of autobiography by the leader of the British communist party, Harry Pollitt. Morgan approaches his subject from a comparative international perspective, one of the two chapters in this book to use this always revealing lens. He locates Pollitt's autobiography in the genre of exemplary communist lives, where the leader is supposed to be absorbed into and subsumed under the party, thus losing individuality. Pollitt departed from and even on occasion defied that set of conventions by refusing to reduce individuals to the social or political role that communist orthodoxy would assign to them. The other comparative study in this volume, by Henk te Velde, uses the concept of charismatic leadership to bridge the gap between high and low politics, a gap that biographies tend to exacerbate by concentrating on leaders.

Churchill has been by no means the only political leader to find guidance from the past in his hour of trial. Michael Foot referred so often to past experience in his struggles against Margaret Thatcher and all her works that he appeared to be locked in the past, unable to move beyond the conflicts of yesteryear. Paul Corthorn, however, shows how acutely Foot used his memories of the 1930s and '40s to criticise Thatcher's violation of the consensus built up between the post-war Labour and Conservative governments.

While I will not again subject myself to the unyielding chains of biography, I intend to go on using it as one of the most useful tools at the disposal of the historian. In fact I will be using ever more of it. For my current project is a family history, a study of the Chamberlains from the mid-nineteenth to the mid-twentieth century. This story will weave together the life histories of the three statesmen who made their family one of the ruling dynasties in Britain during that time: old Joe and his two sons, Austen of Locarno fame, and Neville who, like Pontius Pilate, will always be remembered for one terrible misjudgement. But this time my story will not concentrate on dead white males. The best account that Neville gave of his meeting with Hitler at Munich was in his letters to his sisters. Odd, that. What other prime minister unburdened himself most often to his sisters? Every weekend a long hand-written letter to Hilda or Ida. Historians have begun to appreciate the importance of those letters from Neville Chamberlain. But little attention has yet been paid attention to the sisters and other women in the family who in one way or other prompted, responded to, and hence shaped the correspondence of their men folk.

All of the Chamberlains were addicted letter-writers, the women even more than the men. Joseph set the model for his family after the death of his first two wives by writing lively descriptions of his travels for his motherless children in their nursery or at school. Emulating their famous father as soon as they were able, the children wrote to him, to their eventual American stepmother, and most candidly to each other whenever they were separated. And they treasured those letters, sometimes numbering them in sequences, and saving them. There are literally thousands of these letters in the Chamberlain archive in Birmingham, providing me with closer, more sustained, interlocking information and insight into the life of the family than even the most abundant papers of statesmen on their own can provide.

Family history will, I hope, prove less dictatorial than constructing the life story of a political leader. The activities and interests of individual statesmen on whom there is abundant documentation can be fairly readily identified; and they define their subject. Not so the dynamics of a family. Its membership may be obvious, but not the significance of those members to and influence on each other. That I am beginning to discover is a story full of surprises. Another related dividend of family history is the light that it casts on those whom biographers have commonly marginalised, usually women, and especially sisters - wives fare better among biographers, and mistresses best of all - but unmarried sisters? Yet the sisters of Austen and Neville Chamberlain turn out to have had political significance of their own quite aside from their influence on their brothers. Like the Cecils, the Chamberlains conducted themselves in the political arena as a family, without in any way compromising the individuality of their members.

They can also be observed struggling to ensure that the life stories of their men folk were creditably presented to posterity, a frustratingly long process in the case of old Joe, and doomed to infuriating failure with regard to Neville because Winston Churchill wrote the master narrative of his own Life and Times. Nothing better exemplifies the persuasive power of the way in which a life story can be constructed than this achievement of Churchill's. In spite of the best efforts of innumerable scholars, the Churchillian master-narrative still holds sway at the popular level.

2

Gladstonian Liberalism and the rehabilitation of Robert Lowe, 1866-1868

Kristin Zimmerman

If you want venality, if you want ignorance, if you want drunkenness, and the facility for being intimidated; or if, on the other hand, you want impulsive, unreflecting, and violent people, where do you look for them in the constituencies? Do you go to the top or to the bottom?[1]

With these words, in a speech opposing the extension of the vote to the working classes, Robert Lowe shot to public prominence and became for a time the most hated man in Britain. Reports of his speech were rapidly transmitted around the country by newspapers, and radical groups put his words on posters and read them out at rallies to stir up the crowds. For many supporters of parliamentary reform, he soon came to seem the personal embodiment of the forces of 'reaction', expressing both contempt for the character of workers and a deep-seated unwillingness to share power with them. Reform meetings often ended with the audience giving 'three cheers for William Gladstone and three groans for Robert Lowe'. Lowe himself was hissed at in the street and was sent death threats; he also became an object of fascination and sharp criticism in most of the liberal and radical press. The *Manchester Guardian* noted that the public suddenly seemed to be taking an interest in the 'habits of life and forms of speech' of Lowe as if he were a 'leper, a great criminal, or an utter and avowed unbeliever'. Lowe told parliament in April 1866 that 'no man in the world has been subjected to more abuse than I have been during the last month' in which he had become known as 'the maligner of the working classes'.[2] Public hostility was so great that it was a factor in his decision that year not to separate from his wife, whom he wished to leave; he felt that separating from her while he was so 'unpopul[ar] with the lower orders' would further weaken an already vulnerable political position.[3]

However, just two and a half years later, a still unapologetic Robert Lowe became Chancellor of the Exchequer in William Gladstone's first administration. Even more remarkably, his appointment was welcomed by much of the liberal and radical press as a positive sign of Gladstone's commitment to creating a more progressive type of Liberal government. How did this turn-about in Lowe's reputation occur, and what does it tell us about the emergence of Gladstonian liberalism?

These questions have rarely been asked—in part because they are best illuminated through newspaper reports and commentary, sources that remain under-used in examining mid-Victorian politics. This gap is related to our still limited understanding of how national political life was affected by a rapidly expanding sphere of public communication in which politicians, members of the public, and the press participated, and in which newspapers had a central role both as reporters and commentators. How did this sphere influence perceptions of political personality and shape public expectations of politicians and parties? How great was the press's role in this process? Certainly the press was becoming more influential on national politics during the 1850s and 1860s as it experienced a dramatic growth in its size and public authority—a transformation linked to parliament's repeal of the taxes on newspapers, the press's critical coverage of the Crimean war, and expanded newspaper reporting of political meetings, including the new proliferation of speeches given by MPs during the parliamentary recesses.[4]

The effects of greater 'publicity' on mid-Victorian politics are here examined through the career of Robert Lowe in the 1860s, as he was catapulted into the public sphere, and as interpretations of his personality and actions became important to the debate over parliamentary reform and reconstruction of the Liberal party from 1866 to 1868. Public characterizations of Lowe—over which he had only limited influence—took on different political implications at different points in these crisis-laden years, first making him more vulnerable to sharp attacks by the Liberal progressives, then adding to his credibility in criticizing Conservative reformers, and finally allying him with many radical hopes for Gladstonian government. In examining the construction and reassessment of his political reputation in the limelight of mid-Victorian publicity, this chapter draws extensively on sources that have not received much attention: in particular, speeches by Liberal politicians outside parliament in the mid 1860s, and the comments of the liberal and radical press on Gladstone's new government in December 1868.[5]

In the mid-Victorian parliament, Robert Lowe was a politician who constantly eluded conventional political categories. This was true even on a physical level. Lowe was an albino, a condition that his colleagues found exotic and curious, and which was often seen as placing him outside the basic dichotomy of youth and age: his face and body those of a fit man in his fifties, but his hair as 'perfectly white' as if he were 'an old man'.[6] He also had severely impaired vision, which meant that he had great difficulty in reading print and recognising faces. This forced him to declaim his speeches from memory, and largely excluded him from normal clubbable relations with other politicians; the latter were mostly unaware of the extent of his blindness and often perceived his 'avoidance' of eye contact and collegial chitchat as evidence of an unconvivial personality. This view of Lowe was reinforced by his aggressive debating style and acerbic wit, which sometimes crossed into rudeness.

Lowe was also unusual in his previous career experiences. A formidable classicist, he was for many years a highly regarded examinations coach at Oxford before he became a barrister; he then spent most of his legal career and the start of his political career in Australia. After considerable success there, he returned to England in 1850 and soon entered parliament, where he became known for his very atypical mixture of radical and establishment politics. As a backbencher, he rapidly made a name for himself as a radical administrative reformer and trenchant political economist who frequently denounced aristocratic patronage and jobbery. However, he also proved quick to accept minor office in Lord Palmerston's not very radical administrations, and often made speeches attacking radicals on behalf of the government. Even more atypically for a radical, he made parliamentary speeches arguing from Benthamite principles against extending the vote to the working classes. Furthermore, in 1859 he broke with every canon for radical conduct when he became MP for the pocket borough of Calne with the support of its aristocratic patron. (In taking this seat, he was influenced by having nearly died in an election riot, in which bricks were thrown at his head by a crowd shouting 'Kill the pink-eye!', at his previous, and more democratic, constituency of Kidderminster.)[7] But perhaps the most controversial aspect of Lowe's position from the perspective of other politicians was his dual role as an MP frequently in minor Liberal office and as a writer of editorials for *The Times*—many of which excoriated fellow Liberals. Palmerston tolerated Lowe's dual role, in part to placate the editor of *The Times* and in part for its occasional uses for the government. Other Liberals, including some ministers, were less forgiving of the 'MP for *The Times*' known for directing '900 lashes from *The Times*' against those he disliked or disagreed with.[8]

This was Lowe's reputation around Westminster before 1866. Outside parliament, he did not attract much interest in the liberal and radical press. Perhaps the high point of such interest was during a minor scandal in 1864, when he somewhat rashly resigned as an education minister after accusations that he had made improper use of school inspectors' reports to promote controversial educational policies. He was later exonerated, on the grounds that poor eyesight had prevented his adequately supervising activities in his department, but meanwhile he was out of office, with questions raised about his judgement and administrative competence. And even after this not very flattering controversy, he remained a little known figure.

Lowe's position changed in the wake of events following the death of Lord Palmerston in October 1865. Lord Russell became the new Liberal prime minister, with William Gladstone Liberal leader in the Commons, and soon drew up a parliamentary reform bill that would extend the suffrage to parts of the working class. This measure immediately provoked controversy among Liberal MPs, as it was considered very moderate by some but dangerously radical by others. Robert Lowe spoke for the latter in his March 1866 speech in the House of Commons, in which he denounced the bill and questioned the fitness of the working classes to exercise the vote properly. Although the speech received a rapturous reception from many MPs, outside parliament the response was, as we have seen, largely hostile.

In the months immediately after the speech, the press was overwhelmingly negative in its assessments of Lowe's personality and judgement—with the radical press particularly severe. (The *Daily Telegraph* for example pointed to Lowe's 'insolent intellect', 'detestation of "the common herd"', lack of 'self-respect' or 'dignity', bitterness, and sense of 'personal resentment'.)⁹ Lowe was also criticized by Liberal MPs. Those who agreed with his anti-reform sentiments generally did not make speeches outside parliament and often took ambiguous positions in the Commons, in part because Lowe's outspokenness had clearly harmed their cause by angering popular opinion and drawing public attention to the issue. In contrast, Liberal advocates of reform were very public in their criticism of Lowe. This was not unexpected from a veteran radical and parliamentary reformer like John Bright, who told an audience at Birmingham that Lowe's words should be 'printed on cards, and … hung up in every factory and in every workshop, and in every room of every factory and in every club-house', for 'let us raise the spirit of the people against these slanderers of a great and noble nation'. But Liberal ministers also went on the attack in speeches outside parliament during the Easter recess. A.H. Layard declared at a reform rally that 'it was from the very corrupt borough [of Calne] that came the voice which told them that the people of the country were not fit to possess the franchise', while W.E. Forster described Lowe's opinions as a specimen of 'old English Toryism' incompatible with liberal principles. Nor did G.J. Goschen approve of Lowe's call for Liberal MPs to oppose the government bill regardless of electoral pledges to support reform:

[In 1865] Mr. Lowe challenged those who did not believe in Reform to throw down their false colours and do their duty to their country by breaking their pledge to their constituents. Well

> ... now that Parliament has sat seven weeks, and not seven years,
> for any one to come to the House of Commons and say, 'Your
> pledges are insecure and hypocritical, and you should listen to me',
> is a piece of political seduction of the most extraordinary
> character.[10]

Under the pressure of events, though, perceptions of Lowe began to
change. Liberal MPs who disliked the government reform bill (often
called the 'Adullamites') sought to undermine it not so much by explicit
opposition, such as Lowe had offered, as by more evasive tactics. In
particular, they demanded that it be combined with a bill for the
redistribution of seats bound to divide the government's supporters, and
insisted that the bill's rental franchise be replaced by a rating franchise
(seemingly a minor technical distinction, although many MPs believed
the latter less democratic than the former). Dissident Liberals, supported
by Conservative votes, forced the government to concede a
redistribution bill, but when the bill's rental franchise was defeated on 18
June, the government chose to resign. The Conservatives then formed a
government, with Lord Derby as prime minister and Disraeli as party
leader in the Commons. Change of power did not, however, end talk of
reform; late summer and autumn brought intense public activity by
reform associations, large reform rallies, a minor 'riot' in Hyde Park, and
rumours that the Conservatives were drawing up their own reform bill.
Many Liberal MPs reflected on these events in speeches outside
parliament that autumn, seeking to explain what had gone wrong for the
Liberal government and who was responsible.

These speeches showed that Lowe's reputation as a liberal was not as
badly damaged as had seemed the case earlier in the year. Historians have
often assumed that from a liberal and radical perspective, Lowe was
widely considered the worst of the Adullamites throughout the reform
crisis. This was more true of radical reformers than of other Liberals,
particularly as the Liberal leadership came to blame its problems in great
part on the evasiveness of most Adullamites in claiming publicly to
support reform while seeking indirect means of blocking it. Liberal
reformers denounced the Adullamite strategy as insincere, hypocritical
and dishonest—especially since some of these MPs had expressed
support for reform in previous elections. Thus, many moderate Liberals
and former ministers, speaking outside parliament in 1866 and 1867,
pinned the blame for the failure of the 1866 bill primarily on evasive
Liberals.[11] The chief whip told his constituents that 'the bill ... was
defeated, not so much owing to the attacks of its open enemies as to
those of false friends', while Sir Robert Collier attributed the demise of
the government bill to that 'latent hostility which does not meet you in
the open field, but lies in ambush ready to obstruct and defeat this and,
possibly, every other Reform Bill by every indirect device'. Likewise,

W.E. Forster denounced a parliamentary culture that had become 'utterly unsound, insincere, and untrue' on the issue of reform, which meant that 'all those [MPs] who claimed the credit of being Liberals, while they carried out and supported the Conservative policy', were bitter against 'Mr. Gladstone because he had forced them to choose their side'. So pervasive was the culture of 'insincerity', Forster charged, that 'sincerity in the House of Commons, especially upon this question, was generally considered bad manners'.[12]

This political case not only allowed moderate Liberals and party leaders to distance themselves from the Adullamites and blame the latter for the failure of the government's bill, but also offered the public a diagnosis of what had gone wrong in the reform crisis. A moderate liberal emphasis on the importance of political character and sincerity contrasted with the views aired by 'democratic' radicals such as John Bright and the Reform League, calling for more drastic reform of parliamentary institutions. While radicals denounced parliament for having frequently promoted class and sectional interests at the expense of those of working men and the country as a whole, many liberals asked the public to judge MPs according to their consistency and sincerity in promoting progressive reforms. What was needed was not greater popular accountability or more drastic institutional change, but more MPs of zeal and high character. Some Adullamites further added to the credibility of the liberal critique by trying to convince constituents that their undermining of the government bill in 1866 had been intended to secure a yet more radical and sweeping reform act. As the *Scotsman* said of such an MP, 'there is enough of difficulty in excusing a *soi-disant* Liberal for speaking in Parliament as a Tory—but there is more than enough of difficulty in excusing or tolerating the same man reappearing before his constituents as a Radical'.[13]

In this context, Lowe appeared not the worst of Adullamites but one of the best. He had been consistent, open and public about his opposition to reform from the start, despite the obloquy this brought upon him and the damage he (unintentionally) inflicted on the anti-reform cause. Characteristic of this view of Lowe was a speech by Sir Robert Collier, a former Liberal minister, at a reform rally in November 1866. Collier denounced most Adullamites for blocking reform while pretending to support it but defended Robert Lowe. In response a shout of 'Lowe' followed by hissing, he asserted that while he 'entirely disagree[d]' with Lowe's opinions,

At the same time, we are in a free country, in which a man has a right to express his views, and if he sincerely entertains the opinions that he utters, I, for one, will not attack him for uttering them. I respect Mr Lowe more than I do those who in their hearts agree with him, but are afraid to say so.[14]

The liberal critique of the Adullamites as insincere and hypocritical proved unexpectedly useful to the Liberal leadership in attacking the Conservatives, after the Conservative government brought forward a reform bill that, in its extension of household suffrage, was more radical than many Liberals thought wise. This bill of course inspired considerable disarray among Liberals, which meant that in August 1867 it passed into law in an even more radical form as the Second Reform Act. This act posed a serious challenge to the Liberals in the run-up to the next general election, as they sought to win back public support and to challenge the Conservatives' claim to have proven themselves as progressive legislators.

In this situation, many Liberals, led by the party leadership, argued that the Liberals were the only sincere and trustworthy party of progressive government. They pointed out that the Second Reform Act was far more radical than was consistent with the Conservative party's previously stated principles, election pledges or speech about the 1866 reform bill; this disparity, they suggested, showed the Conservatives to be inconsistent, insincere and hypocritical. Furthermore, they claimed that the Conservatives had passed an act opposed to their party's principles simply to gain power and popularity, and without a sincere intention of pursuing liberal reforms in the future. In contrast, the Liberal party would be earnest, sincere, progressive, and honest in its commitment to progress and reform, its governments united in reforming zeal.

This Liberal position was articulated in a number of ways during the long campaign leading up to the general election of 1868. One leading radical voice, John Stuart Mill, declared that Liberal MPs should be consistent, sincere and progressive on policy, and should avoid the 'tactics which made the last House of Commons a spectacle of dissension and want of principle'. The public should reject all candidates who did not meet the test of sincerity and zealousness, whether Conservative or Liberal.[15] Many other Liberals, and particularly the party leadership, put more emphasis on attacking the Conservatives and less on criticism of party colleagues, while identifying the party with calls for greater honesty and consistency from politicians. For example, the former Lord Advocate of Scotland, James Moncreiff, told a public meeting that MPs should advocate consistent political principles and act openly according to them. The great danger of the reform crisis was that it could

lead to the idea that political principles and political opinion[s] are mere words: that it is open to a man to profess one day or one year a thing which he discards the next ... [This] seems to me to be out of sight the most serious matter in connection with the events of the last Parliament—far more important than the

events of the last Parliament—far more important than the
carrying of the Reform bill - though that was a great and important
measure ... but what we depend upon in this great free country ...
is the honour of our public men. When faith in that goes, you may
make your machine as liberal as you please, you have lost the life-
blood that gave it energy.[16]

Similar claims about the importance of political sincerity and consistency
were characteristic of Gladstone's torrent of speeches in 1868,[17] and the
liberal and radical press proved widely responsive to this case. Thus the
radical *Lloyd's Weekly News* decried the 'immorality' and lack of 'public
honour' shown by the Conservative government, claiming that Liberal
victory would bring 'a return to virtuous and prudent ways, and to
political progress, to be shaped by candid and honourable public
servants'. Likewise the arch-Whig *Edinburgh Review* denounced 'the utter
abandonment of political principle' and 'political dishonesty' displayed
by the Conservatives, which had disgusted the country and which
contrasted with the far higher character of the Liberals.[18]

In terms of this Liberal message, Robert Lowe's outspokenness and
relative consistency on reform made him once again not the worst but
the best of the Adullamites. His speech and actions in regard to reform
were more consistent during 1866 and 1867 than those of many other
Adullamites or the Conservatives. As a result, he could accuse the
Conservatives of inconsistency and hypocrisy on reform without
appearing a hypocrite himself. Indeed, Lowe directed much vitriol
against the Conservatives along these lines with considerable
effectiveness. (One such speech was described by an observer as almost
unequalled in parliamentary history for its telling use of 'acute criticism,
caustic severity, and pungent, biting, if not brilliant, wit—for the use,
indeed of every oratorical weapon that can be employed to punish an
antagonist'.)[19] Moreover, Lowe's speeches were listened to with more
respect than had been the case before 1866, as his reform speeches,
though much criticized for their content, had been widely admired for
their oratorical skill and eloquence. Thus, it was the reform crisis that
first made Lowe's reputation as one of parliament's greatest orators—
and when he used these newly-acclaimed powers to attack the
Conservatives, he became useful to the Liberal leadership that had
condemned him in 1866.

Lowe further increased his acceptability to the Liberal leadership by
taking progressive positions on a variety of other social and political
issues in 1867 and 1868, thus reminding everyone of his earlier
credentials as a radical and administrative reformer. In parliament, for
example, he spoke in favour of legislation increasing married women's
property rights and fiercely denounced the Irish church establishment.[20]
Outside parliament, he gave a series of speeches on reform of education

in which he criticized the curricula of public schools and Oxford University as overly traditional, and recommended the development of a national system of education funded in part by local rates.[21] These speeches were generally described as forceful, well informed, eloquent, and progressive by most of the liberal press, although they met a stormier reception within education circles. The speeches certainly facilitated his return in the 1868 general election for one of the only constituencies in the country to contain few working-class voters: that of the University of London, which he won easily. And when Liberal success in the election brought the party into government, Lowe felt confident that he would gain office under Gladstone—particularly as he had severed his controversial connection with *The Times* earlier that year.[22]

Historians have frequently described Lowe's appointment to the exchequer as one that surprised contemporaries and represented a rather eccentric choice by Gladstone. It is generally attributed to Gladstone's respect for Lowe's intelligence and efforts to reform education in the early 1860s, his approval of Lowe's doctrinaire commitment to political economy and retrenchment, and his belief that Lowe would be willing and able to bully other ministers into reducing departmental expenditure. Thus, it is implied, Gladstone decided to overlook Lowe's role in the reform crisis in 1866 and 1867. This explanation of the appointment, made for example by Richard Shannon in his biography of Gladstone and James Winter in his biography of Lowe, undoubtedly has much merit.[23] It is also true that many political insiders had doubts about the appointment—not least as they knew Lowe to be a man who was often disagreeable to his colleagues, difficult to control, and controversial in his speech. However, this account of Lowe's appointment does not make clear that much of the liberal and radical press approved of Lowe's appointment and saw Lowe as central to their hopes for the new Liberal government.

The press did express surprise about Lowe's appointment, but this was not because the arch-opponent of reform had a berth in Gladstone's cabinet. The liberal press had widely anticipated his placement in the cabinet and accepted that his oratorical abilities, intelligence, and zealousness in administrative reform made him a natural choice. (This assessment of Lowe's potential was rather higher than had been prevalent in the years immediately before the reform crisis). The press's surprise was due more to Lowe's lack of known interest or expertise in finance, in contrast to his established reputation as an administrative reformer and expert on education; as a result, many had expected him to be placed in education or the war department (the latter perceived as in urgent need of administrative improvement).[24]

Although Lowe's appointment to the exchequer was unexpected, it was praised by much of the liberal and radical press, with some journals very enthusiastic. Thus the *Scotsman* claimed that Lowe's appointment 'is a surprise to everybody; and it is a great compliment to Mr Lowe that, though nobody expected it, almost everybody at once assents and approves'. The *Dublin Evening Express* asserted that it would be difficult to find a chancellor who would be 'a harder worker, a more vigorous administrator, a more steadfast and implacable foe to jobbery and extravagance, a public servant more resolved that the nation shall not throw its treasure away on privileged incompetence'. The *Manchester Guardian* suggested that 'though his previous successes have not been gained in the field of finance, if business habits, sound economical views, and unflinching firmness are qualifications for a Chancellor of the Exchequer, it would be difficult to think of a better man'. The *Leeds Mercury* agreed that Lowe was a good choice, as he was a man who 'will hear of no reasons founded on old custom or departmental convenience for an unnecessary expenditure of public money', and would press department chiefs for economies despite their wrath: indeed in his 'ears the wrathful whistling of the tempest will only discourse rather agreeable music'. And the *Daily Telegraph* welcomed Lowe's appointment because of the zeal he would bring to retrenchment: 'He is not a man likely to be at any loss for means to secure his ends ... he will not tamely walk along old paths which have been failures, while original genius can strike out a new path'.[25]

Not only did much of the liberal and radical press think that Lowe would make a good chancellor, but some journals also saw his appointment as a sign that Gladstone was committed to a more earnest, active and reforming brand of executive politics than Disraeli or Palmerston had provided. Some of the more radical journals warned Gladstone that the public wanted a government that would be more efficient and legislatively active than recent Liberal governments had been. The new government should be less aristocratic, less Whig, and less moderate in aims, and staffed by men chosen for eloquence, talent and intelligence rather than for aristocratic connections or past possession of high office. The government should be more vigorous in retrenchment and avoiding jobbery, while also being more responsive to the ideals and needs of ordinary people and to issues of morality. Thus the *Examiner* called on the new administration to be more radical than Palmerston's administration, which had been too 'moderate and insusceptible of impulse from without'. Likewise, the *Spectator* argued:

> The country may trust the incoming Administration,—may at least implicitly trust its chief,—for a Liberalism that will not be disfigured by the slightest taint of that jaunty indifference which Mr Disraeli has anxiously copied from Lord Palmerston; for a

Liberalism that has its roots deep in sympathy for the whole people, British and Irish ... for a Liberalism that will be grave, conscientious, and compassionate; for a Liberalism broad from equal esteem for the many sides of the popular character,— broad not through indifference to moral and religious distinctions, but through respect for them.

The *Daily Telegraph* put it somewhat differently: 'The name and the insignia of Liberalism must be taken up again from the limbo into which they had been thrown by Lord Palmerston's "jauntiness" and Mr Disraeli's "truly Liberal policy"...[for] the gay old Premier laughed the meaning of "Liberal" away; and Mr Disraeli stole such words'. The *Telegraph* continued, 'All this must be sternly set right again. "Liberal" must mean "Liberal", and the great army which bears the honourable name must be drilled to march and counter-march in a fresh and serious sincerity' — a 'sincerity' to be marked by measures such as abolition of the Irish Church, 'Education, Economy, Sanitary and Social Reforms', and revision of taxation.[26] Thus radical newspapers linked Liberal language about the importance of zeal, sincerity and consistency to a more radical policy agenda than previous Conservative and Liberal governments had delivered.

Many newspapers found evidence for Gladstone's commitment to this type of reforming government in a 'triumvirate' at the heart of the administration composed of Gladstone, Lowe, and the outspoken radical John Bright.[27] These three were seen as sharing many important qualities. They were frequently identified as the party's three greatest orators (although some journals pointed out that Lowe's oratorical reputation was very recent in origin). All three were described as commoners and self-made men who were earnest, assertive, intelligent, and willing to make personal sacrifices in order to say or do what they thought right. (Again this quality of disinterestedness was closely linked to Lowe's actions on reform.) All three were perceived to be firmly committed to political economy and retrenchment, highly critical of the Irish church, and progressive on most legislative issues, although this was seen as less true of Lowe than the others. None of the three were considered Whigs, and Bright and Lowe were seen as hostile to aristocratic privilege and jobbery (despite Lowe's recent possession of a seat in an aristocratic pocket borough).

In other ways, Lowe and Bright represented the two poles of progressive liberalism. John Bright represented radical tendencies in the party and was believed to possess a keen attunement to moral and popular sympathies that could help to provide a moral compass for the cabinet. However, there was a fear that he might not prove a very effective administrator or developer of policy—a view confirmed by his insistence on the relatively minor office of the secretary of the board of trade.[28] In contrast, Lowe was described as deficient in moral and popular sympathies, but was expected to be a highly effective administrator, with a ready grasp of the details of policy making and a willingness to apply boundless energies to retrenchment and efficiency in all departments. Given his high office, it was thought likely that his restlessness and strenuousness would help to make Gladstone's government more effective and active. As the *Daily News* said, 'Mr 'Lowe's incessant energy must make him a force in any Government of which he is a member', and *The Times* asserted that the placement of Lowe, with his 'energy of character', in such a leading post would increase the government's commitment to retrenchment and administrative reform. The *Dublin Evening Express* particularly praised Lowe's 'ferocity', which it saw as his most pronounced quality and one highly useful in invigorating the government.[29]

The liberal and radical press's approval of Lowe and Bright was in many cases not extended to all the cabinet appointments. There was broad approval of the fact that Gladstone's cabinet was on average a little younger than Disraeli's,[30] especially as many of Gladstone's younger appointments were radicals or moderate Liberals who were thought to be more efficient, zealous, progressive, and earnest than the norm in Liberal administrations; they also were more likely to lack aristocratic connections. However, several journals criticized Gladstone for placing most of these men in junior posts. And Gladstone's appointment of older Whigs and aristocrats to senior posts evoked regret or hostility in much of the press, with many journals claiming that these ministers had little to offer except influence in the House of Lords, that they were too reminiscent of the Palmerstonian era, and that they were likely to slow the pace of progressive government. The composition of the government thus failed to satisfy many journals.[31]

Such press expectations for the cabinet do not seem, with hindsight, very prescient. The older ministers, with their tolerance and experience, helped to hold the cabinet together as it embarked on a round of major legislative changes.[32] Bright proved not only a poor administrator but often had serious difficulties in predicting—and appealing to—popular and radical opinion. Lowe frequently appeared rude and arrogant, and his relentless commitment to retrenchment came to seem excessive and distasteful to the public (although Gladstone continually criticized him for not pursuing retrenchment yet more strenuously).[33] Lowe also came to seem incompetent after errors in the 1871 budget, disastrous publicity surrounding his match tax, and minor financial irregularities revealed in his department in 1873; after the last, Lowe was shifted to the home office. Furthermore, several of the young radicals turned out to be poor administrators, narrow in priorities, or needlessly rude to the public and parliament; A.S. Ayrton, one of the radical hopefuls of 1868,[34] exhibited all three faults and offended just about everyone. (One of W.S. Gilbert's first productions, a burlesque in which Gladstone, Lowe and Ayrton lectured to the fairies in fairyland about efficiency and economy, had sold-out audiences ecstatic with laughter in 1873—a bad sign for the administration.)[35] A tendency to be zealous, aggressive, and progressive was thus not a particularly good predictor of ministerial success in Gladstone's first government. And many policies which much of the press advocated in 1868 and which the government pursued in its term—such as greater legislative activity, sharp budgetary retrenchment, institutional reforms for Ireland, and broad-ranging educational reforms—by 1874 no longer attracted the same enthusiasm or praise.

The story of Lowe's rehabilitation and his relationship to Gladstonian liberalism is interesting on several levels. Firstly, it shows how rapidly a political personality and reputation could be reassessed and reconstructed in the public sphere. It is ironic that Lowe, 'MP for *The Times*' in the fifties and early sixties and known for his *ad hominem* style of debate, so spectacularly fell foul of the press and public in March 1866. The less familiar sequel to this episode, traced here, also has its ironies. The very qualities that initially seemed to damage Lowe's political position—his outspokenness, his lack of moderation in making his case against reform, and his apparent courting of unpopularity—helped to mark him out as an embodiment of political zeal, enthusiasm and sincerity. The popularisation of this view of Lowe's personality and its growing resonance with the Liberal leadership's rhetoric and public identity helped to boost a career that had seemed doomed in early 1866, and saw him rise to the exchequer after an election which ended the political careers of most Adullamites.

Changing attitudes towards Lowe among the press and the Liberal leadership are also revealing of the process by which new expectations for Liberal government, associated with Gladstone, emerged from the reform crisis and the 1868 election campaign. As we have seen, these were closely associated with greater retrenchment and administrative reform, legislative activity, and responsiveness to 'popular sympathies', and were perceived by parts of the press as a distinct break from the approach of earlier Liberal governments, and in particular Palmerston's. What was needed, such journals argued, was less Whig and aristocratic influence on governments and more bold legislation on complex and controversial issues. This suggests a more negative view of the Palmerstonian era than has been offered by several recent works on liberalism,[36] and perhaps adds to our understanding of Gladstone's later career. Some historians have criticized Gladstone for showing too little respect for moderate Whig values, forming too close an alliance with a demotic politics of enthusiasm, and pushing through too many controversial legislative changes without sufficient party agreement. But one of his goals in his first administration was surely to not be Palmerstonian, and in 1868 much of the press gave him reason to think that the public endorsed that goal. Indeed the press warned him against taking too much advice from the party elite in Westminster: 'It is for the newspapers and the public in whose name they speak, to inform the new Premier of what the country expects'.[37] Lowe's 1866 speech, if it had failed to persuade in terms of its immediate object, had established the future chancellor as a powerful public personality, a fact that made him valuable to Gladstone in meeting such expectations in 1868.

3

'Squiff', 'Lliar George', and 'The McKennae'

The unpersuasive politics of personality in the Asquith coalition, 1915-16

Martin Farr

'These personal things are more exhausting and life-taking than a multitude of political and strategic problems.'

H. H. Asquith to Pamela McKenna.[1]

'The two who came out really worst were Ll.G ... & McKenna ... it will take me a long time to forget and forgive their attitude.'

H. H. Asquith to Venetia Stanley.[2]

'You and I make a pretty strong team both pulling together: but pulling different ways we have several times risked overturning the cart altogether.'

Reginald McKenna to David Lloyd George.[3]

The Asquith coalition of May 1915 to December 1916 was formed by the Prime Minister, H.H. Asquith, on grounds of political expediency when the Liberal government that had taken Britain in to the war in August 1914 was unable to sustain the confidence of the country. Going to war was a significant moral as well as political issue for Liberals; the methods necessary to prosecute the war were even more problematic, and in the eighteen months of the Asquith coalition were found to be irresolvable. This impasse might have been negotiable were the differences only political, but they were to an exaggerated extent also personal. David Lloyd George, as Minister of Munitions, then Secretary of State for War, had a strong personality, as did Reginald McKenna, the Chancellor of the Exchequer, and neither personally could bear the other. Outside the Cabinet, Margot Asquith was actively hostile towards anybody who threatened her husband; while Pamela McKenna, who was the confidante of the Prime Minister, was a more effective politician than her own husband, while Frances Stevenson chronicled Lloyd George's thoughts with equally partisan diligence. To the sound of doors slamming ran statesmen, soldiers, diplomats, civil servants, journalists, wives, mistresses and children in that season's premier Whitehall tragicomedy.

It can be argued that the Asquith coalition first failed properly to function, and subsequently broke down, as a result of personality, and, specifically those of Asquith, Lloyd George, and McKenna. Relations between those three successive Chancellors radiated and affected every area of the war effort, were reflected in the course of the ministry, and were exaggerated by the methods adopted by each in seeking to influence the conduct of the war. Most obviously these were: the debate over the prosecution of the war, centring on conscription, which climaxed in the first December crisis, of 1915; the suzerainty sought by Lloyd George over – and then from – the War Office; and the increasingly strident role of journalists. Those events culminated in the second December crisis, of 1916, which resulted in Lloyd George becoming Prime Minister, and Asquith and McKenna leaving office. Until then governance lay in the hands of a fraught triumvirate; as Churchill observed from France, 'LG and McK and the old block are far away and look like the mandarins of some remote province of China.'[4]

As with all good stories, that of the Asquith coalition has been told many times.[5] It has, however, never been told with the benefit provided by the papers of his closest auxiliary. That Reginald McKenna has been so neglected by historians is testament both to his personality – unprepossessing when compared to those of his opponents – and to the importance of archival material in the understanding of high politics. It is through the complete papers that one can see the role played – generally but most particularly during the 1915-16 coalition – by McKenna's wife, Pamela. 'Mrs McKenna, before her marriage, was [Asquith's] old love', Lloyd George told his entourage. 'Then he became enamoured of Venetia Stanley, who has recently married Montagu, much to Mr A's annoyance. Now he has returned to Pamela McKenna.'[6] The Asquith letters to Venetia Stanley offered a new perspective to the formation of the government when they appeared in 1982,[7] and the correspondence between the Prime Minister and the wife of the Chancellor of the Exchequer reveals more fully the nature of the clash of personalities that broke it.

Though it was a coalition, it was really the Liberal Government of 1910 with knobs on. The tensions were exacerbated by the disagreeable presence of Tories, but lay in essence in the nature of a Liberal administration. Any government would have found dealing with the related issues of economics, strategy, politics, and diplomacy – to say nothing of philosophy or morality – a perplexing task, but a radical government had a peculiar challenge. Whatever the doctrinal and electoral concerns, around the cabinet table sat men who had worked together for, in some cases, ten years; worse, there also sat men who had not been able to work together for as long. H. H. Asquith was a Prime Minister so clearly first among equals that it was very hard for anyone – least of all himself – to imagine another. As Chancellor from 1908, Lloyd George had served as the motor for the ministry: unparalleled oratorical genius, organizational élan, and a singular and highly charismatic public persona; reason enough, therefore, for him to have been handed the nascent, belated, and central, Ministry of Munitions. Taking over at the Treasury was the antithesis of charisma, Reginald McKenna. What he lacked in flair, however, he made up for in intellectual rigour, stubbornness, and courage. With Asquith in charge, Lloyd George charged with procuring the materials to fight the war, and McKenna paying for them, the divergence of interests between Asquith's principal lieutenants almost inevitably led to strategic disagreements of escalating seriousness. What made matters irrecoverable, however, was the fact that Lloyd George and McKenna loathed each other. This mattered more than it might since Lloyd George believed 'we were now living under a McKenna regime'.[8]

The feud between the two reached a malevolence exceptional even for the ill-tempered and antagonistic coven of which it was the centre, and is still not fully realized.[9] Years later Margot Asquith admitted McKenna's 'hostility was foolish and overdone',[10] while Walter Runciman's father berated his son: 'You tied yourself up too much with McKenna's prejudice against Lloyd George'.[11] The Chancellor's antipathy was, however, far from incongruent. 'McKenna is the only person whom D. really detests', Frances Stevenson wrote.[12] 'D. literally hates him & I do not think he will rest till he has utterly broken him'.[13] For his part, McKenna said he was 'an acknowledged authority' on 'ruining Lloyd George',[14] though events ultimately proved the opposite. George Riddell likened McKenna to Robespierre;[15] Viscount Esher thought Lloyd George a Girondin.[16] Temperamental opposites, McKenna and Lloyd George's personal rivalry and mutual antagonism became almost obsessional, and destroyed both a Government and a party of government in the Thermidor of December 1916.

The friction had real political provenance, but was perhaps in origin superficial. It was enriched with jealousy, and was shaped by, and illustrative of, each man. Margot rued 'What is charming and *amusing* like Lloyd George, not what is ... ugly and loyal like McKenna is preferred'.[17] It was certainly a distinction of which Lloyd George was aware, and, testifying to its accuracy, drew upon: the mind that saw everything in pictures was compared to one seeing everything in figures;[18] intuition against empiricism; the demonstrable against the measurable. The dichotomy was ageless: Lloyd George's Pitt to McKenna's Grenville,

Canning to his Liverpoool, Disraeli to his Gladstone, Churchill to his Attlee, Bevan to his Gaitskell. As in other incarnations, each man drew upon the weakness of the other. While he appreciated Lloyd George's value as a demagogue,[19] McKenna spoke of his 'defective education ... details were beyond Lloyd George's comprehension'.[20] For Lloyd George there was no greater calumny than that a colleague was held to lack an impulsive streak. He would even venture into the quantitative to prove it: 'Simon has a quixotic strain, say 20%. But it is there. McKenna has no 20%!'[21]

The two had circumstances in common. Both were born in 1863 of the Celtic Fringe; they died only eighteen months apart. Both were elected for Welsh constituencies in the 1890s. The two were associates in opposition, radicals of note, Lloyd George defending the Boers, McKenna attacking Protection. Both became ministers in December 1905. Both left the cabinet during the life of a government; neither to return. Neither ever really left the margins of Westminster life even when notionally at the centre; neither was regarded as a 'Commons man'. Both retained something of the outsider: McKenna's Irish roots and foreign education, Lloyd George's Welsh language and foreshortened education. Neither evoked indifference, sitting together as they did in the Commons, J.A. Spender's 'able and brilliant freelances under the gangway'.[22]

The central contradistinction was that while Lloyd George was not of politicians, he was decidedly of politics: an MP for fifty-five years, McKenna endured for half that before ennui anticipated his constituents. McKenna's disillusionment was felt before the war, and would have survived the war intact even if he had not been forced from office. He regarded politics as a mission increasingly requiring dishonesty, to which 'Lliar' George's success testified: 'I don't want to fight anyone – Lloyd George or anybody else – but I am all for backing whoever I believe has truth on his side.'[23] Lloyd George's acknowledged factual inexactitudes were excused by peers and historians as necessary flaws inevitable where there can never be perfection, and rarely inspiration.

A related difference was Lloyd George's pointed sociability, and ensuing retinue. Lloyd George pioneered personality politics through a concern with appearance that heightened popular recognition. It was a pointed metaphor that while Lloyd George dyed his hair, McKenna had none to dye. Similarly, Lloyd George's means of support rested more with individuals outside the Cabinet, and to an extent, outside parliament: the electorate, among others. Nor was Lloyd George averse to undermining friendly colleagues as required, as Churchill could attest.[24] McKenna recognized Lloyd George's contradictions did not 'injure him in the minds of his admirers so long as he says today with picturesque force what they are now thinking'.[25] His admirers were seen most vividly in the 'Garden Suburb' where he let a hundred followers blossom; McKenna was content with brother Ernest and Spender at the Reform Club. Ernest and Pamela provided him with all the support he required, another contrast with Lloyd George, who was so approving of the value of the family he had more than one.

Both McKenna and Lloyd George discerned that the methods of the other reflected wider concerns; their view of the war reflected the man: the one preoccupied with probity, the other with victory. McKenna suspected Lloyd George's application of rhetoric and the cult of personality constituted ends as much as means, and since he could not be certain as to Lloyd George's intentions, he thought caution in the prosecution of the war the surest path to revelation; Lloyd George saw in this approach at best indecision and at worst defeatism. The manner of politics was incompatible even if the ends were not necessarily at odds. The state of personal affairs was such that neither was free from ulterior purpose when the political initiative was taken, and the presence of Unionists in cabinet distorted motives and perceptions further.

The war effort could only suffer in this light, the more so given the weaknesses inherent in the qualities of the Prime Minister, whose almost Olympian disdain for the improvised requirements of coalition government during wartime gave the ministry the air less of an interregnum than an *ancien régime*, and one it did McKenna no harm in being closely associated with: the Prime Minister to Asquith's President. 'For comfort and confidence we all look on the Prime Minister and McKenna, both looking happy, sleek, and complacent',[26] Clementine Churchill wrote to Winston. Whatever his importance for the Prime Minister, for McKenna Asquith was the difference between office or backbench, and McKenna had no interest in serving merely as an MP. Asquith did not write to him as often as he did Grey or Crewe; or bemoan him as he did Lloyd George or Churchill; instead, the Prime Minister appointed McKenna Chancellor in spite of many compelling reasons not to.[27] Unlike the position of Lloyd George, that of McKenna was not the result of a strong personal or political following; but, and just as important for a Prime Minister, McKenna had 'characteristic efficiency',[28] and other qualities 'particularly courage (of which, with all his limitations), he is a shining example'.[29]

Perhaps as importantly, Asquith had introduced McKenna to Pamela Jekyll, the young and beautiful daughter of a fairly wealthy and highly cultured family. It was an incongruous pairing, and nothing short of an induction for the somewhat shy ascetic, with Pamela filling a role similar to that which Margot Tennant performed for Asquith twelve years before. McKenna immediately found himself in different West End dining rooms during the week, and different country houses at the weekend, his angular and pedantic manner softened. Before long Asquith described him as 'completely Jekyllised'.[30] McKenna in turn became a regular guest at the Asquiths'; the two families holidayed together, Asquith was godfather to McKenna's first son, while Pamela would cut the Prime Minister's hair at the McKenna's new Lutyens-designed house in Smith Square. It did McKenna's career no harm that the Prime Minister could 'spend Sunday in an atmosphere more or less permeated by the McKennae.'[31]

McKenna's sharpness, however, often made governing an even harder task for the Prime Minister than it would otherwise have been. Asquith complained of McKenna's 'gloating' over any Lloyd George misdemeanour, and on one occasion described him as 'a wrecker, pure & simple'.[32] If the Chancellor could have done more to assist the Prime Minister, Asquith was clear where the main responsibility lay. 'Of course Lloyd George is the villain of the piece', Asquith told Kathleen Scott, 'You know what I think of him.'[33] To Crewe he complained of Lloyd George's 'inexcusable' behaviour;[34] to Pamela he conveyed his dread of 'the prospect (now impending) of a talk with Ll.G, who has invited himself here to lunch. "These are my crosses, Mr Wesley".'[35] In this respect, Lloyd George was part of a larger problem. Asquith's continual unhappiness with the course of the government implicitly served as self-criticism for calling the coalition into being. On 10 September 1915, with fifteen months to follow, he wrote to Pamela from No. 10: 'This is a horrible place – full of cross-currents, and smouldering fires, and trimming sails, of bold bad men, and timid good men, and of men who are neither good nor bad. I might add indefinitely to the catalogue, but I will spare you'.[36]

Personalities were more important to the Asquith coalition than to other such assemblages because of the nature of that coalition. While for a 'brasshat' the circling flock of procrastinating Liberal 'frockcoats' were a 'miserable pack of Hesitations and Hiccoughs, the Squiffs and McKennas, and Lulus and Runcimans',[37] Asquith preferred 'a cad with Liberal ideas to a Gentleman with none',[38] and complained to Pamela of having to 'rub shoulders with uncongenial and unfamiliar personalities,'[39] which he sought to view merely as 'disfigurements of the landscape'.[40]

In such uncommon surroundings, the Prime Minister resorted increasingly to more appealing visions. Ironically, for the man who resisted their enfranchisement, Asquith was devoted to women. In addition to a peculiarly strong-willed and proactive spouse in Margot, Asquith also had, in Violet and Cynthia, a highly literate and opinionated daughter and daughter-in-law. Most infamously, however, he had correspondents, confidantes, and intimates – Venetia Stanley, Sylvia Henley, Kathleen Scott, Violet Tree, Ettie Desborough, Diana Cooper, Hilda Harrisson – of whom the least well-known was the most significant to the course of the coalition. Though she was certainly appealing, she was also much more. Lloyd George thought her 'a clever little woman – full of brains'.[41] Through her youth, appearance, and manner Pamela complemented the qualities of her husband by contrasting them, and continued many of his associations by other means; antipathy was similarly shared.[42] 'Mrs McKenna hates Winston with the most deadly animosity', Riddell noted in January 1915.[43] 'I have been impressed by the way in which the McKenna vendetta haunts the scene in all sorts of strange ways. I wonder if Mrs McKenna's courtesies and attentions to me in the past two years have not been made partly with the object of detaching me from Winston';[44] she also had the knack of making Lloyd George 'very apprehensive'.[45]

Pamela was more than merely protective, being a woman of pronounced political views herself. Her politics were in fact more socialistic than they were Liberal, and she was a staunch Labour supporter after the war during which time she was asked by several constituency parties to stand for parliament. In a later age, Pamela might well have experienced ministerial life herself; as it was she did so vicariously. Political wives did not need to emulate Margot Asquith, the 'extraordinary indiscretions' of whom, C. P. Scott noticed, were 'widely reported'.[46] Pamela operated with more subtlety, indeed such subtlety that the essence of her role remained almost unknown. In other ways she more obviously complemented her husband. Venetia Stanley told Violet Asquith: 'I wonder whether Clementine will become as much of a Cabinet bore as Pamela. I don't expect she will as she is too humble.'[47]

It was through their extra-parliamentary relations that Asquith and McKenna forged their political partnership. In that, McKenna found his wife was central. Asquith's correspondence with Pamela was further evidence of the importance of the 'McKennae', and a unique example of its kind, his letters concerning the political but emphasising the personal in a way those to the others did not. Though usually marked 'Personal' the letters were hand delivered or posted to Smith Square, clearly originating in Downing Street, and would have been no secret to his Chancellor. Perhaps that was why they could be so disarming. 'What do you think I did between 12 and 1 last night? As you couldn't guess I will tell you. I filled four sides of a Wharf sheet of paper with pencil writing – of and to you'.[48] In another letter he concluded solemn reflection with:

> there is only *one* person among all my friends who loves me entirely for myself; not with blind eyes ... who knows me as I am, with all my weaknesses and shortcomings; and yet would (I sometimes think) rather be blotted out of the book of life than I should cease to be. That *one* person is *you*.[49]

To the awkward collection of personalities along Whitehall was added those of another thoroughfare: Fleet Street. 'Results only count in the public estimation of politicians,' McKenna concluded after ejection from office, 'and in this connection results mean the public opinion which is formed upon them for the newspaper accounts. Apparent success is as good as real success until the truth is known and it takes a long time to get behind a skilfully manipulated press story'.[50] The Chancellor learnt the hard way: his bête noire was an altogether more skilful manipulator of press stories. The view was common at the time, even to backbenchers: 'LG did little work in the House, and little work in the War Office, but he worked a good deal with the press'.[51] McKenna could not separate the endemic political manoeuvring within the coalition from the concerted actions of what he called the 'maniac press',[52] and the success of each did nothing to enhance his opinion of either. As elsewhere, McKenna felt the need to adapt, so that his words to an editor several years earlier sounded more than anachronistic: 'Expression of opinions by ministers for communication to the press are against all precedent'.[53]

'It is foolish to ignore the "good press" as Asquith did', Runciman wrote after the fall. 'Had the Liberal Press been as well-informed as the Unionist Press, the outcome may well have been different'.[54] At least the Chancellor tried. The problem was, as Riddell noticed, that 'McKenna is kind-hearted but angular and not genial. It is amusing to watch his clumsy and elephantine attempts to emulate LG's genial and attractive ways'.[55] Spender, a genuine and close friend of McKenna, was altogther too fastidious an editor to have been of much use during wartime, while Lloyd George could call on such disparate figures as C.P. Scott and Northcliffe, Robert Donald and H. A. Gwynne: an unbeatable coalition.

The two key pressmen were George Riddell, proprietor of *The News of the World*, a Lloyd George confidante, and, for McKenna, Hedley Le Bas, proprietor of the Caxton Press, and creator of the most famous image of the war: 'Your Country Needs You'.[56] That Le Bas did not remain well known or his name widely remembered would not have been the case if he had been an ally of Lloyd George rather than of McKenna, though the former thought him a creature of procurement. 'Le Bas is like a whore', Lloyd George told Riddell.[57] McKenna had clandestine needs, and it was more than mildly ironic that, when he employed Le Bas to advertise war loans, Lloyd George, of all people, pronounced: 'This expenditure of public funds is certain to lead to corruption'.[58]

There were unlikely links. Lloyd George and McKenna were both members of Walton Heath Golf Club, as were Riddell and Le Bas. In June 1915 it was still possible for the improbable rubber of Lloyd George and Riddell against McKenna and Le Bas; on a later occasion Riddell and Lloyd George were busy between shots berating Donald for listening to McKenna, when McKenna and caddy appeared, taking Donald with them.[59] As if relations were not already bad enough, in 1915 Riddell sued Le Bas having been accused by him of fraud, and responded by accusing Le Bas of blackmailing him over his divorce; as two former colleagues consumed with the denigration of the other, and marshalling as many interests as were required to that end, McKenna and Lloyd George were not disinterested observers.

The peculiar effects of the coalition on the ability of strong personalities to work together were evident at the outset. As, respectively, Home Secretary and Chancellor prior to May 1915 there was little reason for the interests of McKenna and Lloyd George to cross. When McKenna was appointed Chancellor, Lloyd George was charged with first creating, then sustaining, a war-winning munitions industry. Overnight was created both the largest spending department in government and the one that, owing to the working methods of its head and the unprecedented nature of its task, was the most ill disciplined. This coincided with the appointment as Chancellor of a man with every credential required by the Treasury, and especially an aversion to high spending and profligate government departments. Thus was a fundamental divergence of departmental interest grafted onto already poor personal relations. So in his two most significant appointments Asquith either had in mind the merits of creative tension or had simply misjudged the nature of the enterprise.

Henceforth the two clashed continually in the various committees charged with executive control of the war. Lloyd George felt that the Chancellor should be excluded, on institutional as much as personal grounds, and McKenna's continued presence left him 'much annoyed. He says that McKenna worried the PM into appointing him and that in doing so he had not played the game'.[60] Lloyd George identified the real 'soft underbelly' of the war effort: 'The PM has been spending the weekend with the Jekylls and has no doubt been subjected to much feminine influence', Riddell wrote. 'Mrs McK, LG thinks, has been working hard in the interests of her husband'.[61] Pamela was not alone. Margot had to decided keep the Prime Minister out of town 'as the gossips will say that Mr McKenna 'got at' H[enry]...[McKenna's] well advertised hatred of Ll.G make it highly important for us all to be silent – not a word'.[62]

Whether or not his prophecy was self-fulfilling, Lloyd George found the committee 'very unpleasant ... McKenna opposes almost every project [of mine]'.[63] The diffusion of opinion within the expanding committee had the effect of further disorientating the Prime Minister as to the nature of the challenge. As late as 16 December, he told Pamela 'I am just going to face a large anti-conscription deputation – not (I hope and believe) Ephesian Beasts, but nice, more or less, peace loving specimens from our old pre-Coalition menagerie'.[64] Reality was soon evident – the first December crisis – and Christmas 1915 for Asquith was 'in the fullest sense of the word a Hellish week: one of the worse even in my storm-tossed annals'.[65]

'A wife can play a big part in a great crisis like this,' Margot told Pamela. 'If [Reggie] whom I love[,] really cares for Henry and believes him necessary to our country just now he must stick to him ... That is the whole question + by this he will be tested'.[66] Two days later Henry wrote 'we had a Cabinet in the morning which may or may not be fateful'.[67] The consequences, were all ministers to act as they had intimated, were clear to the Prime Minister when, with mandarin celerity, Hankey fashioned the government-prolonging formula, and only one minister – Sir John Simon – resigned. 'Asquith has thrown over his friends in order to placate hostile colleagues', Runciman grumbled,[68] and Margot told Pamela 'Thro Ll.G's treachery and baseness yr husband and Mr Runciman + others feel that Henry has come down on the wrong side ... I sympathize'.[69] Her husband was in fact equally disgruntled, also telling Pamela: 'Listening to Simon's [resignation] speech this afternoon, I felt rather like a father who has been publicly hit in the face by his son. These are the things one really minds.'[70]

The Prime Minister then compounded the institutional clash between Lloyd George and McKenna, by acceding to the former, who demanded an even greater influence on the direction of strategy. 'About teatime (this is secret)', Asquith briefed Pamela, 'I received by special messenger a kind of ultimatum from Ll.G to wh. I did not reply'.[71] Lloyd George had threatened to resign unless Kitchener was dismissed. 'Happily I have got the habit of *mens aegna in arduis* and slept peacefully ... I summoned the writer ... then (as I dare say you know) we had a Cabinet...'.[72] During the meeting McKenna alone had opposed the move to unseat the Secretary for War, as much for tactical as for strategic reasons, though by way of another compromise, Kitchener was sent off on a spurious mission to the Mediterranean until December. A precedent had been established: it was the first, but by no means the last, 'Kitchener dodge'.

At an improbable dinner party convened by Stevenson for Lloyd George and McKenna, the latter suggested the two 'bury the hatchet'.[73] Any such efforts were undermined by Kitchener's death in June 1916. With Lloyd George anxious to replace him, Riddell thought 'it is certain that McK did his best to prevent him from being appointed'.[74] 'Directly I heard of Ll-G's ultimatum', McKenna told Runciman, 'I wrote to the P.M. that I earnestly hoped before coming to a decision he would give the Cabinet an opportunity to consider a matter so gravely affecting Robertson's position'.[75] The Prime Minister sought to dissuade him. 'The P.M. said to Ll-G that he would have been obviously the right man for the W.O. if the powers of the S. of S. had not been so seriously curtailed for Robertson's benefit ... To this Ll-G replied that he could not take the post with its present limitations ... Otherwise resignation.'[76]

At the end of June McKenna told Runciman that the Prime Minister was 'to appoint Ll-G on Kitchener's terms. He knows the appointment is a bad one but has not the strength to resist. Ll-G's friends say "how

magnanimous the P.M. is," which means, as I interpret it, that LI-G has
been given assurances.'[77] Assuredly, Lloyd George continued the
marginalization of William Robertston. Recognising that Robertson was
both sympathetic to his own concerns as Chancellor, and that as Chief of
the Imperial General Staff he provided a serious counterbalance to Lloyd
George, McKenna promoted his case. Lloyd George re-employed his old
policy with Kitchener's predecessor. Robertson complained in
November how 'L.G. tried to shove me over to Russia. The King took
up the matter strongly & it was dropped. The idea was to let L.G.
become top dog here & have his wicked way. Like he used to get rid of
poor old K'.[78] Lloyd George's enemies were likely friends of McKenna,
a reasoning that led Lloyd George and his friends to see McKenna as a
source of intrigue as well as of obstruction. In Cabinet on 21 November,
Lloyd George complained that 'he had lost influence with Robertson
owing to the fact that someone had poisoned the latter's mind' with the
'K Dodge'. When a Tory chorus demanded he name his accuser, Lloyd
George proclaimed: 'Very well, then I will tell you. It is the Chancellor of
the Exchequer!' When he was asked later how he knew it had been
McKenna, Lloyd George chortled 'that was pure bluff ... !'[79]

Lloyd George's next coup underlined his mastery of modern
statesmanship. In an interview to the *New York Times* he rejected
American peace overtures, and proclaimed Britain would 'fight to the
finish'. McKenna was furious, regarding Lloyd George's 'affront to
America [as] sheer lunacy", and having 'no doubt Lloyd George had
written the whole thing – very likely written it interpolations and all'.[80]
The interview precipitated a financial crisis, as Asquith told the King in
what would prove to be his last Cabinet report.[81] His disenchantment,
revealed to Pamela McKenna as it was to no other, was by then almost
absolute, and when his son was killed he told her 'I feel, for the first time
at any rate, bankrupt in pride and life.[82] A disgusted McKenna told C. P.
Scott, 'Lloyd George risks little: his sons are well-sheltered'.[83]

Raymond's death, compounding his father's exhaustion, and the
increasing effectiveness of Lloyd George and the Unionists, placed
McKenna and the other Asquithians in a serious dilemma: only through
Asquith remaining Prime Minister would they retain any purchase on the
policy of the government, and it was Asquith remaining Prime Minister
which became the prevailing concern, especially as the Chancellor would
have seen Asquith's extraordinary letter to Pamela days before the fall.

> In case I do not see you again, this is to assure you of my deep and
> everlasting gratitude for unceasing and always understanding love.
> It is to me a priceless possession and will (whatever happens) be a
> lifelong and death-surviving memory ... Whatever may come, yours
> ever loving and wholly devoted, HHA.[84]

Twelve days later Lloyd George demanded a new war committee, which
would omit both Robertson and McKenna.[85] McKenna duly complained,
and Asquith duly rejected the proposal, though with little hope of
closure: 'Alas! the whirlwinds are blowing, and the windmills are
whirling: in short I am in the centre of an aerial tornado, from which I
cannot escape'.[86]

'I don't think during the war, I have had a worse 48 hours', Asquith
told Pamela on 1 December.[87] Lloyd George's next organizational
gambit actually omitted the Prime Minister, and was presented to
Asquith for his refusal on 1 December.[88] Balfour thought that, once
again, 'LG had put a pistol to the head of the PM'.[89] McKenna knew his
fate in the event of Lloyd George being appointed chairman, and, even
in Asquith's own compromise, there appeared to be no room for the
Chancellor. With Northcliffe personally intent on undermining the
Prime Minister's authority, McKenna mobilized his own, rather less
prepossessing, pressman, and Hedley Le Bas was spotted around
Westminster throughout the day. Riddell heard of 'a message from the
poisonous Le Bas stating that McKenna would resign unless he is
included in the war council'.[90]

Asquith, convinced that Lloyd George had sought to pre-empt his
decision by briefing the press, rejected the proposal in toto, and refused
to see Lloyd George. McKenna spent much of that day with the Prime
Minister. Asquith had initially been content with the revised proposals,
but, after meeting McKenna on the morning of 4 December, refused,
and on 5 December, himself resigned.[91] Whether this confirmed the
infirmity of the Prime Minister in the eyes of Lloyd George and his allies,
or the apparently disproportionate influence of the Chancellor, the effect
was further to reinforce their sense of purpose. While the Prime Minister
would better withstand McKenna's departure than he would that of
Lloyd George, it was never clear quite how close he came to abandoning
McKenna. Asquith's draft memorandum of 25 November omitted
McKenna from a civilian General Staff; others maintained that that was
Asquith's position as late as 1 December; the consensus was certainly
that McKenna would go, which, of course, in the end, he did. To the
despair of some of his colleagues, he took the Prime Minister with him.[92]

The Asquith coalition was hardly government as Liberals knew it, though
it more closely approximated governance as it would come to be known.
Lloyd George, in that sense, was the first twentieth century statesman.
Asquith, meanwhile, could reflect, during his first Christmas as an
ordinary MP for eleven years, that he had followed the advice of those
closest to him, only peremptorily to find himself first among erstwhiles.
This may explain a starchy letter written to McKenna shortly after,[93] and
far fewer than before to Pamela. Yet in his last two years as Prime
Minister, Asquith, deaf to the overtures of those who were to prevail,

remained wedded to a man as isolated at the time as he has been by subsequent consideration. Spender made the judgement, as obvious in retrospect as it was unhelpful, that if McKenna and Lloyd George 'had been rolled into one, McKenna's cool judgement and political rectitude, added to Lloyd George's impetuousness and eloquence, an incomparable statesman would have resulted.'[94] As it was the two Welsh MPs were driven apart, as much by the changing nature of modern politics as by their own mutual antipathy. Asquith's tragedy was that, having considered personnel politically, he had not realized that the personal could be quite so political.

4

Charismatic leadership, c. 1870-1914
A comparative European Perspective

Henk te Velde

When we speak about the role of personalities in politics, sooner or later we use the word 'charisma'. Usually this word just means that a politician has a strong media presence and, implicitly, that personalities matter in particular to the public side of politics, albeit in a rather superficial way. Often we use it in a rather casual way, describing a politician who has just a bit more magic than the next civil servant. Originally, of course, the concept of 'charisma' had a much more powerful meaning. When the German sociologist Max Weber imported the term from religious studies into political science at the beginning of the twentieth century, he had in mind politicians who were really capable of arousing the masses.[1] Weber distinguished between 'traditional', 'legal' (or 'rational') and 'charismatic' authority or rule. Traditional rule rested on the legitimacy of 'old' habits, such as the loyalty to a king, and in general on the common belief in the sanctity of existing traditions, while legal rule was based on the legitimacy of 'rational', bureaucratic rules, and yet they both presupposed an element of continuity. Charismatic rule, on the other hand, rested on an uncommon devotion to the sanctity or heroism of an individual. It only developed in times of crisis, was something inherently instable, and completely dependent on the position of the charismatic individual.

According to Weber, the important thing was that the public attributed to the charismatic leader the supernatural powers necessary for the fundamental social changes they wanted. Charisma, then, was not something a politician possessed irrespective of circumstances, but rather an almost religious, cult-like relationship between a leader and his adherents in a specific situation. Charisma was not a quality inherent in a politician – though not every politician could become a charismatic leader – but rather something that the public ascribed to him. Even the type of political leadership that seemed to exclusively concentrate on the extraordinary qualities of an individual appeared in reality to have quite strong social aspects.

Charisma is not confined to a particular period of history, even if you take the strong Weberian sense of the word as the point of departure.

When Weber introduced the concept of charisma at the beginning of the twentieth century it did not become popular overnight. In the 1930s, the word became current when it was used to describe the Hitlers of the age,[2] and charisma was regarded as a diabolical quality that bewitched people and made them do terrible things. Weber's first examples and the examples he used to exemplify his theory, however, were not totalitarian but rather democratic popular leaders, such as the first major leader of the German socialist party August Bebel (1840-1913) in Germany and, in particular, the popular liberal leader William Gladstone (1809-98) in Britain.[3] This type of leader was prominent during the last decades of the nineteenth century, a period in which charismatic leaders seem endemic or even ubiquitous. Apart from Bebel and Gladstone, one could mention, among others, the early socialist leaders Ferdinand Lassalle (1825-64) in Germany, James Keir Hardie (1856-1915) in Britain, Ferdinand Domela Nieuwenhuis (1846-1919), the first socialist leader who had been a Lutheran priest and later turned anarchist, and Pieter Jelles Troelstra (1860-1930), the leader of the social-democratic party in the Netherlands. But there were also the right-wing Catholic leader Karl Lueger (1844-1910) in Austria (Vienna), the Dutch neo-Calvinist leader Abraham Kuyper (1837-1920), the republican populist leader Alejandro Lerroux (1864-1949) in Spain (Barcelona), or the flash in the pan of General Georges Boulanger (1837-91), who for a short period mobilized radical conservative sentiments in France but then was frightened out of his wits by what he caused and committed suicide. I will briefly describe a few of these leaders, and examine the metaphors that were used to praise or characterize them.[4]

However, I would first like to say something about the different aspects of popular leadership in the late nineteenth century. Popular leaders had existed previously of course, but this was a period of democratization during which they managed to bridge the gap between formal parliamentary systems and the country at large, and during which they changed from critical outsiders or revolutionary rebels to centre stage political figures. John Bright, for example, had still been a relative outsider, but Gladstone became the 'people's premier'.[5] Their function was the mobilization of the people in a period when mass politics and political parties outside parliaments were beginning. Often they were transitional figures, marking the transition from older forms of politics – based, for example, on local patronage systems – to institutionalized party politics.[6] Charismatic leaders stimulated political participation and national integration or 'the nationalization of the masses', and they bridged geographical or social distances. According to William Edwin Adams, a contemporary leftist commentator (1880), Gladstone 'found the people who live in cottages hostile to political parties and succeeded in uniting them with the rest of his countrymen'.[7]

There were at least three different types of new popular leaders. The first was the real charismatic leader, the prophet who led his people and was an extraordinary individual without many ties to party or bureaucracy. This pure type was represented by Gladstone in Britain, the early bohemian socialist Lassalle in Germany and the socialist turned anarchist Domela Nieuwenhuis in the Netherlands, who did not manage a well-organized party but were the centre of a dynamic 'movement'. They were also writers, but their success depended on their oratory, they personified rather than belonged to their 'party', and they became mythical figures. The second type was the party manager, for example Joseph Chamberlain in Britain, or Bebel in Germany, whose main contribution to socialism was the organization of the party in the difficult years of the Bismarckian oppression before 1890 and who became the grand old man of the party. And finally there was the city administrator, the man who as a modern entrepreneur organized public utilities and a kind of social policy at a local level. Once again we can think of Chamberlain in Birmingham, or Lueger in Vienna, and Wim Treub, the radical, in Amsterdam.

When we look at this list, we see at once that the new political style ('politics in a new key' in the well-known phrase of Carl Schorske about Vienna)[8] was not confined to one political current. Prophets and party managers could be liberals, for example Gladstone and (before his defection) Chamberlain in Britain, but also socialists, for example Lassalle and Bebel in Germany, or neo-Calvinists, for example Kuyper in the Netherlands, or even Catholics, for example Lueger in Austria, or anticlerical, for example Lerroux in Spain or Paul Janson, the famous radical orator, in Belgium. The new style appeared in different places and was not usually directly affected by foreign examples. Because there were so many similarities, one biographer of Lueger, for instance, assumed that Lueger in Vienna had been inspired by the example of Chamberlain in Birmingham, but in his research he could not find any support for this whatsoever.[9] The Dutch Protestant leader Kuyper, on the other hand, referred to Gladstone and was compared to him on a regular basis, but he had established a position for himself as a party leader that differed in important ways from Gladstone's position.[10] There were many international parallels but not many direct influences. However, Gladstone was the best-known international leader of his kind. Apparently, he was compared to aspiring politicians in countries as far apart as Japan and Canada.[11] It was no coincidence that Weber used Gladstone as his prime example of charismatic leadership. He had been Prime Minister and had become a real popular leader in the country that many Europeans regarded as an example in politics.

The three types, prophet, party manager and city administrator, could also occur in all possible combinations. Gladstone was a prophet but not a party leader in the sense of a manager of an organization, whereas

Chamberlain was a party manager and city administrator but not really a prophet like Gladstone. Chamberlain's position always rested more on his organizational and administrative positions than on his rhetorical skills, even if he was able to deliver great oratory. 'Into the tones of his voice he threw the warmth of feeling which was lacking in his words; and every thought, every feeling, the slightest intonation of irony or contempt was reflected on the face of the crowd. It might have been a woman listening to the words of her lover!', according to the perhaps not completely objective testimony of Beatrice Potter, though only a few years later according to the same commentator the 'statesman had overcome the demagogue'.[12] Kuyper, on the other hand, was a prophet and a party leader, who founded the first Dutch modern political party in 1879 (the orthodox Protestant party ARP), a protestant newspaper and a protestant university, but he was not a city administrator. He was the leader of the cabinet on one occasion, but that was not his greatest success and he never served on a local government board. Seen from a British perspective, he was a combination of Gladstone and Chamberlain. The Austrian Lueger was a city administrator and a prophet who founded his own Catholic 'Christian-Social' party, but he was not really a party manager, and due to poor management, his movement fell apart after his death. This is all at least partly a matter of personal qualities. As we all notice daily in our work, not everyone is a good manager, nor is every manager an inspiring prophet, and the combination of the two is even rarer. No one person combined all three aspects of the new popular leader, but internationally the prophets and party managers made the biggest impression.

The emerging modern political parties could hardly do without prophets and party managers in their initial phase. Indeed, in particular the need for prophets as symbols and uniting forces was so strong that even a quiet and modest manager type like August Bebel had to serve as one in the German socialist party. Bebel himself had to struggle with the cult of Lassalle, who had, quite romantically, died young in a duel, and who had been the leader of a competing party.[13] After Bebel's own death at a ripe old age, the writers of his obituaries used expressions such as 'pilgrims in search of a preacher' to describe the relationship between Bebel and his devoted followers,[14] but he was not a figure like Lassalle or Gladstone. Unlike those patrician leaders who maintained a delicate balance between distance and identification with their followers, Bebel had sprung from a working class background, stressed the importance of party discipline, and also lacked the bohemian aspects of someone like Keir Hardie.[15] Unlike those 'heroic exotic' figures, he was admired as a common worker who had risen to a leadership position but remained true to his background.[16] His friends and admirers often said that he did not subscribe to the emotional and verbose French style of oratory, but instead employed a simple, almost scientific German style. This seems to be a euphemistic way of saying that he was not a moving orator at all. The Belgian socialist leader Camille Huysmans said that Bebel was not a spellbinder who captivated the masses. He spoke plainly, clearly, and without large gestures.[17] Nevertheless, he did move his audience because they wanted to be moved. This explains why charismatic leaders did not necessarily have to be great orators.

An adherent of Kuyper's party in the Netherlands once explained the mechanism. The first time he went to a meeting to hear Kuyper speak, he was so excited that he saw the great man rather hazily, surrounded by a kind of halo, but the speech was not what he had expected. The next time, however, as he put it, he did not have any criticism. He said that he had learned how to listen to Kuyper, and now, of course, he was carried away.[18] Everybody was moved before the speech had even begun, as soon as Kuyper entered the hall, and this is the point. The audience wanted to be moved, almost independently of speech or occasion, and this is what happened to Bebel when he grew older.

In his old age, Bebel personified the struggles of the socialist party, its culture and traditions. In fact, he embodied the party. He had been there from the start and had built up its organization; 'I have grown up with the party', he said, and the party members were his 'children'.[19] In those early days, joining the socialist party was almost like joining a religious sect. In these circumstances the party leader could hardly be just an ordinary politician. He had to have at least some saintly or prophetic qualities. Nevertheless, some obituaries stress quite different aspects of Bebel's public appearance. The workers called him 'our Kaiser', according to contemporary comments he was the 'Gegenkaiser' (counter-emperor), and according to a more recent biography the 'shadow emperor of the German Empire'.[20] He was the son of a soldier, and he had a kind of military precision and rigour. Army metaphors abound in contemporary descriptions of the socialist party, and Bebel was 'Oberfeldherr' and 'Generalissimus'.[21] 'Volk, dein Führer ist tod!', an anonymous poet wrote when Bebel died.[22] The socialist party was two things at the same time. It was a world of its own, with its own atmosphere, lifestyle, and rules, an almost religious community that needed a prophet. But it was also meant to be an organization for battle, an army fit for the political struggle in need of a general. Like Bebel, Kuyper was also admired as a general and commander-in-chief, and his party was often described with army metaphors, but in the case of Bebel in particular, it was the foundation of his position. So if even his orations could produce 'a sort of religious mood', and if even someone like him was called a 'prophet',[23] it is obvious that the period was craving for charismatic leadership. He was the personification of the party.

Weber imported the term 'charisma' from religious studies; the word actually means a gift of grace, a gift from God.[24] The religious link is no coincidence. The end of the nineteenth century saw the emergence of religious parties in many European countries, and also a revival of religion, for example the Salvation Army – the name alone a combination again of religious and battle metaphors – and American revivalists travelling around Europe. Incidentally, Weber compared the style of modern politics to 'the means the Salvation Army also exploits in order to set the masses in motion'.[25] But in the context of this contribution something else is more important still. Much more than before, politics acquired what you could call a 'religious' function in the life of the political activist. On the continent, where politics used to be mainly a matter for parliaments composed of notables and lawyers who rejected direct contacts with their voters, political parties introduced a new element to politics. Politics was no longer a matter of parliamentary debate but of identity and belonging. Dutch neo-Calvinist activists felt that Kuyper's party was taking care of their most fundamental beliefs and needs. Workers joining Bebel's party often thought that for the first time politics really mattered, and the new party also boosted their self-esteem. Political parties acquired a role similar to that which religions often have: they provided a sense of purpose, a sense of belonging, a sense of a shared fate.

Leaders were very important in this situation because they gave shape to the new party, determined its course, and established the connection between the movement and the national political system. Most importantly, the ordinary members could sympathize and identify with them. This could happen for different reasons. Bebel was originally an ordinary worker and was still regarded as 'one of us' by the lower classes, even if he was now a member of parliament, party president and also the owner of a small company. But the real charismatic leaders were different. They were extraordinary personalities, often from the middle or upper middle classes – such as Gladstone, Lassalle or the Dutch socialist leader Domela Nieuwenhuis – and fraternising with the workers did not come naturally to them. Lassalle in particular abhorred shaking the sweaty hands of workers. But they were idolized because they demonstrated a populist solidarity with the common people that you did not expect in the class-ridden nineteenth century. 'If you will permit me to identify myself with you', Gladstone said to a mass audience, and then he would use the word 'we'. 'I am one of yourselves', he shouted. On the other hand, he also presented himself as a 'stranger' to politics, someone who had lost his faith in the ruling classes and was now looking for virtuous passion among the common people.[26] Other charismatic leaders used similar expressions.

The British socialist leader Keir Hardie was routinely called 'the prophet, priest, and patron saint of his class'.[27] Hardie himself preferred the word agitator, but there is no doubt about the religious quality of his political work. He admired the Salvation Army and called Labour a religious movement. He particularly liked meeting an audience, and (in 1903) described his experience in mystical-religious or even erotic terms: 'I absorb and am absorbed by my audience ... we seem to melt and to fuse into one, and I am not speaking to them, but through them, and my thoughts are not my thoughts but their thoughts'.[28] The experience of the Dutch socialist and atheist Troelstra was almost identical. 'At some point during my speeches', he writes, 'there often came a moment when I wondered who is speaking now, they or myself?'[29] It was a radicalization of Gladstone's well-known early description of the oratorical process: the work of the orator 'is an influence principally received from his audience (so to speak) in vapour, which he pours back upon them in a flood [...] his choice is, to be what his age will have him, what it requires to be moved by him, or else not to be at all'.[30]

The interplay or even symbiosis between leader and audience was a typical element of charismatic leadership. The audience needed the leader but the leader needed the audience just as much. In the cases of Hardie and Troelstra, words such as addiction or intoxication (by their own rhetoric) have been used by contemporaries and historians alike.[31] This could perhaps even be generalized to include most charismatic leaders: most of them were, as Gladstone, 'addicted to *bains de foule*', even though Gladstone himself tried to avoid the 'flattering' but also 'intoxicating' effects of mass meetings.[32] Keir Hardie and Troelstra both realised that they were leaders of a particular kind. Hardie said that he was no leader in the normal sense but a pioneer who followed his intuitions; Troelstra said that he would not have made a great member of the cabinet. He was a 'tribune of the people', a popular leader of the 'heroic age' of his party; when he had retired he said that in the established party the 'prophetic' element had waned.[33]

Charismatic leaders actively transformed their own lives into political symbols. In their lives nothing happened by chance. Gladstone famously detected the hand of the Almighty in every twist of his fate, and liked to think of himself as a chosen tool of a divine project. Other leaders compared their own suffering to the suffering of Christ. When Domela Nieuwenhuis was convicted and sent to prison, he compared his fate to the 'Via Dolorosa' of Christ. At the beginning of the First World War Keir Hardie said: 'I now understand the sufferings of Christ at Gethsemane'. He also identified and was identified with Moses.[34] This was perhaps the most common comparison during this period; it would be hard to find a charismatic leader who was not compared to at least Moses if not Christ himself. Strong emotions stimulated the use of religious metaphors. In France, Boulanger's followers distributed pictures of the maverick general as a Christ on the cross, and words such as 'prophètes', 'missionnaires', 'prêcheurs', and 'apôtres' permeated the language of socialism.[35]

If the use of religious language is something to go by, Josephine Butler, who led the campaign to repeal the Contagious Diseases Acts, should definitely be included in a list of fin-de-siècle charismatic leaders. *Personal Reminiscences of a Great Crusade* is the title of one of her books, and in it she compared her own sufferings to those of Christ. The element of quasi-religious self-sacrifice was an important element of her feminist leadership.[36] She was also a powerful orator. According to her ally James Stuart 'she touched the hearts of her hearers as no one else has done to whom I have listened'; another supporter wrote that 'it was surprising and refreshing to men to find themselves spellbound by the passionate eloquence of a gentle sweet-voiced woman.'[37] Another sweet-voiced woman was also a charismatic leader. The 'suffrage army' of the Women's Social and Political Union (WSPU) did not have a clear written constitution, but was held together by the charismatic power of Emmeline Pankhurst, the leader of the suffragettes, who was sometimes accused of acting as a despot. She was a 'spellbinder' holding her audience in the palm of her hand. She preferred speaking to writing and thrived on the immediate response of an audience.[38]

The similarities in descriptions of leaders and their charisma is striking. They were 'interpreters' of the real opinion of the people, they awoke the 'sleeping' masses, or made them 'conscious' of their power and real ideas. Abraham Kuyper was famously called the piano player of the 'keyboard of the popular conscience'; Bebel 'played the people as if they were a noble instrument'.[39]

Religious metaphors and charismatic leaders abounded in politics, but there were important differences between Britain and the continent. In Britain, it could be argued that popular interest in parliament had always been stronger, and that the gap between parliamentary politics and 'the people' could be bridged more easily. Moreover, the Gladstone period saw the culmination but also the beginning of the end of a strong evangelical presence in politics. Elements of evangelicalism still pervaded early British socialism, but during the twentieth century there was a marked decrease in the evangelical influence. In countries such as Germany or the Netherlands, it was virtually the other way round. There, a dry liberal Protestantism had been present in politics during the nineteenth century, but it could be argued that the religious element in politics grew from the end of the nineteenth century, not only in the sense that denominational parties began to appear but also that political parties took the shape of religious communities or even almost churches. The most important charismatic leaders were the inspiration of these moral communities, milieu parties as they were called in Germany or 'pillars' in the Dutch case. Without Kuyper, it is hard to imagine the Dutch Neo-Calvinist moral community in the twentieth century, and without Bebel, according to one of his biographers, the German socialist moral community would hardly have come into being.[40] In Britain, on the other hand, the political work of the charismatic 'Grand Old Man' resulted in a split in the Liberal party. Both on the Continent *and* in Britain, however, charismatic leadership marked the beginning of mass politics and the transition to political parties instead of parliament as the centre of politics. And this is what counts. In the initial phase of organized parties, the 'religious' elements were equally strong in the style of atheist socialist parties as, for instance, in the Dutch neo-Calvinist party.

In the twentieth century, after organized political parties had been established as the dominating force in politics, a resurgence of populist and charismatic politics implied criticism of party politics. Populism became another word for bypassing parliaments *and* political parties, and concentrating instead on a direct, emotional bond between a leader and 'the people'.[41] In this respect the period from about 1870 to the Great War is very interesting because the emergence of organized political parties went hand in hand with the appearance of charismatic leadership, and this leadership was clearly populist: biographers often use this word in passing,[42] but it is also true in a more fundamental sense. Many key themes that run through populism, such as criticism of the existing representative system, identification with an idealized 'heartland', reaction to a sense of crisis and to 'corruption', and a quasi-religious tone may be found in late nineteenth-century charismatic leadership.[43]

Almost all leaders wanted to broaden the existing representative system and identified with a heartland of, for instance, common workers (socialist leaders) or neo-Calvinist 'little people' (Kuyper) as the true or only real nation. With respect to his ideas about the importance of 'the people' and the 'vox populi' as a 'vox Dei', Gladstone was rather typical.[44] But the charismatic leaders of the age obviously did *not* criticize party politics from the start, as most of them founded or supported a party themselves. Because charisma and organization do not go together well permanently, the combination was inherently unstable. There was a clear though uneasy relationship between the two. This may be illustrated by the role of Gladstone in the National Liberal Federation (NLF). This was of course Chamberlain's creation, but in the late 1870s Gladstone had the same objective of mobilising the common people, and both politicians followed the same course in the Bulgarian agitation, which propelled Gladstone back to leadership of the Liberals. Against the wishes of the Liberal parliamentary leadership, Gladstone consented to speak on the occasion of the founding assembly of the NLF in Birmingham, and Chamberlain had arranged for a general half-holiday in the city in order to guarantee Gladstone 'an almost Royal welcome'.[45] But after this Gladstone did not have many dealings with the organization. He remained the idiosyncratic charismatic leader.

In socialism there were tensions between charismatic leaders and their parties. Lassalle died early, but Domela Nieuwenhuis, the Dutch socialist leader, eventually turned anarchist because he did not like the discipline of organized parties and, even if he had wanted to, he would not have succeeded in submitting to a party line. He was the unpredictable, messianic and charismatic leader of the 1880s, who did not succeed in parliament, and afterwards lost the battle against the disciplined social-democratic party. Keir Hardie sympathized with Domela Nieuwenhuis;[46] he remained within the party, but at times also felt ill at ease in the organized world of political parties. Bebel identified completely with the party, but all 'really' charismatic leaders had their difficulties with the organized party they were supposed to lead, let alone follow.

At the end of the nineteenth century, on the other hand, populism was not an enemy of organized mass parties but often accompanied their emergence. The obvious though uneasy relationship between charismatic leaders and democratic parties distinguishes late nineteenth-century charismatic leadership from most of its twentieth-century successors. There is yet another difference. In the shape it assumed in the period between the wars, populist charismatic leadership has often been presented as synonymous with totalitarian propaganda and hysteria. It cannot be denied that certain elements in late nineteenth-century politics bear resemblance to these aspects. And in particular some charismatic leaders of a slightly later period, such as Lueger, the anti-Semitic Catholic mayor of Vienna, seem to foreshadow things to come. Lueger used propagandist tricks to seduce his audience. Arguably, however, all great orators do, and when one of Troelstra's biographers tried to contrast the 'true', 'authentic', in fact even 'unconscious' rhetorical power of his hero with the artificial effects of a Hitler, this was patently untrue.[47] More importantly, Lueger's speeches were powerful for a live audience but lost their power entirely when read in private; their emotional power was not matched by intellectual content. Hitler later used Lueger, the mayor of the city he was living in at the time, as an example. He admired him precisely for targeting the lowest common denominator among his audience, and for only trying to arouse the emotions of the common people, not their intellect.[48]

If this assessment is taken as a characterization of the effect of charismatic leadership in general, it clearly was a pernicious force. But at the end of the nineteenth century charismatic leadership also stimulated political involvement, national integration and emancipation, and it appealed to the intellect of the electorate, too. In order to assess the meaning of charismatic leadership, I would like to return once more to Weber's prime example, William Gladstone.

In his biography of Gladstone, Richard Shannon focuses on 'Peel's inheritor', the executive politician, who is not using 'demagogy' to flatter the people but rather uses his rhetorical power for reasons of '*étatist* manipulation'; who had, according to Walter Bagehot, 'the same sort of control over the minds of those he is addressing that a good driver has over the animals he guides'.[49] The Bulgarian agitation of 1876, which brought Gladstone back to power on a wave of popular support, was the real beginning of the charismatic man of Midlothian. It is clear that there already was a movement before Gladstone decided to join the mass agitation. According to Shannon this was an exception to the rule that Gladstone led, or even manipulated the people, instead of the reverse.[50] Seen from this perspective Gladstone seems to resemble Bismarck, with 'one-man government' based on the idea that 'the multitudes love to worship a political idol'.[51]

The German historian Wehler calls Bismarck a charismatic leader, though with the caveat that his political position was not built on the fanatic community of adherents that is normally assumed to be part of charismatic leadership.[52] It is possible to read Weber in this way – if only because Gladstone *was* an executive politician, which was rather rare in the case of charismatic leaders. However, it is perhaps revealing that Weber does not mention Bismarck as an important example of charismatic leadership in the strict sense of the word. He describes charisma as a social phenomenon, something the followers ascribe to their leader. He himself, however, was mainly interested in leadership, in particular in the possibility of powerful leadership in a democracy. Democracy was just a means to select leaders, and leaders should dominate the masses. He therefore focused on the 'Caesarist plebiscitarian' element in politics[53], on the mass support for populist charismatic leaders, which would allow them to remain in control, to rule without really binding them to their followers. This fits Wehler's description of Bismarck – who, according to Weber, was indeed a 'caesarist figure'[54] – and Shannon's description of Gladstone.

However, the popular leadership this contribution is dealing with is not primarily the manipulative power of the executive politician, it is the interplay and reciprocity between leader and followers that results in a strong emotional attachment.[55] In this sense the Bulgarian agitation was not just an exception to prove the rule that Gladstone was in control but an essential step in the development of his charismatic leadership, according to Matthew even 'a conversion of Evangelical intensity'.[56] Many charismatic leaders knew a comparable moment, when their later adherents took the initiative. It took a famous open letter from workers to get Lassalle to become socialist leader, and Domela Nieuwenhuis later wrote that he was 'drawn into' the movement, he did not know how.[57]

Gladstone's description of the orator – 'his choice is, to be what his age will have him' – should be taken seriously. Not in the sense that the charismatic leader is simply flowing with the tide; there is more to leadership than either domination or flatter and follow. If one considers the charismatic relationship of the age as a kind of interplay, Colin

Matthew's approach to Gladstone as both charismatic and rational has much to offer.[58] Gladstone took his audience very seriously and gave it a sense of importance, purpose and belonging. But he also had his own agenda that he explained clearly but without pandering or talking down to his audiences. For his purposes, speaking to live audiences at mass meetings, and to the newspapers, which spread and explained the news, were equally important. The same holds true for socialist parties of the period. Mass meetings were very important for the actual 'conversion' of new members, but newspapers and other written media made sure that this did not remain a one-night stand but became a permanent relationship with a clear and rational content.[59]

The concept of charisma was and is still being used to analyse totalitarian leadership,[60] but its ambiguous qualities could also be used to analyse aspects of democratic leadership. If it is true that modern representative governments contain an 'aristocratic' as well as a 'democratic' or populist element,[61] charismatic leadership will have its chance once the aristocratic element becomes too oppressive. At the end of the nineteenth century charismatic leadership contributed to the broadening of the suffrage and the democratic aspect of representative systems and announced the era of mass politics, and as a result on the continent the fear of populism was often strong. In Britain there was a tradition of popular election politics and of single-issue movements using popular methods, which provided a basis on which Gladstone could build his charismatic leadership, so that he could be a 'heroic minister' and a popular leader at the same time. On the Continent the transition from parliamentary to mass party politics was often more sudden. A whole industry of mass psychology emerged, and Weber is only one of many German and especially French analysts who worried about the arrival of mass politics. In Britain the mood was less pessimistic, and Graham Wallas wondered if the pessimism of French mass psychology, or 'the exaggeration which one seems to notice when reading the French sociologists on this point may be due to their observations having been made among a Latin and not a Northern race.'[62] Nowadays not many people would attribute this kind of difference to national character, but the comparison between Britain and the continent shows once more the ambiguous qualities of charismatic leadership.

The ambiguities are mirrored in Weber's work. His concept of charisma was a social and relational concept, and he seems to have been well aware of the reciprocity between leaders and followers in the charismatic relationship. Politically, however, he was mainly interested in dominant leaders, in Caesars and their plebiscitarian rule. For several reasons the first approach seems to be more promising for historians, and recently it has been noted that Weber himself focussed on the 'anti-authoritarian re-interpretation of charisma' and that Weber's work provides important keys for understanding the reciprocal and democratic elements of modern political leadership.[63] If we take the second approach, charisma can be dismissed too easily as a quality that is dangerous for democracy. The first approach, on the other hand, will show the inherently ambiguous qualities of charisma: it is a means to mobilize the people, and this can lead to either democratization or populist manipulation – and it is not easy to distinguish between the two, if only because the evaluation will depend on political preferences. The early socialists were convinced that their leaders were virtuous democrats and martyrs for a just cause, but according to their opponents they were dangerous and irresponsible populists.

There is a second reason why the relational approach seems to be more fruitful. If historians concentrate on the reciprocity of the charismatic leadership they will be able to avoid the pitfalls of either a great-man-theory or the neglect of the personal element in political history. The recent revival of political history has contributed to a new interest in political personalities. It is obvious that the history of British liberalism or Dutch Neo-Calvinism would have been different without William Gladstone or Abraham Kuyper. But this does not mean that these 'great men' could have made their mark in another period just as well. The times called for their type of leadership, and they made the most of the opportunities.

The case of socialism is also interesting. Apparently, charismatic personalities were almost indispensable in the first phase of modern mass politics, and if Keir Hardie or Domela Nieuwenhuis had not been available, it is not improbable that more or less comparable figures would have emerged, who could personify socialist protests. After all, socialism emerged almost everywhere in this period, and British or Dutch socialism had also come into existence without the two leaders, but they both nevertheless left a mark on the development of socialism in their countries. In the past the existence of the working classes plus the wake-up call of socialist ideology seemed to provide a sufficient explanation for the development of a socialist movement. Politics seemed to be a mere reflection of structural social forces.

But after the cultural turn in historiography, which challenged the idea that culture or politics were socially or economically determined, historians have become more aware of the creative power of politics. For better or for worse, politics can create new realities and charismatic politics are a potentially disruptive and creative form of personal politics. The distinction between a superficial level of personalities, incidents and anecdotes, and a 'deeper' level of structural developments is no longer convincing. If the concept of charisma is really applied in a relational sense, it may also partly bridge the gap between the study of high politics, mainly interested in leading personalities, and the study of low politics, mainly interested in the masses and in grassroots movements. In this way it is a typical example of the political culture approach, which has recently become popular, and at the same it is very useful for international comparison.[64]

5

An exemplary communist life?
Harry Pollitt's *Serving My Time* in comparative perspective[1]

Kevin Morgan

Traditionally, biography has been one of the weakest genres of communist historiography. In a country like Britain, where the communist party (the CPGB) had a peak membership in the 1940s of perhaps 55,000 and never elected more than two MPs, its leading figures held few obvious attractions for the conventional political biographer. Moreover, if proximity to power was not an inducement to explore their lives, personality and persuasion offered little compensation either. Not only were private papers rarely accessible, but also the public face of communism was one relentlessly prioritising the collective over the individual, even in respect of the life histories which communists constructed. Though there did exist a public genre of exemplary party lives, these were notorious for their reticence and even mendacity and in Britain at least have received little scholarly attention.[2]

Nevertheless, because the issue of personality and its suppression was so central to the culture of communism, the study of these narratives can provide crucial insights into the construction of both individual and collective party identities and the interconnections between them. Already in France, with its well-established traditions of prosopographical research, they have given rise to an extensive, sophisticated literature including important published colloquia of international scope.[3] What nevertheless remains somewhat undeveloped is the comparative dimension of this literature. Apart from the obvious practical considerations, a possible reason for this is the perceived uniformity of communist political culture. Like other aspects of the communist experience, the creation of a standardized party 'life' and personality has sometimes been seen as essentially transnational in character, with communism constituting a 'unitary system' which in the Stalin period was becoming not only politically but to some degree sociologically homogenized.[4] Where variations are acknowledged, these tend to be of a secondary or parenthetical character, insufficient to sustain meaningful comparison. However, if the standardized components of such a system seemingly offer no real basis for a comparative methodology, perhaps the corollary can also be proposed: that to the extent that such a methodology can be effectively employed, universalizing narratives of communist history may themselves be seen to be in some key respects partial or inadequate.

Without entering into the larger debate of which this forms part, these questions are explored here by revisiting the published memoirs of the British communist leader, Harry Pollitt (1890-1960), and comparing them with the analogous productions of his French counterpart, Maurice Thorez (1900-64), and the American party chairman, William Z. Foster (1881-1961).[5] Born into a socialist household in Droylsden, Lancashire, and joining the CPGB on its foundation in 1920, Pollitt was the party's general secretary almost uninterruptedly from 1929 to 1956 and a seasoned working-class activist embodying the qualities of proletarian authenticity thought indispensable in a communist leader.[6] In this respect, he was a stock figure of the Stalinist era, and the emblematic significance of his memoirs is such that one might expect them to conform rather closely to the conventions already established in Thorez's and Foster's texts. Indeed, the very appearance of these accounts in close succession has been taken to show the simultaneous or mimetic development of local Stalinist personality cults, here given the common form of the inspirational memoir.[7] Thorez's *Fils du peuple*, published in 1937, has attracted extensive commentary as just such a 'master narrative' of the exemplary communist life, and Claude Pennetier and Bernard Pudal have suggested that the French communist party (PCF) conformed particularly closely to the Stalinist canons of the time.[8] Foster's *From Bryan to Stalin*, dating from the same year, shares with it a number of defining features with which we can identify the master narrative. I shall discuss them here under the three broad headings of anonymity, teleology and combativity.

Both *Fils du peuple* and *From Bryan to Stalin* were published in British editions, and Thorez's account carried an effusive introduction by Pollitt himself. This itself suggests a degree of cultural and political proximity to British communism: if any parties might have displayed the homogeneity of popular-front era communism, it was surely those in the three leading western democracies. It is nevertheless argued here that Pollitt's *Serving My Time*, published three years later than the others in 1940, reveals significant differences in tone and content: at least as marked, for example, as those which Stefan Berger recently found in comparing British and German labour autobiographies.[9]

Such a divergence reveals more than something of their respective authors' personalities. Both *Fils du peuple* and *Serving My Time* had an explicit 'exemplary' function, providing a mirror to the party of the ideals with which its members were also to identify themselves. Pollitt's book was even subtitled 'an apprenticeship to politics', written so that its readers 'should so conduct themselves' as to fit themselves like him for political leadership.[10] Previously Pollitt had presented Thorez's account in much the same light, and in France its lessons for party activists were systematically promulgated.[11] Such productions do not therefore belong to some marginal realm of cultural autonomy, but have been held to encapsulate a sense of political identity whose significance was clearly understood by author, reader and party alike. In this perhaps lies the relativizing value of comparison. If, as is argued here, *Serving My Time* in some respects subverts the Thorez-Foster master narrative, then the exemplary party life has in this instance a more ambiguous significance. For, if the argument is accepted that the suppression of the individual personality acted as a mechanism of the 'total institution', then so, by extension, must the expression of personality have implicitly delimited it.

The identification of such productions with anonymity must at first seem perverse. It used to be held by some commentators that leaders like Thorez and Pollitt wielded an 'absolute power' within their parties analogous to that of Hitler, Mussolini or Stalin.[12]   The premature appearance of their memoirs – Thorez's when he was only thirty-seven – seems to confirm their standing as party satraps requiring appropriate literary expression, like the idealized portraiture then emerging as a favoured genre of socialist realist painting.[13] Nevertheless, as Pennetier and Pudal demonstrate, the individualization of the form was in many ways misleading. Even at the apex, Stalin was presented as the creature as much as the creator of the party, and the ideal-type communist leader lacked not only charisma but also any personal history or character traits that could set them apart from the party.[14] In the post-war people's democracies, autobiographies were initially not sanctioned at all as detracting from the collectivity; and after *Fils du peuple* it appears that no authorized autobiography of a living French communist appeared for another thirty years.[15] Equally, however, a biographical format could mask the effective subsumation of the individual personality in the larger collective myths of the party. As a Soviet art journal put it, also in 1937: in Stalin's portraits 'the "personal" and the "social" merge into one'.[16]

Fils du peuple conforms to these conventions in every detail. As Pudal, Stéphane Sirot and others have demonstrated, Thorez's life history provides no more than a vehicle for the party's collective values, embodied in its leader while at the same time assimilating him to the bureaucratic persona of the party. It is not so much that matters like Thorez's illegitimacy are dissimulated, for such conventional omissions would hardly distinguish the model communist biography from those of British Labour leaders.[17] Similarly, the falsification or evasion of political embarrassments is hardly without parallel in the lives of active politicians. Instead, what Pennetier and Pudal call the volume's 'anti-individualism' lies in the absence of almost any personal inflexion, whether true or false, and whether or not of any moral or political sensitivity. It has been aptly said that Thorez's 'I' is at no point 'a lived "I"', and is totally displaced by the 'we' of the party on his attainment simultaneously of manhood and party membership.[18] Everything is renounced, even in his origins, 'that might set him apart or single him out'.[19] Essentially, his ghost-written narrative is one of powerful collective myths with which its author's life is identified in a purely formal fashion.

Foster was born nineteen years before Thorez, in 1881, and nearly half of his *From Bryan to Stalin* is devoted to the forty years of his life before the communist party existed. Nevertheless, it is equally with Thorez's an exercise in anti-individualism, to which, by virtue of Foster's longevity, it adds an even stronger sense of the teleology by which the party as destination shapes the narrative almost from the cradle. Foster's basic object was to portray his progression from an honest but misguided syndicalism to the higher form of revolutionary consciousness which communism was held to represent, and which he repeatedly identified with the agency of the Russian Revolution and its leaders. His adhesion to the party was thus the hinge on which the narrative hung, in this sense resembling the 'second birth' which has been identified as a distinguishing feature of the lives of French and Italian communists.[20] To borrow Sandro Bellassai's expression, Foster's narrative epitomizes the 'exemplary presentation of one's own life story divided into "before" and "after" entering the party … [which] alone marked an existential watershed between the kind of hazy and defective personal "prehistory" and a new sense of completeness and maturity …"'[21] In this respect, the only fundamental variation in such narratives was in the point at which they began. Thorez's great political asset, as one of the 'Leninist generation' of the 1920s, was that politically speaking he had virtually no prehistory by which to have been contaminated.

Foster, meanwhile, was evidently made aware of his limitations as an autobiographer, for two years after *From Bryan to Stalin* he produced a second volume of purportedly more 'personal' reminiscences, *Pages From a Worker's Life*.[22] As his biographers note, though the narrative focus does shift from 'party' to 'class', the author's self remains obstinately submerged in the larger collectivity.[23] Moreover, Foster's dessicated attempt at a personal perspective was evidently incompatible with a developmental or even continuous narrative. Instead, what was effectively no more than a scrapbook of loosely connected sketches concluded with a section in which Foster the individual disappeared completely, to make way once again for 'Socialism Victorious' in the USSR.[24]

My third defining characteristic, 'combativity', is one which Pudal has identified both with *Fils du peuple* and with other contemporary biographical materials generated by the PCF.[25] Here I use the term in a more restricted sense than Pudal, meaning not just the 'struggle' to which every communist was theoretically committed, but the qualities of discipline, firmness and intransigence towards the 'class enemy' which Thorez himself used to invoke.[26] The significance of these attributes was further impressed upon communists by the cadre autobiographies collected by all communist parties, whose questionnaire format itself provided a sort of template for the model communist life, and which were used in France to record all compromising associations, including those with forces of the state, agents or police inspectors, journalists and 'members of enemy parties'.[27] This posture of total implacability is clearly displayed in *Fils du peuple*, where almost the only 'personal' anecdotes of the adult Thorez convey 'combativity' in this sense. In one scene, perfectly capturing the volume's utter unreality, Thorez is described ejecting an examining magistrate from his prison cell.

> Calmly and firmly I said to him: 'Excuse me, but I must ask you to get out at once. ... You may be a magistrate. ... But I am a Communist and a worker, a political prisoner with whom you have nothing whatsoever to do. Get out!'
> And without more ado he went.[28]

Foster, who was more credible in such a role, also punctuated his memoirs with constant clashes between communists and the forces of authority, as one can be sure that his life was also so punctuated. Replete with scabs, spies and gunmen, an entire section of his *Pages from a Worker's Life* carried the heading 'Agents of the Enemy'. Others, on 'Strikes' and 'Prison', conveyed the same basic message.

In contrast to the cadre biographies, there were no established procedures for the production of such narratives. Whether it is really true that their authorization came from Stalin, there was scope for a degree of autonomy that did not exist in matters of formal party policy. Even so, the basic parameters were clearly understood. In 1937, a first official CPGB history, written by the veteran Tom Bell and casually approved by Pollitt, came in for fierce criticism both from Moscow and within Britain and was withdrawn.[29] Repeatedly the demand was made for the closer scrutiny of all such works before publication, and for the wider dissemination of pro-Soviet materials.[30] Criticisms were routinely made of the CPGB paper the *Daily Worker*: that books by renegades were favourably reviewed, or party congress proceedings shown with empty seats, or an ex-policeman allowed to serve as ballet critic.[31] There were, in theory, no nooks and crannies in the Stalin era.

However, Pollitt's *Serving My Time* departed from the master narrative so far described in clearly signalled ways. From the handful of surviving draft chapters, it is clear that his text was worked over to remove inappropriate allusions or emphases, always in a sense that brought it closer to its international prototypes. Nevertheless, even the published version presents a narrative conforming to the wider conventions of British labour autobiography at least as much as to the special requirements of a communist party life. Of these, it may even be regarded as a somewhat heterodox vehicle.

Least of all could it be described as anonymous. On the contrary, Pollitt's autobiographical persona was delineated in a highly personalized narrative style drawing on the literary models of his own formative years. Foremost among them were Robert Blatchford's *Clarion*, with its occasionally rather overdone eschewal of pomposity, and the plebeian life histories of H.G. Wells, on whose *Kipps* Pollitt mentioned having once spent his 'last tanner'.[32] A characteristic Wellsian device, entirely foreign to the conventions of the communist life, was Pollitt's use of bathos, intruding incongruous details into solemn narratives, often with a sense of the ridiculous. This may be compared to the 'readiness to crack a joke in the midst of the most serious discussion' that even adversaries recalled as one of his most engaging, but also politically effective, skills.[33] Formally, there was nothing incompatible with Stalinism in the purely personal details with which he embellished his walk-on parts in History. Nevertheless, the accumulation of such details made for a more individualized account, with a vivid sense of time, place, occupational and associational culture. Consciously or otherwise, Pollitt projected himself very much as a personality distinguishable from his party.

At the same time, bathos was inimical to teleology. This is best illustrated by what should have been a political contest of considerable symbolic significance: Pollitt's 1929 Seaham election campaign, his first as party leader, against his ultra-moderate Labour counterpart, Ramsay MacDonald. It is true that references to popular indifference to his campaign have been excised from Pollitt's published text, and an admission that 'somehow or other we never seemed to get the votes' is transformed into the formulaic pronouncement that 'in every case these electoral fights have led to the strengthening of the fight of the workers against capitalism'. Nevertheless, even the published account depicts not so much the groundswell of inexorable social forces as a battling minority making little or no impression on the population at large. It is encapsulated in the story Pollitt tells of his humble Baby Austin, pelted with rotten fruit, confronted with MacDonald's glistening Rolls Royce and then suffering the final indignity of its wheel coming off. The scene closes with the candidate and his entourage pushing the car to the nearest garage to hoots of derision.[34] Told with a note of self-mockery entirely foreign to the canons of socialist realism, it is a long way too from the rhetoric of martyrdom and persecution associated with Labour pioneers like Keir Hardie.[35]

Such an anecdote calls to mind Arthur Koestler's perplexity on arriving in Britain to discover communists who were 'English' even more than they were communist, 'and, even more bewilderingly ... tended to indulge in humour and eccentricity – both of which were dangerous diversions from the class struggle'.[36] Pollitt was certainly aware of this self-perception of the 'English democracy' as, in G.K. Chesterton's words, 'the most humorous in the world'. Cited in a Labour memoir circulating in Pollitt's youth, Chesterton ascribed this to the English being 'quite undignified in every way', contrasting them in this respect with the Scots.[37] It was a well-established theme, and perhaps there is an echo of the old antagonism between Hardie and Blatchford in Pollitt's easy-going depictions of the wider populace and its foibles, including a shared fondness for drink. Perhaps these cultural distinctions need to be fed into generalized discussions of labour biography. Just as Scots have figured prominently in discussions of socialist 'martyrdom',[38] it is intriguing that Pollitt nowhere mentions even Hardie among his several glowing references to English socialist pioneers.

More than this, however, the communist teleology of Pollitt's memoirs was not merely attenuated by eccentricity but in some respects inverted, as Pollitt depicted his own 'glorious salad days' as a sort of golden age of working-class activism. Here there is no hint of a conversion narrative, or of anything 'defective' either in his personal 'pre-history' or in the social contours of the northern England in which he grew up. On the contrary, his induction into the socialist movement is conveyed with a nostalgic fervour confounding the expected development from lower to higher stages of political consciousness. Recalling the innocent salutations of the *Clarion* cyclists of his youth, Pollitt even defended these from the 'clever people' – obviously other communists – 'who today have fallen under the spell of phrase-mongering and scoff at such "sentimental stuff"'. Comparing their artless greeting of 'Boots!' and 'Spurs!' with the communists' clenched-fist 'Red Front' salute, Pollitt added that 'personally' he had 'never been enamoured of salutes, slogans and badges' – an extraordinary observation at the height of Stalinism.[39] In another passage, he commended the superior moral ardour of socialists like William Morris, citing Morris's pastoral utopia *News from Nowhere*.

There is not half enough of this type of propaganda today. We have all become so hard and practical that we are ashamed of painting the vision splendid – of showing glimpses of the promised land. It is missing from our speeches, our Press and our pamphlets, and if one dares to talk about the 'gleam', one is in danger of being accused of sentimentalism. Yet ... [this] gave birth to the indestructible urge which helped the pioneers of the movement to keep fight, fight, fighting for freedom, when it was by no means as easy as it is today.[40]

Pollitt might have added that the promised land already existed in the shape of Soviet Russia, and that communists were meant to be foremost in propounding its achievements. That he did not, as we shall see, will not have gone unnoticed in Moscow.

The honouring of Pollitt's formative influences even seeped over into his account of the party itself. Particularly in the aftermath of the Moscow show trials, 'renegades', that is, those who for any reason had broken with the party, were routinely traduced or else written out of party histories. In Italy, for example, references to the early 'leftist' communist Amadeo Bordiga were expunged from a 1940s reprinting of Giovanni Germanetto's memoirs, and 'Bordigism' was retrospectively constructed as a Trotskyist deviation.[41] In France, later editions of *Fils du Peuple* appeared with defectors or expellees removed from the photographs reproduced.[42] In Britain too, a passing allusion to Trotsky was removed from a speech reproduced in *Serving My Time*, and Pollitt had no hesitation in depicting as careerists the 'big-wigs' who had broken with communism. It was not, however, a blanket proscription, for Pollitt warmly recalled the suffragist and left communist Sylvia Pankhurst, expelled from the CPGB almost at its foundation and the nearest British equivalent to Bordiga. Far from dissimulating his own close involvement in Pankhurst's Workers' Socialist Federation, he pointedly described its members as 'the most self-sacrificing and hard-working comrades' he had ever associated with. For Melvina Walker, who like Pankhurst appears to have abandoned the CPGB for a more leftist alternative, he claimed to have had the same deep regard as that so eloquently attested for his own mother.[43] Given that one of the complaints concerning Bell's history had been its recognition of figures like Pankhurst at the expense of the CPGB's current leaders, Pollitt can hardly have been unaware of the unorthodoxy of this presentation.[44]

There is one alteration to his text that is particularly revealing. Describing how in the 1920s he was regarded 'more as a militant trade unionist than as a Communist', Pollitt's original draft contained a direct rebuttal of this allegation with the promise of a fuller explanation in a later chapter. This later passage was not published, and does not survive in a draft version. Nevertheless, the allegation itself remained and it is instructive to see how his text was now 'corrected' to concede the limitations of his trade union outlook and depict a formulaic progression to revolutionary maturity under the influence of Bolshevism.

All my activity had necessarily been in the workshops and trade unions, and naturally had influenced my outlook and way of looking at things. I was only beginning now to have the chance of studying the fundamental works of Marx and Lenin and, of course, the experiences of the Russian Revolution and the Bolsheviks were invaluable in helping me forward from an outlook based on militant trade unionism to Communism. [45]

This inserted passage has all the hallmarks of the master-narrative, for essentially Foster's memoirs are no more than a book-length elaboration of the same basic theme. Interpolated in such a fashion, it shows how Pollitt's life might have been constructed in more conventional terms.

The most singular feature of *Serving My Time* is the repeated transgression of the boundaries defining the model party life. As well as labour movement big-wigs, stock images were provided of political faint-hearts, and of the mill-owners and 'big nobs' for whom Pollitt's hatred even as a child was powerfully evoked. Interspersed with such passages, however, are episodes depicting individuals acting outside of their prescribed roles, often assisted by the Blatchfordian social lubricant of laughter. A favourite device is the depiction of individuals from opposing sides of the class or political battlefield, who nevertheless establish contact at a basic human level. Deployed so often as to suggest a sort of tacit political credo, it precisely recalls the Blatchford who taunted Hardie that his opponents were always 'malignants', and that Hardie was 'incapable of imagining such a person as an honourable soldier, sailor, or Tory'. [46]
     Examples from within the political left may be passed over as befitting the current communist rhetoric of working-class unity. This could not, however, be said of the foreman whom Pollitt described as securing him a job, because 'he was a member of the Salvation Army, and did not believe in punishing a man for his activity on behalf of the workers'; or of the Conservative Party worker who, in the Seaham campaign, inadvertently gave Pollitt a lift, only discovering his true identity on pulling up at his own destination. 'He stared for a moment in amazement, then burst out laughing and said, "Well, the joke's on me. Jump in. I'll drive you to Blackhall!"' This, by common consent, was the most embattled and sectarian period in the entire history of British communism. [47]
     Not only enemy parties but even 'bosses' could be caught in such moments of fraternization. Recalling his first expedition to workers' Moscow, Pollitt described in approved accents how irresistibly his loathing for the exploiters was further aroused by moving amidst their former surroundings. On the other hand, he also described having befriended on his outward voyage one of these self-same exploiters, whose family owned one of the London shipyards in which Pollitt worked. 'Well, to think that such a nice young man as you should be that man!', exclaimed his interlocutor, like the denouement in a West End play:

After that it was plain sailing ... and we had many interesting conversations about the Labour movement, the conditions of the workers and Socialism. When I returned from Russia I found a pile of books at my lodgings which had been sent by Mr Fletcher, and until he died he used to send me boxes of apples and pears grown on his estate. But they did not succeed in diverting me from my aims![48]

Told for some unexplained literary effect, the story has an echo in a private letter from one of Pollitt's employers of the 1920s describing him as 'an excellent workman and ... one of Nature's gentlemen'.[49] After his death, a former Special Branch detective even wrote to the *Times* to recall how Pollitt would invite him over for a drink, sit next to him on the top of the bus and if necessary protect a colleague from physical violence.[50] One of the curiosities in turn of Pollitt's recently released MI5 files is the almost benign tone in which 'Harry' and his activities are depicted, even down to his impromptu music-hall renditions at communist social gatherings.

Pollitt's depictions of the police themselves therefore require special mention. For both Foster and Thorez, police figured as brutalised symbols of class oppression, exposing the fraud of the rule of law and the disposition of state and employers to open violence. Pollitt's very different imagery may be illustrated by the contrasting tableaux which he and Thorez presented on the first page of their autobiographies. Thorez's opening scene is of a pit disaster, a socialist realist image with police portrayed like sentinels at the local colliery gates, keeping out the 'screaming crowds' as if oblivious to their common humanity.[51] Pollitt, by contrast, evokes a 'solitary dim light' in the mean, unpaved but seemingly placid street in which he was born, before adding irrelevantly that it stood near 'the house of the local policeman (whose wife proved a good friend to our family during many hard times)'. Seemingly gratuitous – for neither policeman, nor wife nor streetlamp are mentioned again – the allusion imperceptibly invokes a sense of community and of what Orwell would have called 'decency'.[52] The two other references to the police in *Serving My Time* are of a similar character. Even Pollitt's arrest on trumped up sedition charges, just four days after his wedding in 1925, gives rise to a notably indulgent recollection of how the detective set to interview him turned out to be the same 'pleasant gentleman' with whom he had unknowingly exchanged toasts during a weekend's honeymoon in Surrey. 'I can only say that my sense of humour got the better of me and I had a good laugh at having been so thoroughly taken in', Pollitt writes. By now this may perhaps be described as a characteristic emphasis.[53]

Police brutality in Britain was never on a par with what took place in France or the USA: these were not simply differences of literary effect.

Even so, more or less continuously up to the time at which Pollitt was writing, communists had been subjected to an arbitrariness of treatment as if beyond the pale of Britain's unwritten constitution. Consequently, it is the use that Pollitt made of such incidents that is significant. Even in prison, though he described conditions as degrading and brutalising to those who administered them, he also drew attention to exceptional figures who stood out for their 'really fine character'. One apparently was the prison governor, whom Pollitt asked for special leave to send his mother a birthday letter. 'He listened, quite unmoved, but, when I had finished, said to the warder, in as gruff a voice as possible: "See that A.44 has a special letter."'[54] In contrast to the standard communist memoir, Pollitt seemed set on depicting individuals as ultimately irreducible to the social or political roles with which they were publicly identified.

Harry Pollitt was an old hand. Experienced in his dealings with Moscow, he was fully aware that his book would nowhere be more closely scrutinised than by the hard, clever people of the Comintern: just as he knew that every comment he made at the CPGB's central committee, and every letter he sent to its Moscow representatives, was subjected to the same careful scrutiny. He knew perfectly well how to 'talk Bolshevik', or 'talk Stalinist'; and he also knew when he was not doing so. In explaining the differences between these autobiographies, variations of indigenous political culture therefore provide only part of the answer. The further question remains: why was Pollitt's indigenous culture allowed some authenticity of expression, when Thorez's in particular was not?

Several reasons may be suggested, all in some way linked with the peculiar circumstances in which the book was written. Though *Serving My Time* was constructed as an exemplary life history, culminating in Pollitt's becoming CPGB general secretary in 1929, it was commissioned and written at the time of his temporary removal from the party's inner leadership because of his resistance to the Comintern's initial line of opposition to the war. Relations for a time were badly strained, and the signing of the contract with the communist publishers Lawrence & Wishart would have signalled to both Pollitt and the party his continuing standing as one of the party's foremost leaders. This would tally with his restoration to the party's political bureau, against the initial instincts of the Comintern, just a month later, in January 1940, and by the failure to replace him by any single individual as the party's main figurehead.[55] According to intelligence reports, his fellow leaders understood that his 'popularity with the rank and file was such that expulsion or severely disciplinary action would have a serious effect upon the membership'.[56]

The signing of the contract is itself an interesting detail, as if party and individual were separate legal entities and even a general secretary's life remained his own intellectual property.[57] It also reminds us of the significance for these exemplary lives of their respective markets. In contrast to the 'protected market' of the much larger PCF,[58] the CPGB's literature had always circulated in quantities exceeding the party membership, creating a material dependency on this domestic market as well as on the Comintern. If communists like Wal Hannington started publishing authorized memoirs long before their French counterparts, and even before Thorez himself, this was partly because they depended on the income generated to support their activities as political campaigners.[59] With the apparent discontinuation of Comintern subsidies at the beginning of the war, and the return to their trades of a number of communist functionaries, eventually including Pollitt himself, *Serving My Time* may thus be linked with other activists' memoirs produced in circumstances of financial need.[60] In any case, if it was written for a 'Labour movement' readership and not just a communist one, both commercial and political considerations of the party's marginality must have been among the factors involved.[61]

A further consideration was that Pollitt more than any of his colleagues had the ability to reach this wider readership. After the CPGB's damaging display of subservience over the war, *Serving My Time* may thus be seen as an attempt to reaffirm the party's British credentials through its most plausible indigenous leadership figure. It was precisely this aspect, in opposition to the 'fable of "Stalin's agents"', that Pollitt's de facto successor, the austere pro-Moscow theoretician R. Palme Dutt, stressed in his *Daily Worker* review of the book.[62] In this sense, Pollitt's was a usable history serving the party's wider interests. Nevertheless, there was still the contract to be signed: exploiting Pollitt's personal qualities was only achievable by projecting him as an individual distinguishable from the party in a way that seems never to have been true of Thorez. One striking illustration of this phenomenon comes from the 1940 Labour Party conference held just a month after the book's publication. There, the veteran trade unionist Frank Rowlands, like Pollitt once a founder of the communist-sponsored Minority Movement, stood up to denounce the communists' latest efforts to undermine the war effort only to add the significant caveat: ' I pride myself on my friendship with Harry Pollitt – one of the best fellows I have ever met in my life – but he is in the wrong party.'[63] Nobody ever said that of R. Palme Dutt.

A final and more speculative conjecture is that Pollitt consciously used his memoirs both to project an image of Britain as a relatively tolerant and humane society and to articulate a vision of communism informed by the same values. The plausibility of this interpretation rests upon two bitter political disillusionments which Pollitt had suffered in the preceding two-and-a-half years. One was that over the war, and it is not difficult to see how the image Pollitt constructed of British society cut through the conflation of fascism and the 'bourgeois' democracies displayed in communist propaganda at the time he was writing. In many ways more disturbing was the arrest as a British spy in 1937 of Pollitt's former inamorata, Rose Cohen, who had moved to Moscow with her Russian communist husband in the late 1920s. Pollitt cannot have known that Cohen had immediately been shot. Nor can he have known that he was himself tentatively lined up for a Comintern show trial. He was, however, aware of what he believed to be Cohen's disappearance into a labour camp, and is said to have made strenuous representations on her behalf.[64] Already at this time, unspecified changes in the party leadership were apparently mooted.[65] It is a world away from *Serving My Time*, and is an aspect of Pollitt's life that is nowhere alluded to there.

Sadly, over this issue, as over the war, Pollitt always upheld the formal positions of his party, and in the longer term his concessions to *realpolitik* were to leave a deep residue of cynicism. For the time being, however, Comintern archives reveal how a note almost of national defiance entered into his internal communications with the Comintern. A few months earlier, in March 1939, he had responded to slighting references to British communists at the congress of the Soviet communist party with an apparent allusion to the Cohen affair, noting how 'if one crosses swords on a personal question there are all sorts of ways of getting a dig in later'. Addressed to J.R. Campbell, the CPGB's representative in Moscow, the letter ended unambiguously: 'One thing let me say Johnny, you have no need to be ashamed of your section of the C[ommunist] I[nternational]. The more I see of some others ... the more proud I am of our own Party. Forgive me for being British.'[66]

In the debate over the war in October 1939, Pollitt even described the Soviets as having been 'compelled ... to do many things which none of us expected ... at the price of antagonising very important sections of the working class movement':

I say this, and I only say what [other] comrades ... have themselves said but won't say for a book. That the thing that has disturbed them in recent months has been the disappearance of internationalism in the pronouncements that have been made from Moscow. ... I tell you there is enough thinking about the poor German people and not enough about the poor British people.[67]

No such comments were made in public: the 'book' – the stenogram that was made of all such deliberations – was only accessible to Comintern scrutineers in Moscow. Nevertheless, it is not difficult to find encoded in *Serving My Time* something of the same identification with the 'poor British people' and the values he saw as threatened by fascism. Perhaps, too, his presentation had a more personal resonance. Implicated as he was in the fate of Rose Cohen, it may be that subconsciously Pollitt needed to convince himself that not only gaolers and employers but also revolutionaries like himself retained their basic humanity in spite of the public roles they took upon themselves. Possibly it was not so much the honourable Tory as the decent communist in which Pollitt needed both author and reader to believe.

Comintern documentation about *Serving My Time* must rest in Pollitt's closed personal file. However, there is accessible a Comintern report on a newspaper article he wrote for May Day 1940, just a few weeks after the book was published. Perhaps this can function as a surrogate commentary, for the article is here described as requiring 'special attention', having appeared 'very unnecessarily' when an official manifesto was already in preparation. Furthermore, like Pollitt's concluding peroration in *Serving My Time*, it omitted any reference to the USSR and passed over the most obvious opportunities to invoke Lenin and Stalin.[68] The whole piece, the rapporteur concludes, 'sounds like the call of a – shall we say – *British revolutionary movement* (which ignores the Soviet Union)'. 'British' is underlined three times, with heavy disapproval. Its limitations as a dissenting text notwithstanding, re-reading *Serving My Time* one may speculate that this was precisely Pollitt's intention.[69]

6

A Mosleyite Life Stranger than Fiction
The Making and Remaking of Olive Hawks

Julie Gottlieb

Few without a specialist interest in the history of inter-war British fascism are likely to have heard of Olive Hawks (1917-1992). She was a young woman who rose to the position of Chief Women's Organiser of the British Union of Fascists (BUF, from 1936 British Union, abbreviated as BU) in 1940, and began her career as a novelist while interned in Holloway Prison under Defence Regulation 18B 1(a). Only sixteen years old when she joined the BUF in 1933, Hawks rose up rapidly through the movement's sex-segregated hierarchy as a result of both her firm and fanatical commitment to Sir Oswald Mosley, and of her talent for literary expression. After nearly four years interned, first in Holloway Prison and then on the Isle of Man, Hawks seemed to have emerged from her war-time experience with her reputation almost unscathed, and refashioned herself as a novelist, publishing four novels between 1945 and 1950.[1] In the light of the BUF's anti-Semitism and relentless mockery of the 'Jewish sciences' psychoanalysis and sexology, it was paradoxical that after the war Hawks also co-authored a practical guidebook for the young woman with Harley Street psychiatrist, gynaecologist and sexologist Eustace Chesser.[2] Her relationship with Chesser was one of many incongruous friendships and collaborations in her post-war story, prompting the historian to unravel the mystery of Hawks' political, psychological, and literary formation and various reconfigurations.

This chapter seeks to use Hawks' biography as a means to mine a more subterranean layer of women's political history, and to elaborate on an alternative version of female political leadership that, it would readily appear, could not jar more with the ideologies, ambitions and accomplishments of the noteworthy or even 'heroic' female politicians discussed in other chapters included in this collection. While this investigation of Hawks is by no means meant to be a celebration of her life, it does provide the opportunity - and the challenge - to put into practice the methods and theoretical concerns of women's history, and to test and contest the boundaries of feminist political biography. Therefore, on the one hand, this chapter makes no claim to the affect that Olive Hawks deserves a place in the pantheon of exemplary British political women. It does, however, claim that a study of a woman on the political margins can reveal much more about the dynamics of women's political inclusion and their self-representation in the so-called mainstream. On the other hand, it does not claim that Hawks was a Feminist, and it is important to differentiate feminist political action in the cause of the furtherance of women's emancipation within a democratic framework from female political action in the service of fascism, an anti-democratic, racist and even misogynist creed. Nor am I suggesting that the practical effects of her political work had great historical significance or consequence - no matter how much she and her follow Blackshirts would have hoped to see the dawn of a Mosleyite Britain in which they would have been rewarded with positions of power. However, it does claim that we can gain insight into the practice of feminist political biography by taking as I do here a subject who inspires little sympathy, and a woman with whom this biographer has more than some difficulty identifying.

Taking a methodological cue from Mark Rosen's outstanding *The Past in Hiding* (2000), I am likewise attempting to bring out of obscurity a past that has been in hiding. Olive Hawks' story is hidden in many archival and literary nooks and crannies. Nonetheless, certain key elements of her story will have to remain forever undiscovered; perhaps they are undiscoverable, most obviously because Hawks died in 1992 and does not seem to have left any personal papers or a memoir. Her personal story is so difficult to discover partly because it has only recently been in vogue to retrieve the lives and drives of the political 'losers' in the highly polarized and emotionally and ideologically charged street battles of 1930s Britain. A plethora of Mosleyite autobiographical accounts and personal testimonies have emerged in the past decades once former members felt confident that they could finally come out of political hiding, and could use the opportunity to set the record straight as they saw it.[3] Further, these fresh sources emerged at the same time as historians of British fascism began to archive the sources more systematically, and the Mosleyite-produced personal accounts were thus regarded as part of the record and of historical consequence. It has been the case even more recently that historians have become interested in the lives, the gendered experiences, and the narrative constructions of those British women who played roles on the losing side of these conflicts. Mosleyite memoirs and oral testimonies collected by researchers included those by women. Similarly, the appearance and the collections of these sources motivated historians to think more deeply about the gender dimension of the movement.

Olive Hawks' story is not represented in this swatch of documentary material. She did not write her memoir, and, as far as can be established, she was never interviewed by an historian. Nonetheless, the methodological and analytical questions that these other sources have inspired can still be applied to the study of her case. Furthermore, as will be detailed later, Hawks did leave a unique body of source material in the form of her novels, and one can thus attempt an analysis of personal narrative and examine the construction of memory by looking at her literary expressions. The literary documents provide clues to subjectivity and personality that would normally only be brought to light in oral testimony or explicit memoir.

Olive Hawks' story reflects and refracts several phases in the history of the British Union of Fascists and the British far Right. First, the initial surge of youth support that Mosley's movement exploited upon its formation; second, the mobilization and promotion of women in the ranks of the sex-segregated hierarchy of the movement; third, the communal life, and the social and sexual comradeship engendered by an extremist movement that also functioned as a thinly veiled secret society; fourth, the personal, psychological and intellectual crises experienced by many of the 747 British Union (BU) members who were interned under 18B during the Second World War; fifth, the diverse processes of physical and psychological recovery necessitated by the readjustment to civilian existence after the trauma of political imprisonment, especially the immediate response in the early post-war years when former-internees were regarded as virtual pariahs; and sixth, the ways in which former members of the BUF either regrouped or made the conscious decision to fall away and start anew.

Jeffrey Wallder, an associate of the Friends of Oswald Mosley (its resident amateur historian, in fact), has conducted valuable detective work on the lost years of Olive Hawks' life. As he wrote to me in 1997: 'I could write a book about my 15 year "Quest for Olive Hawks."' Like a good private investigator, Wallder has made the best of the laborious job of finding out what happened to Hawks after she left the movement, and still later after she emigrated to Australia in 1964 and fell off the face of the Mosleyite earth. However, Wallder's investigations have a clear motivation that is not shared by this writer. Wallder inflates the potential the movement had for escaping from the political margins, and he shares with other Friends of O.M. enthusiasts a counter-factual faith that had the right circumstances been in place, either during the crisis of the 1930s or during the crises catalyzed by the fraught racial politics of the post-war years, there was a real potential for Mosley to come to power. In this worldview, someone like Olive Hawks, who rose to the position of Chief Woman's Organiser by 1940, is seen to be the lost woman's leader of a plausibly imaginable Mosleyite Britain, the female counterpart - the British version of Gertrude Sholtz-Klink (the Nazi woman leader), if you like - to the British fuehrer and to Britain's lost dictator. He repeatedly refers to her as 'the Number One woman fascist in Britain', and concludes his revelations of her post-war life by saying: 'quite an obscure ending for someone who would have become the most powerful woman in Britain had a Mosley Government come to power.'[4] Thus an organization like the Friends of O.M. would like to find out what happened to a woman who they consider might have become Britain's *Fuehrerein*. However, even if I do not share Wallder's motivations, and while I diverge markedly from the Friends of O.M.'s ideological preoccupations and their desire to provide what they regard as corrective rehabilitating accounts of the BUF and its stalwarts, I have nonetheless embarked on a similar course of detective work.

Consequently, the question is how can the historian unweave the web Hawks herself wove to obfuscate her past, to camouflage her political origins, and ultimately, to go into virtual hiding and exile. I would argue that an important phase of this personal odyssey was to hide herself in her literary production of the late 1940s and early 1950s. The next phase was more explicit, and she almost completely disappeared from the public record, emigrating to Australia, and - to the best of my knowledge - made no attempt to either pursue her literary career or to remain in contact with her former comrades in the BUF. Other former members, and certainly many of her counterparts who were the more prominent members or who were holders of significant ranks in the movement, were to maintain these channels of communications well into the post-war period, culminating in the institutionalization of the old members' network and the memorialization of the 'good old days' in the Friends of O.M in the 1980s. Why did Hawks distance herself from this? How did she attempt her great escape? How can the historian gain access to her story as well as to her frame-of-mind?

While many literary critics have long rejected the notion that an author can reveal herself in her writing, or that the reader can claim any confidence in trying to discern the intentions governing the author's literary production ('the intentional fallacy'), the historian can nevertheless attempt a reading of Hawks' oeuvre as a means to locate the author herself. I am not asserting that Hawks' novels are explicitly autobiographical, but they do contain elements of only thinly fictionalized accounts of the author's own experiences, both what she witnessed and participated in as an activist in the BUF, and how she felt about and psychologized those experiences. This is especially true of her first novel *What Hope for Green Street?* (1945), but also more subtly true of her other novels, as well as of her collaboration with Eustace Chesser.

A related issue to consider is the generic and artistic significance of her writing. Hawks' novels, while of historical use and interest, are not of outstanding artistic merit. (However, having said that, they are not painful or excruciating reading either, and are remarkably readable and structurally fluent, evidenced by the facts that they were published at all and by mainstream presses, and elicited decent reviews). It should thus be possible to be more instinctive and intuitive when reading these novels, and put into practice a historically informed reader response theory when interpreting the novels.

Olive Hawks' novels were praised by the critics for their sincerity, honesty, strong psychological observation, as well as for being 'instructive and easy to read.' Hawks' life, on the other hand, is anything but easy to read. The questions that interest me are how she transformed herself from leading British fascist to post-war novelist; how Hawks managed the monumental shift from enemy of the state to mildly prolific post-war novelist, travelling in a circle of conspicuously anti-fascist writers; whether Hawks' novels reflect her fascist experience and continue to betray sympathy for the British fascist cause; whether her novels reflect this personal transformation, and subtly evoke themes of masquerade or imposture; and whether one can see a consistency between her fascist gender politics and her post-war concern for women's issues.

Clearly, Hawks' progress through life did not follow a predictable or a coherent path. What we can know about her comes from diverse sources. Up to 1945 her story can be pieced together from the articles she wrote in the fascist press, and from Special Branch and MI5 files which reveal more about her personal affairs, including her marriage to fellow-fascist Frederick Burdett, and her romantic entanglement and infatuation with the married Alexander Raven Thomson, one of Mosley's 'right-hand men.' According to the biographical notes contained in her post-war novels, Hawks was the daughter of a well-known architect. She spent her early childhood in East Thurrock, Essex. She was educated at Eltham Hill Secondary School. By 1950, either she or her publisher chose to gloss over the next phase of her life. The dust jacket of her 1950 novel, *A Sparrow for a Farthing,* euphemistically explained how 'she has been writing since her schooldays, but has also worked at a variety of jobs while studying social conditions in many parts of the country.' In fact, Hawks' experiences during the dozen years between 1933 and 1945 were a fair bit stranger than fiction. We know that the social conditions she studied, she studied through the eyes of a staunch Mosleyite. Still in her teens, Hawks did secure employment in the editorial department of the Amalgamated Press, as well as a post as reader for the Wellington Press, but by 1937 she merged her literary interests with her political convictions, and she was employed in the Research Department of the British Union.

Hawks' gender and generational profile made her a typical member of Mosley's BUF, a movement that made a pronounced appeal to the youth of Britain, and in which women accounted for 25 per cent of the membership.[5] The common presupposition of an antagonistic relationship between women and fascism was undermined in the British case by the fact that Miss Lintorn-Orman – a young, unmarried, ex-servicewoman – founded the first British fascist organization in 1923, and further complicated by the fact that three former suffragettes became leading figures in Mosley's movement during the 1930s.[6] Indeed, one of these former suffragettes, Mary Richardson, held the post of Chief Woman's Organiser of the BUF's Women's Section a few years before Hawks rose to that office. Perhaps we might even speculate that the political and ideological transformations implicit in each of these former suffragettes' journey from Edwardian feminist militancy in the name of inclusive democratic citizenship, to the desire to see the realization of a Greater Britain built upon the foundations of racially exclusive citizenship and dictatorial rule by the 1930s, provided a precedent and license for Hawks' own radical metamorphosis after the Second World War.

Nor was Hawks atypical among her female comrades for harboring literary ambitions. Other prominent women members belonging to the same generation who published their poetry in the BUF press included Joan Bond and Nellie Driver, and Anne Cutmore was also an aspiring poetess (using BUF headed note paper to jot down her verse).[7] Of the older generation of BUF women supporters, Mary Richardson had published a volume of poetry, and Dr Margaret Vivian was an aspiring novelist. Vivian published a first novel titled *Dr Jaz*, which she explained 'sold very well and so did the book on Antique Collecting.' Accompanying a letter to Mosley after the war, she sent her manuscript for *The Only Man*, which was presumably a fictionalization of her fascist beliefs. She asked Mosley: 'Do you think you would consider publishing it when the paper is more plentiful? Or shall you confine yourself to political treatises only? The general public reads mainly fiction, and a novel is, I think, the best way to make people understand what BU members went through in this "free democracy".'[8]

Olive Hawks was one of a handful of woman journalists readers of the British fascist press would have come to know. Throughout the 1930s, her contributions to the BUF's *Blackshirt*, *The Fascist Week* and *Action* were easily as frequent as those of the aforementioned three ex-suffragettes (Mary Richardson, Norah Elam, and Mary Allen), and as regular as the articles written by other fascist women leaders, such as Anne Brock Griggs or Olga Shore. Hawks' articles covered a number of issues, and she was a strong advocate of the position that only through fascism could the British woman realize herself politically. As a woman with literary aspirations, she was perhaps less critical of modern art and Modernist art forms than the aggressively Philistine fascist journalists who wished to see a return to a pre-modern ideal of Spartan manhood and aesthetic austerity. Nonetheless, Hawks conceived herself to be a social revolutionary. As far as this revolution would transform gender relations, she identified a moderate position: 'after centuries of oppression [women] are often going to unfortunate extremes to prove their independence from economic and moral custom. Fascism in this as in everything else, upholds neither the reaction nor the anarchy.'[9] She predicted that 'the fascist woman of the future will be neither narrow Victorians, nor sexless "arty" spinsters. They will be afraid neither of their brains nor their womanhood, but will dedicate both to clean wholesomeness of Fascist morality, and the service of the State which they are helping to bring into being.'[10]

Hawks did not confine herself to fascist prose, and she contributed poems too. 'We Live' and 'Chant for the People', the latter meant as an inspirational marching song, both put into verse the BU's anti-war position. They both spoke of the dead of the Great War, and the urgent need to save the youth of Britain from a repeat of the tragedy. They both expressed a deep and fanatical faith in Mosley's movement and its aims, and excitement at the use of revolutionary methods to prevent war:

> We are alive. Our scarlet banners flash in the wind,/ The symbol of unity floats o'er our lifted heads./ We hold ourselves straight like arrows eager for flight./ We are the fire-chastened instrument of revolution./ We are alive. In British Union, Britain shall live./ We are alive. We are revolutionaries cast in the ancient mould./ Much is asked in endurance, but we shall not fail./ We clutch to us our faith; we defend it; we challenge the world./ Not for us the peace of stagnation, the calm of surrender./ We will make Britain great again.– WE LIVE.[11]

They both considered the role of women in war and foreground women's suffering as part of the emotive appeal to prevent war: 'The Women./ Our hearts are dead;/ They died in vain/ When our men were killed,/ If our sons go again./ Our homes were broken;/ We toiled on our knees/ To keep our children – / For what ends but these,/ That like their fathers of twenty years past/ They should answer your call, and that thought be their last.'[12]. While not so explicitly anti-Semitic as to describe the coming war as the 'Jews war', Hawks nonetheless evoked the code words for undue Jewish influence, and the victimization of the British people at the hands of the Jewish profiteers, as exemplified by these lines: 'We will not go through the fire again/ For bankers and broker and confidence men.'[13] Hawks thus made every attempt to serve her political faith with her poetry and prose, although she was not merely a fascist of the pen, as evidenced by her inclusion in nearly every administrative aspect of the movement.

The British Union of Fascists consistently strove to be more than a paramilitary movement and to become a political party that would attain power constitutionally. With its origins in Mosley's New Party, which failed miserably to win any seats in the 1931 general election, the BUF was conceived as a more aggressive alternative to the 'old gang' parties. The starry eyes of party stalwarts were always pointed in the direction of inevitable parliamentary victory, which was the prerequisite for the reordering of the British state into the Corporate State of the utopian fascist future. Due to financial constraints and organizational weakness, the BUF did not run candidates in the general election of 1935. By 1936, however, the thrust of the movement was to prepare for the next general election by building election machinery, and by embarking on a vigorous canvassing campaign. The role and utility of women members became increasingly important once the BUF began to consider trying its electoral fortunes. The women were entrusted with most of the canvassing work, as the presence of a female Blackshirt on the doorsteps of the nation tended to dispel certain apprehensions of the BUF's hooliganism and violent temper.

Ten of the first one hundred British Union prospective parliamentary candidates were women, a savvy propaganda ploy as the three mainstream parties each ran less than 10 per cent women in the 1935 election. The BUF thus could, and repeatedly did, claim that its commitment to sexual equality and its dissimilarity from Nazi policies towards women were substantiated by the high rate of women parliamentary candidates. These preparations for the next general election were in vain, of course, as the outbreak of war in 1939 forestalled another general election until 1945.

As one of the starry-eyed enthusiasts, Hawks was easily enlisted to perform both roles in the fascist movement. First Hawks became the Women's Organiser in Lewisham in 1934. In June 1937 she became the British Union's prospective parliamentary candidate for Camberwell (Peckham), and in November of that same year she was appointed Women's Canvass Organiser for the 11th London Area. Her prospective candidature might have been merely nominal, but for the fact that Hawks did become embroiled in local politics in Camberwell. It seems that she actually instigated some controversy, and in line with the BUF's Jew-baiting, in June 1938 she was applauded by the fascist press for her role in preventing Lewis Silkin, 'Jewish MP,' from opening the new Odeon Cinema in Peckham High Street by writing letters of protest both to Silkin and the Press.[14]

As in the case of so many other young people who devoted so much of their spare time to the BUF, the movement simultaneously gave vent to Hawks' political convictions and to her social concerns in private life. Just as Hawks advocated a position against sex war in industry, so too did she participate in the pacification of sex war within the movement by fusing her political and love interests. Hawks' male counterpart in the Peckham Branch was a young man by the name of Frederick Edward Burdett. Burdett (born 1917, the same year as Hawks), had joined the BUF in 1933, and he became the District Leader for the Peckham Branch in September 1937. He was a commercial traveller by profession, but it was clear from his schooldays where his political sympathies lay.

As a schoolboy, Burdett wrote an essay about Mussolini 'which his headmaster sent to Italy, and in return for which he was given an autographed photograph of Mussolini, he then wrote a similar composition about Hitler and got back a letter from the German Embassy who pointed out that they could not possibly give him an autographed photograph of Hitler, but they rewarded him with a black and white printed etching.'[15] This early success encouraged Burdett to try his hand at pro-German journalism, and part of the Government's case against him when he was interned under DR 18B was that he had also been in touch with Konrad Henlein, leader of the *Sudetendeutsche Partei*, in order to obtain information for a book he proposed to write about Germany. He also contributed articles to the *Blackshirt* under his own name, and to the *Saturday Review* and other right-wing newspapers under the pen name Frederick Edwards.[16]

In Olive Hawks, Burdett found a genuine ally in love and 'anti-war', and the couple married in September 1939. He was open about his opposition to war well before such a position carried serious legal consequences. In an article entitled 'British Youth Refuse to Fight for the League of Nations,' he wrote: 'I watch events closely; should war come, I could be called upon to put on asbestos clothing and gas mask and pump fire and gas upon my fellow men, letting loose certain death - and yet I am not considered old enough to vote. I am old enough to be a pawn in this game of war, to become a perpetual cripple, to die a living death - but I am allowed no part in the choice of Government at whose command I am to endure all this.'[17] Burdett's enthusiast endorsement of Nazi Germany bolstered his anti-war stand, and in December 1939 he registered as a conscientious objector, appearing before the C.O. tribunal at Fulham Town Hall in April 1940, when his objection was disallowed. Only one month later his personal quandary about how to serve his beliefs in wartime were resolved for him, as he was arrested and detained under Defence Regulation 18B. After his first appearance before the 18B Advisory Committee, the Committee concluded that 'Burdett was a man of unstable character whose whole outlook was against the present democratic form of government in this country, and whose views are mostly tinged with sentiment in favour of Germany and the German method of government.'[18]

Hawks and Burdett shared this strong aversion to a war that would be fought against an enemy with whom they had profound ideological sympathies. While Hawks' post-war story would provide such a striking contrast to her dedicated involvement with fascist during the 1930s, she did, in fact, remain true to her fascist convictions until the bitter end of Mosley's British Union. Unlike others who prudently renounced their political diversions through British fascism once the war began in the interest of self-preservation, Hawks' remained true to the fascist cause even after war broke out. Indeed it was only in 1940 that she finally rose to the highest and most coveted office in the BU's women's hierarchy, becoming Chief Women's Organiser, after Anne Brock Griggs was 'dismissed from her appointment since the war on grounds of inefficiency.'[19] Hawks was a leading figure in the BU's Women's Peace Campaign, wrote the campaign's main propaganda pamphlet, and was consequently interned under Defence Regulation 18B 1(a).[20] At 3pm on 23 May 1940 Mr. and Mrs. Burdett were arrested at the headquarters of the BU at Sanctuary Building, Great Smith Street, London – she was conveyed to Holloway Prison, and he to Brixton Prison. A photograph of the young couple upon their arrest, their arms raised in the fascist salute, appeared in the *Daily Express*, the *News Chronicle* and the *Daily Mirror* (under the headline 'Britain Swoops on Fascists') on 24 May, 1940, thus insinuating that they were important members, even if their hand raising and hair-raising publicity stunt might also account for the coverage they received. Further, Hawks was among the very first group of the British Union's leadership to be arrested and interned in Holloway Prison. This was the same London women's prison that had once held another notorious group of women political prisoners, the Suffragettes, and was now commandeered to hold British fascists and enemy aliens.

In her autobiography, the BU Women's District Leader for Nelson, Nellie Driver described some of the ways in which the women 18B internees whittled away their hours of idleness in Holloway Prison. In the spirit of cultural exchange, Driver remember how on one occasion, 'our Wing gave scenes from Shakespeare, and we hoped the aliens would understand them. They would certainly have understood the joke if they had known that the balcony had given way under Juliet (Olive Hawks) and that she was hanging on with great self control and little else to support her.'[21] There was certainly something Shakespearian about Olive Hawks. Like Juliet, Olive lived her life from adolescence in an intense and romantic manner, giving her youthful energy to the fascist movement. Not unlike Juliet, Olive also had a forbidden love. Her Romeo was the much older and married Alexander Raven Thomson, and their relationship aroused a Montague-Capulet-like rivalry when both Olive's husband and Raven Thomson's family entreated the Home Office to intervene and prevent the two wayward lovers from indulging in their taboo expressions of affection. However, complementing the 18B women's farcical performance of Shakespeare's *Romeo and Juliet* in Holloway Prison, Hawks' story also betrayed elements of melodrama and tragic comedy.

There can be little mystery to how Oliver Hawks met and established a relationship of intimacy with Alexander Raven Thomson. They both worked at the BU's National Headquarters and they would have had ample time to get acquainted, as well as the opportunity to move beyond a working relationship, given their inclination. But the question of inclination is an intriguing one, and the solution to this secret has no doubt died with these seemingly mismatched lovers. Alexander was much older than Olive, and from the beginning of the BUF he was a figure of authority and high stature. He has been regarded as the 'intellectual' of Britain's fascist movement; he wrote books that provided the blueprint for the British Corporate State; and he was a frequent contributor to the movement's newspapers in which he outlined the form and organization of a fascist Britain. From 1934 he was Chief of the Research Department, the very same department that employed Hawks in 1937. He was also the BU's prospective parliamentary candidate for South Hackney. In March 1937, however, he was struck off the BU's pay roll together with some 70 per cent of the paid staff, but still opted to remain as a voluntary worker. He was also among the first BU leaders to be detained under Defence Regulation 18B, and he was one of the five leaders of the BU who were the last to be released in 1945. Thomson's wife was German by birth, and she ran a business in Haymarket called the Anglo-German Agency for Domestic Servants, which placed German women in service in English homes. Raven Thomson must have adopted his wife's daughter by a previous marriage, as it was Helga Thomson who was the most vociferous in condemning Olive as a vile home-wrecker and the grand manipulator of her vulnerable stepfather.

It is not clear whether Olive and Alexander consummated their love before they were each interned. All that is certain is that they conducted a regular correspondence while they were in different prisons. The impact of this correspondence was far-reaching, and it is also evident that Olive and Alexander were something less than discreet in the manner in which they conducted their affair, leading Thomson's step-daughter to describe Hawks in letters to the Home Office as an 'unscrupulous woman' who is 'driving her husband slowly insane with jealousy.' Indeed, Helga Thomson's letters to the Home Secretary, in which she sought to secure the release of both her stepfather and the man he had cuckolded, reveals a great deal about Olive's temperament and character as well as her firm position in the BU's inner circle. Helga wrote to advise the Home Secretary that Burdett's wife, 'the main woman leader of Mosleys[sic] organization—the only woman member with a big following, was the only one in Mosleys [sic] confidence...Hawks attended all secret meetings together with [Francis] Hawkins and Capt. Donovan.' Helga depicted Hawks as a dangerous and conniving woman:

> Hawks is driving her poor husband slowly insane with jealousy – her long love affair - easily proved by her correspondence with my stepfather - Raven Thomson is affecting Burdetts [sic] brain seriously ... Raven Thomson in the hands of this unscrupulous woman might become a danger to himself and his country -

removing her influence - he would revert to his old ... self - backed by his family - their same outlook on life and an non Fascist wife ... [R]emove Hawks' bad influence over him and so avoid a tragedy for the good of so many innocent people.[22]

By January 1942 all actors in this love triangle were still interned, and Olive had made it clear to the authorities that she did not want to be reunited with F.E. Burdett in the married camp on the Isle of Man. Olive had communicated this to her MP, Archibald Southby, who proceeded to explain to the Home Secretary that she was 'anxious for her case to be considered in conjunction with that of a certain Mr. A. Raven Thomson, now in Brixton Prison, whom she hopes eventually to marry.'[23]

But it was not chiefly this scandalous behaviour that resulted in Hawks' long internment under DR 18B. Indeed, Hawks was one of the last of the ninety-six British fascist women internees to be released. Her continued detention after appeal was assured by her unwavering political attitudes and her stated commitment to anti-war and anti-government activity if released. As a Home Office report of 1942 explained:

She has not only a devotion to BU but a personal reverence for Sir Oswald Mosley, and is now in a state of complete infatuation with Raven Thomson ... [S]he presents in her attitude all the most unsatisfactory manifestation of British Union ideology. All the nonsense of 'Mind Britain's Business' and the conclusion of peace without sacrifice of prestige or territory is still expounded by her. She assured the Committee that she would not do anything to hamper the war effort and Miss Skene, of the Women's Internment Camp, who had a long interview with her, is satisfied that she is a person who would keep her word if she gave it. Much time, however, was devoted by her before the Committee to explaining that she could not possibly give an undertaking ... to refrain from doing anything legally or illegally against the British Government. She argued that it was not right to ask her to give any assurance other than that she would keep within the law because if the law was inadequate then [sic] the law should be amended ... The Committee have reached the conclusion that she should be released 'not without moments of hesitation' and their recommendation is based on the view that the risk of her injuring the war effort by speech or otherwise is very small indeed ... On the other hand, so long as we maintain a policy of detaining any of the women Fascists, it seems to me difficult to accept the Committee's view that Mrs. Burdett, with her intransigent Fascist ideas and infatuation for the leaders of the movement, is a proper case for release unless we are to take refuge, as the Committee apparently do, in the view that she is a silly young woman and full of nonsense which it is to be hoped will subside in her mind after a few weeks of freedom. To release the husband without the wife will merely perpetuate the unfortunate domestic situation which the husband is anxious to remedy and may even have a bad effect on the husband's declared intention to assist the war effort. The alternatives are either to release both or to detain both. On the whole, though with some doubt, I think that we must disagree with the Committee and maintain detention for the present in both cases.[24]

Olive Hawks was still under detention in 1943, and she must have been released in 1944 or thereabouts. We know that her marriage had broken down by the time of her release as, rather pathetically, in a letter to Mr. O. Peake of the Home Office, requesting that he should be permitted to be employed as domestic help to the Mosleys after their release, Burdett made clear that 'in doing this I am prepared to submit myself to the same restrictions as those imposed upon Sir Oswald. I have no relations to whom I would wish to write and so have no objection to being cut off from the rest of the world.'[25]

It is at this point that we lose the colorful and spicy documentary trail, and from hereon the only traces of Hawks are subjective fragments conveyed through her novels. From her strained political and romantic 'bedfellowship' with Thomson, Hawks seems to have established more unpredictable associations shortly after the war. It is a perceptibly very different woman, still young, whom we encounter as the omniscient narrator in the four novels published between 1945 and 1950. By considering those she identified as her literary and personal mentors, we also encounter an appreciably refashioned woman in terms of political complexion and cultural influence. Each one of her novels is dedicated to a person of some note in British politics and letters, but most surprisingly, only one of these is dedicate to a fellow-Mosleyite. Her 1947 novel, *Time is My Debtor* is dedicated 'gratefully' to the novelist Henry Williamson, best known as the author of *Tarka the Otter*. Hawks' only novel with overt political content, *What Hope for Green Street?* (1945) is dedicated to Ethel Mannin, the sex reformer, anti-fascist anarchist and pacifist. Her 1948 novel, *These Frail Vessels*, is dedicated 'affectionately' to doctor, sexologist, and future literary collaborator Eustace Chesser. What Hawks and Chesser may have had in common in intellectual and temperamental terms is not entirely clear. However, one could speculate that Chesser's encounters with wartime legal strictures and censorship was not an experience that was completely dissimilar from Hawks' experience of internment. Chesser's *Love Without Fear: A Plain Guide to Sex Technique for Every Married Adult* (published in 1941, and selling 5,000 copies by June 1942), a study of sexual difficulties which included frank discussion of oral sex, was prosecuted under the Obscenity Act in 1942. In the end, he was found 'not guilty'.[26] Finally, her novel of 1950, *A Sparrow for a Farthing* is dedicated to Robert Lantz.

The dust jacket for *A Sparrow for a Farthing* explains that Hawks' first novel, *What Hope for Green Street?*, 'was discovered and launched by Henry Williamson, with the sympathetic backing of Ethel Mannin. Of her debt to these distinguished writers, she is always strongly aware.'[27] While it was well known that Henry Williamson was a Mosleyite, writing for the *Blackshirt* during the 1930s, and offering a very sympathetic portrayal of Mosley (fictionalized as Birkin Hereward) in *The Phoenix Generation* (1965), the other inspirational figure for Hawks was anything but an admirer of Mosley. Ethel Mannin was a novelist and political polemicist who articulated strong opposition to fascism during the 1930s. In Mannin's *Women and the Revolution*, Joannou has identified the 'orthodox Marxist view that gender was a secondary matter that ought properly to be subsumed into class.'[28] Mannin wrote that 'women alone cannot fight Fascism; the need is not for a new feminist movement, but for the cooperation of women in the general struggle for workers' power against capitalism of which fascism is only an advanced form.'[29] As was the case for many politically active women during the 1930s, resistance to fascism transcended feminist concerns. While Olive Hawks was rising up the rungs of the BUF's ladder during the 1930s, Mannin (1900-1984) was securely placed among British leftist revolutionaries, anti-imperialists, anarchists and pacifists. In 1937 Mannin married Reginald Reynolds (1905-1958). When an anti-fascist organization was formed for Spanish relief in 1937, Emma Goldman was appointed as its English representative, and Mannin its treasurer.

However, Mannin broke with her former associations, became particularly skeptical about the merits of the Soviet Union and expressed great irritation with the Communist Party of Great Britain, and even came to express opinions in her novels and letters which implied some sympathy for Germany. Mannin's letters to Allen Lane at Penguin, who published some of her novels, is revealing of her steps along this ideological broken road. Already in 1938 she complained to Lane that 'there are altogether too many labels handed out these days, and altogether too many rumours current in the literary world - as no one knows better than myself.'[30] In April 1940 she wrote to Lane to enquire why the publication of her latest novel was being held up: 'Are you holding up publication for *Cactus*? I hope not until this disgusting war is over.'[31] In June 1940 Mannin wrote to Lane that she felt 'it might be well to abandon the idea of doing *Cactus*. The "hun-hate" is now so acute that the heroine's love for a German prisoner-of-war in the last war might not be particularly acceptable!'[32] Thus, Mannin's own experience of personal and political dislocation and remaking was not completely dissimilar from that of Hawks.

The intriguing question is how Mannin and Hawks came into contact, and how they established their mentorship. Their initial contact must have been made during the war when Reynolds and Mannin regularly visited 18B internees in Holloway Prison. As Reynolds explained:

> Ethel and I detested fascism, but for the same reason we also detested this barbarous business of interning people against whom no charges could be brought which would have satisfied any court of law. It was only by degrees that we learnt of the grosser injustices and of the infringement even of their own regulations by the highest authorities. Ethel and I found ourselves, step by step, drawn into sympathy even with self-confessed fascists who were the victims of the system. At least they did not pretend to believe in democracy and were to that extent guiltless of hypocrisy.[33]

While Hawks is nowhere mentioned by name in this evidence, the couple did come across a fascist prisoner who was kind to Resi, the young German Jewish girl interned under the Emergency Regulations whose case had initially interested the couple in conditions in Holloway under the defence regulations. 'A fascist fellow- prisoner, such is the paradox of shared suffering, was kind to Resi. And when Resi left Holloway she asked us to visit this woman sometimes, as she had nobody to care for her. Apart from feeling gratitude, we were willing enough.'[34] This woman might not have been Hawks, but these visits to Holloway must nonetheless have brought Hawks and Mannin in contact. It is also perhaps no coincidence that Hawks' first novels were published by Jarrolds, Mannin's own publisher.

At first glance, the political polarization between Hawks and Mannin could not be more striking. However, Mannin and Reynolds were pacifists first and foremost, associated with the Society of Friends, as well as staunch anti-Zionists. In 1939-40, Hawks was a leading figure in the British Union's Peace Campaign, and through her intellectual interaction with the BU's anti-Semitism, she was also likely to have been keenly anti-Zionist. Upon closer analysis, Hawks and Mannin were coming to share more political common ground as the war wore on, political sympathies that no doubt facilitated a degree of personal empathy.

What might have Williamson, Mannin, Chesser, and Lantz seen in Olive Hawks and what spark of originality and talent did they discern in her that they might have hoped to stoke? In the last part of this chapter I discuss two of Hawks' novels. I have chosen to concentrate on *What Hope for Green Street?* and *These Frail Vessels* because, on the one hand they contrast with one another in terms of theme and content, and, on the other hand, because they are both nonetheless typical in terms of structure, genre and style of Hawks' entire literary oeuvre. Neither of these novels could be considered overtly fascist, even though *What Hope for Green Street?* is set during the 1930s in the BUF's East End stronghold, and ends with a Mosleyite critique of social conditions in the present, and an epiphany of Mosleyite hope for the future.[35] Nor should either novel be considered feminist in ideological outlook nor in motivation, although *These Frail Vessels* is concerned with 'displaced' and 'unfulfilled' women, questions the significance of women's liberation in the lives of the 'normal' and unremarkable women who must work for their sustenance, and who are shackled by the dream of wifely domesticity which remains outside their reach. Both novels rely on social and psychological observations, with generic similarities to social realism; they are, essentially, both theatrical ensemble pieces, with large casts of protagonists drawn in with thumbnail character sketches. Indeed, we could speculate that the psychological impressionism this entails might well be a form of evasion, an escape from the individual into the quasi-anonymous mass, and a process that runs parallel to Hawks' own recasting of her own personality, and her endeavor to return to normality after the politically and romantically intense moments in her recent past.

What Hope for Green Street? is the only one of Hawks' novels which engages with what might be considered her own past and her own experience of fascist politics – in fact, it is the only one among the four novels that deals with politics at all.[36] Set in the 1930s in Bethnal Green, the East End of London, the novel focuses on one working-class family during the depths of the Depression. Through a family saga, it is an attempt to represent and psychologize the recurrent themes in the BU's propaganda – the fictionalization of working-class life is a vehicle for an illustrated manifesto of and an apologia for British fascist policy. Although Hawks implies a certain intimate knowledge of working-class life in *What Hope for Green Street?* the reader is left with the indelible impression that the omniscient narrator is actually an outsider, a middle-class stranger peering in the window of a typical Green Street terrace. The narrative tone is meandering, undecided, and distant, and fails to penetrate beyond the surface of caricature, and in this sense it has all the hallmarks of blatant propaganda. The very title of the novel, posed as a question, evokes the social investigations (and mass observations) of the 1930s, and suggests a certain non-committal distance from the subjects of her investigation. However, this is certainly not impartial or socially scientific social investigation, and the Mosleyite bias is unashamed. The working class are objectified, their lives used for overtly didactic and polemical purposes. Hawks' does attempt to achieve authenticity by mimicking the dialect and dialogue of the East Ender, but this conceit tends to exacerbate her middle-class condescension.

The main tenets of British fascist ideology are personified through the members of the significantly named Smith family. The Smiths stand as an icon for the common family, for every family. The repression and poverty of young manhood is expressed though the son Charlie who 'had not had a job for three years, since he asked for a raise when he turned sixteen. For that he had been sacked ... So he fooled around with drink and girls.'[37] The precariousness of female employment and the tragedy of non-unionized female labour in the catering trade are illustrated through daughter Alice, a seventeen-year-old girl who works in an East London teashop. One of the main planks of the BUF's women's policy was the capitalist exploitation of female labour. In the novel, at Alice's workplace:

A new girl, who usually kept quiet, spoke from the end of the table, looking up with intelligent dark eyes. 'Exploitation will always go on so long as we don't keep together. That's what's wrong with the working-class – especially the women. No solidarity. 'Oh and that's what you think, is it? Well, how the hell are we going to keep together when there's always somebody ready to step into our job, or take it for less wages if they can? Fine sort of solidarity! And you can't help it. We'd do it ourselves if we was out.'[38]

The wreckage, and courage, of British womanhood is personified by the mother of seven who constantly frets about her struggling offspring, and who comes to support the British Union at election time. The East End working-class sympathy for Mosleyite precepts is personified by the father, who, although a dedicated Labour man, comes to see the sense of British fascism. Inevitable class conflict and the haughtiness and smugness of the British middle class is illustrated by the son-in-law Herbert, who expresses sympathy for the Jews in Nazi Germany, but is immediately shouted down by the powerful figure of his John Bull-like father-in-law, who appears to speak from first-hand experience about Jewish exploitation and corruption in his locality. Significantly, the unsympathetic Herbert is married to Millie, who cannot conceive a child because the effete Herbert is also impotent. Daughter Millie herself is a trope for the racial degeneration of salt-of-the-earth British stock. Millie's doctor laments:

Fine women! ... Fine and healthy bodies, that ought to have mothered fine children! With good homes, into which a child has a right to be born! People who can afford to give them an education, a background and a start in life! And all they do is think of their figures ... What's going to happen to the country, with foreign governments subsidizing the bearing of children? ... What's going to come of it? Extinction! Race suicide! The fit won't bear children and the unfit will breed![39]

While each member of the Smith family functions as a personalized anecdote for the inherent justice and common sense of British fascist proposals, only one member of the family actually joins the movement. Son William Smith, 'of Green Street, shop assistant, saw himself as one struggling against all the evils and the obsolescent system of financial democracy, whereby distressed areas, unemployment, desolate agriculture, the slow sapping of British virility, were perpetual and inevitable.'[40] This passage could well have appeared in the *Blackshirt* itself as it reiterates the British fascist lexicon almost exactly.

Further, it is significant that although Hawks makes many references to a British fascist organization, and to marches, speakers, processions, violence, and the fascist political programme, she never calls the movement by its name and never identifies it as 'fascist'. Even when Bill joins the movement and becomes an ardent member, Mosley's name is never uttered. It is as if Mosley is a demigod whose human nature can never be spoken. There may be a number of possible explanations for this conspicuous nomative absence. First, censorship: Hawks wrote the novel when she was interned and when her activities were restricted under DR 18B. Part of these restrictions was a regulation against internees publishing. Second, the novel is a *roman a clef*, written for those in the know, and she is confident that the ideals of the British Union speak for themselves. Third, when she was writing in the last years of the war, she may also have been trying to expound the philosophy of the BU without giving it the taint of a now discredited and defeated political creed. Finally, and less speculatively, throughout the 1930s and 1940s Mosley and the BUF were fictionalized by an array of prominent writers but never was Mosley or his British Union of Fascists mentioned by name. It was thus already a well-established literary convention by the time Hawks was writing to obscure the identity of the BUF and its leader, as if the BUF was the movement and Mosley was the leader 'that dare not speak its name'. In Aldous Huxley's *Point Counter Point* (1928) Mosley was fictionalized as Everard Webley and his movement was called the Green Shirts. In Nancy Mitford's *Wigs on the Green* (1935) pressure applied by the author's sister and Mosley mistress, Diana Guinness, forced the author's pen, and Nancy had to expunge most references to her Mosley character, Captain Jack, although the novel offers lengthy parodies of Captain Jack's organization, the Union Jackshirts. In P.G. Wodehouse's *The Code of the Woosters* (1937), Mosley appears as Roderick Spode, leader of the Black Shorts. In H.G. Wells' *The Holy Terror* (1939), the Mosley figure is fictionalized as Lord Horatio Bothun, leader of the Popular Socialists. In Winifred Hotlby's play *Take Back Your Freedom* (published posthumously in 1939), the Mosley-like character is given the name Arthur Clayton, leader of the People's Planning Party. Nor was this convention reserved for anti-Mosleyite writers. Even in Henry Williamson's *The Phoenix Generation* (1965) Mosley appears 'undercover', and in *The Mill*, an unpublished novel by Nellie Driver, Mosley is re-christened Manly, leader of the 'Buffshirts'.[41]

Even if Hawks could not bring herself to call the BUF by name for any or all of the above reasons, the novel clearly illustrates her feelings about the movement and its aims. The narrative of *What Hope for Green Street?* closes in August 1939, on the eve of war, when the increasingly tragic hero William Smith is forced to confront the impending doom of war. William Smith also has the last word, and it is his British fascist perspective that gives meaning and interpretation to the social, financial, national, racial and sexual crises of inter-war Britain. Significantly, Hawks' fascist protagonist is male and working-class, and thus differentiated from the author herself by both gender and class. Hawks offers a very different version of working class existence, and evokes an imagined working-class solidarity from the perspective of the extreme right. *What Hope for Green Street?* is a politically inverted *Love on the Dole*, and could very well have been subtitled 'Mosleyites on the Dole.' *What Hope for Green Street?* is just the kind of novel that we could expect from Olive Hawks, feeding as it does on her own political perspective, building on the propaganda themes in the BUF newspapers to which she contributed during the 1930s, and, as the novel reaches its climax with a patriotic cry of despair as war approaches, it also serves as a retrospective apologia for Hawks' own unswerving dedication to the BU's anti-war campaign

Hawks' 1948 novel *These Frail Vessels*, provides a very sharp thematic contrast to *What Hope for Green Street?*. By the time Hawks wrote *These Frail Vessels* it was very clear that her passion for fascism had been translated and transfused into a passion for psychology and the close observation of quotidian human behaviour. It is no coincidence that this novel was dedicated to Eustace Chesser, with whom she was soon to collaborate on *Life Lies Ahead: A Practical Guide to Home-Making and the Development of Personality* (1951). While the novel is set in the immediate post-war period, focusing on a confined social space of a house of women who live a very precarious and uncertain existence at the imperious-sounding No.39 King's Drive in London, there is very little reference to the historical moment or the consequences of the Second World War itself. The house itself is symbolically very important in *These Frail Vessels*. It is a gendered social space which evokes middleness. It has a life of its own. The address is evocative of the middle-of-the road, a middle England, middle age, complementing the mediocrity, the middle age, and the lives in parentheses of the women who inhabit the dwelling. 'Standing secure in the curve of his arm, looking out on the sunlit morning, Fanny [the proprietress] thought how, after all, the life of the house would go on in a similar pattern for year after year yet to come ... Strangers would come. More girls with hopes, sorrows and joys of their own— with lovers or cats and a few pounds a week hard-won in office or workshop as all their endowment. Two more girls in the places of Clare and Louise, and another later for Christine, stiff and awkward at first, but in time good friends of them all. For they'd be the same kind of girls, glad to have somewhere nice to come home to. She and Benny would have a new family, that was all.'[42]

Although the novel begins precisely in September 1946, and ends even more precisely on April 4th, 1947, the historical specificity of the temporal parameters is de-prioritized. Rather, time is a rhetorical construct and a structural device. The time span is clearly defined in order principally to emphasize the cyclical and circular nature of personal, biological, seasonal, and sexual evolution. As I have suggested, the absences in Hawks' literary production are as intriguing and informative as the presences, and no silence could be louder than the complete disinterest in politics, either of the extreme or the mainstream variety, in *These Frail Vessels*.[43]

The protagonists in the novel are half a dozen women who are united by their loneliness, their displacement, and their involuntary deviance from the envied model of the loved wife. Each of their lives has been fractured by the war, and they are either coping with a broken marriage, forlorn spinsterhood, or a broken heart. Yet for their failure to find fulfillment in marriage, in men, or, conversely, in a productive or liberating career, they are meant to represent the average and the overlooked common denominator of female experience. They are the surplus women from another world war who find that marriage is actually 'the natural fulfillment so many thousands seemed somehow to miss.'[44] The omniscient narrator makes a stand for the integrity, the identity and the desperation of these women, and if Hawks' has a politically informed point to propound, it would be that 'the true "career woman" was rare.'[45] If *What Hope for Green Street?* can be generically categorized as a key novel, then *These Frail Vessels* might be described, almost literally, as a 'through the key-hole novel.' The interiors of No. 39 King's Drive come alive as we are invited into each woman's room to listen to chatty conversations about mundane matters, to witness nights of restless sleep and interpret frustrating dreams about treacherous lovers, or to follow, step by step, the rehearsal for a suicide attempt.

However, the novels do not offer the historian an unobstructed view through the keyhole into the author's own life or her psyche. From the perspective of the biographer, it seems as though, with *These Frail Vessels*, Hawks is engaging in a process of imposture, reconstituting herself as an empty vessel, and annulling her pre-war self. I would argue that Olive Hawks' right to notoriety and historical notice owes far less to her rather unremarkable and disjointed prose style conveyed through her conservative, meandering and episodic novels, than to her life story and her own transformations and mystery. Olive Hawks – the adolescent fascist, turned imprisoned *femme fatale*, turned post-war novelist – is far more interesting than fiction, and a far more compelling character and psychological study than the myriad of superficially sketched female protagonists in her post-war novels. Her fictional characters are a pale image and replica of the writer herself.

In this regard it is interesting to note how Hawks' described her temperament and existence by 1950, two years after the publication of *These Frail Vessels*. As the dust jacket for *A Sparrow for a Farthing* explains:

> She now lives in an eighth floor London flat where she is happy with her typewriter and what she claims to be the most striking view in Town. She believes the good life can only be made from within, the individual striving through human errors towards discipline of self and understanding of others.

There is a discernable sense of sadness and personal tragedy in this self-representational passage, mixed with a devotion to the solitary life of the author, a love of England and the London landscape (which she sees from a birds' eye view of the tower of the modern metropolis) and a cry for forgiveness for past indiscretions. She appears to be making an appeal for others to understand her, as well as suggesting that her own views have changed and that she is reformed. However, it is also worthy to note that this inner drama (psychomachea), this personal reassessment, is played out in the public domain and in an open space—she has no qualms about letting the reader into her private and solitary flat on the eighth floor. Hawks' condition is a self-chosen solitary confinement, with no inkling of her past and her rites of passage through Mosley's British Union of Fascists. However, at the very least, she is still visible, no matter how camouflaged and remade.

If we lose the documentary trail after 1945, and catch the last glimpses of the author through her literary persona by the early 1950s, then we completely lose sight of the enigmatic Olive Hawks when she ceases to publish her work. What little we do know of her life after this time is the result of Jeffrey Wallder's relentless detective work. Wallder has discovered that she eventually married a Greek soldier, had two sons, and later moved to Australia. In 1992 she died alone in Perth, and it was some days before her body was found. It is unclear whether she left any other manuscripts, although Wallder assumes that such a woman would have written her memoirs. These have not, however, been found.

In conclusion, there are a number of ways in which the historian can gain access to a figure like Olive Hawks, and not merely retrieve the colorful detail of her biography, and a number of reasons why her particular story has wider significance. Her web of contacts, ranging from significant figures in the medical, the political and the literary spheres, are interesting in themselves, and suggests the permeability of social and intellectual borders, the same permeability that helps us understand the double life that an Oswald or a Diana Mosley could maintain, regardless of their extremist politics. The correlation and codependency between Hawks' political and intellectual endeavors and her love affairs -consummated with Burdett, Thomson, and Chesser (there is a persistent rumor that Hawks and Chesser had an affair) and unconsummated with her idolized Mosley - also suggests that even the most ambitious and independent-minded political woman of that time could not achieve her ambitions in the absence of a male patron and mentor. Therefore Hawks' story gives another meaning to the slogan 'the personal is political'. The ways in which Hawks' transfused her youthful enthusiasm for inter-war British fascism to literary production after the war reveals something about the Romantic temperament of and modes of expression favored by British fascist women, and invites the historian to cast the empirical net wider than official sources and oral testimonies in the attempt to uncover feminine fascist subjectivities. Her post-war career as a novelist also indicates the freedom former-internees had following their release and after the war to reform and remake themselves. It is significant that Hawks was never blacklisted as such, and that there were no constrictions on her freedom to rejoin civil society, and even to engage with members of the pre-war anti-fascist intelligentsia.

This chapter has taken an interdisciplinary approach - empirical investigation and detective work, literary criticism, and psychological analysis -as a means of bringing one woman's past out of hiding. It has also pushed the boundaries of feminist biography, most obviously by taking as its subject a woman who does not elicit much sympathy and who does not stand out as an exemplary feminist life, and more subtly by providing parallel narratives of Hawks's story and the biographer's methodological and even psychological confrontation with the subject. But is Hawks worthy of notice and micro-historical research? There is little doubt that she deserves notice insofar as she craved political power, exemplified by her ambition within Mosley's BUF. She engaged with the media of persuasion, in the form of her propaganda work for the BUF before using her novels, especially *What Hope for Green Street?* as vehicles for her ideological preoccupations. Finally, Hawks possessed a personality that is at once historically significant as well as the stuff of her own fiction and the stuff of 'historical fiction,' the latter, arguably, being an inevitable and inescapable component of biographical research.

Winston Churchill and the 'Men of Destiny'
Leadership and the role of the Prime Minister in wartime feature films[1]

Jo Fox

'I am writing to you to express my warm thanks to you and your society for your kindness during these past years in making so many films available to the Ministry of Information for me to see. They have given me much pleasure and relaxation during the hard times through which we have passed'.[2] Just over one month after the official end of the Second World War in Europe, Britain's wartime Prime Minister, Winston Churchill, took the time to drop a note to Major Baker of the Film Renters Society, thanking him for providing films to the Government for the duration of the conflict. This note exemplifies the importance that Churchill placed on film as a means of information, propaganda and entertainment. As studies have demonstrated, Churchill saw the cinema as a conduit for the representation of leadership, and there is considerable evidence that he himself drew confidence from it.[3]

In a crisis, leadership and inspiration become all the more important and, during the Second World War, the question of confidence and sustained morale was decisive. The home front and the front lines needed to have faith in the leadership's ability to conduct the war, as well as having an inspirational character that could act as a beacon for the values of the nation. As early as September 1939, the Home Publicity Sub-Committee of the Ministry of Information (MoI) noted, 'trust in leadership is an enormous factor in maintaining confidence'[4]. The focus in Britain was concentrated around the figure of the Prime Minister. The aim of the war propagandist was to ensure that the leader of the nation became the embodiment of the core values of the overall war propaganda campaign, outlined by the Home Publicity Committee. These values were justice, strength, efficiency, readiness for sacrifice and toil, commitment to freedom and truth, unity and a determination to be victorious.[5] Winston Churchill quickly became the embodiment of these values for the nation, with propaganda in various media stressing the link between the leader and the war effort. In film, one of the most influential media during the war,[6] the depiction of leadership and the leadership of the Prime Minister became a central issue for both the public and the Prime Minister himself.

This chapter will concentrate on the historical depiction, favoured by filmmakers, propagandists and the public alike for its escapist value, its ability to depict issues of present concern thinly veiled by historical parallel, and its provision of comfort to a population facing intolerable hardships, convincing them that, as the past had shown, they would overcome them. Moreover, the historical depiction of leadership fitted well with Churchill's own strong vision of self-presentation, aware of the political dangers of over-glorification in the public mind. Many studies have already explored the depiction of the past with reference to leadership and its propaganda value.[7] However, this chapter will attempt to interpret Churchill's perception of his own image as a leader and how this was reflected in films during the Second World War and how the historical films of leadership reflected public opinion of Churchill, evidenced by the findings of Mass Observation. Judgements have been made as to the propagandistic success of historical films such as *The Prime Minister* and *The Young Mr. Pitt*. Given that it has frequently been observed that propaganda is most effective when it plays upon pre-existing opinions and beliefs, this chapter attempts to discern whether there is an observable correlation between the filmic images presented and pre-existing popular opinions, and to ascertain whether that 'popularity' in terms of propaganda and persuasion can be related to public opinion regarding politics, leadership and war.

It has often been said that Churchill himself was a 'film fan'.[8] He certainly had a better appreciation of film as a propaganda tool than his predecessor, and a stronger relationship with the film industry, as documented by the contemporary film press.[9] He had particularly good relations with the film-maker Alexander Korda[10] and often assisted in war productions for the industry[11] such as *Desert Victory*[12] and the MoI short film, *The Biter Bit*,[13] although his attempted interference on Powell and Pressburger's 1942 film *The Life and Death of Colonel Blimp* caused much irritation to both his Minister for Information, Brendan Bracken, and the film's producers, Archers.[14] Indeed, the US promotion for the film encouraged filmgoers to 'see the film Churchill tried to ban', in an attempt to increase its potential box-office takings.[15]

There is also evidence to suggest that Churchill used film as a political tool in domestic and international spheres. The Prime Minister recognized the importance of film, as a record of contemporary events, as a means of distraction and as a way of understanding both allies and enemies. To bring film into politics, he suggested to Bracken in September 1941 that the MoI should 'try to arrange a cinema in the

House of Commons', where members might not only see British films, but also German and Russian productions.[16] In addition, Churchill's great passion for the cinema was also shared by other contemporary Allied leaders, prompting the exchange of key films between governments. *Desert Victory* was one such key film that Churchill was keen to distribute amongst Allied and Commonwealth leaders, in particular to Franklin D. Roosevelt,[17] Joseph Stalin,[18] Mr Frazer[19] and Field Marshal Smuts.[20] Films were exchanged between the leaders, who attempted to ensure the distribution of allied films in the individual national cinemas. On receiving *Desert Victory*, Stalin assured Churchill that the film would 'be widely shown [to] all our armies at the front and among the widest masses of the population'.[21] In return, Stalin forwarded the Soviet film *Stalingrad,* which Churchill 'hoped' would 'be shown widely in this country so that all may have a chance of paying tribute once again to the immortal defenders of Stalingrad'.[22] The leader, therefore, provided a valuable means of ensuring theatrical distribution of documentary films and newsreels.

Nevertheless, given his enthusiasm for the cinema, it is interesting to note Churchill's own reluctance to be portrayed in film, and particularly feature film. During the course of his premiership, various producers, particularly from the United States, were keen to capitalize on the Prime Minister's global appeal. *The Cinema*, a popular trade newspaper, reported on 13 November 1940, that Warner's had plans to make a film of Churchill's life, energetically commenting that, 'the Prime Minister's story certainly offers fine screen material – from [his] Harrow school days, through army life to his finest hour, every bit a colourful record of energy and action'.[23] Just five months later, in April 1941, a telegram from Viscount Halifax, ambassador to the United States, to Churchill suggests that the Prime Minister had approved a script by John Colton for a film of his life. The film was to be produced by James Roosevelt,[24] son of the US President, who had already visited Chartwell to see Churchill prior to the outbreak of the war.[25] Halifax noted that 'such a film would be useful under present conditions if it were really well made'.[26] Halifax clearly indicated that any cinematic promotion of Britain's leadership would help sway US public opinion towards a more interventionist stance. But Bracken was not so sure. He warned the Prime Minister that James Roosevelt was 'a tricky creature. He was Kennedy's partner in some rather hot deals … I do not see how he can be prevented from making the film. But I think that it should be made clear that you have not seen the script, nor do you approve the making of the film'.[27] Eventually Churchill agreed to sell the 'film rights of *My Early Life* to Warners for £7,500 in 1941 … they did not proceed and gave the rights back'.[28] It is unclear as to why the filming was cancelled. However, although a favourite of the newsreel and documentary producers, Churchill did not feel comfortable with the prospect of his portrayal on the screen in feature film. The release of the 1943 US film *Mission to Moscow* caused problems for both the British censor and the Prime Minister. The film depicted the build–up to the war in Europe, centring on the diplomatic relationship between the US Ambassador to Russia, Joseph E. Davies, and the Soviet Dictator Joseph Stalin,[29] or as the strap-line for the film stated, it was the story of the world 'cheering a couple of guys named Joe!'[30] Having had a key role in events surrounding this relationship, Churchill would have to be portrayed in the film. Warners claimed that, as the protagonists were so well known to the public, they had to 'find virtual doubles' for the roles of Stalin, Pierre Laval, Haile Selassie and Churchill.[31] In order to stress this, the studio press book placed images of the actors alongside their character. Churchill was played by Dudley Field Malone, 'an internationally famous trial lawyer and orator, former collector of the Port of New York and assistant secretary of state in the administration of Woodrow Wilson', who Warners felt bore 'a marked resemblance' to Churchill.[32] Indeed, Malone had repeatedly pestered FDR, who was informed of the progress of the film, for the part, taking care to enclose photographs of himself in his letters to the President to assure him of the resemblance.[33]

Significantly, Malone's major scene alluded to representations of Churchill in popular memory both in Britain and the United States. Here Churchill appeared as the isolated, radical advocate of a hawkish approach to German expansionism. Flying in the face of appeasement, government and popular opinion, he tells Davies ironically: 'I'm an alarmist. I say things people don't like to hear. Nothing short of a major catastrophe would cause my voice to be heard'.[34] This image, presented in Michael Curtiz's 1943 film, was frequently reflected in the historical representations of leadership in British wartime cinema, ensuring that the public could make the necessary connections to Churchill himself.

The release of *Mission to Moscow* in Britain prompted a controversy. It was passed by the British Censor, despite the depictions of 'living statesmen on the screen'. Under the British Board of Film Censorship Regulations, living characters could not be portrayed without express permission, which was often not forthcoming. As Ernest Betts of the *Daily Express* reported on 22 July 1943

> The censor passed the film with a cut of only 150 feet out of 11,000 feet, but I understand that Warner Brothers, the producers, were unwilling to release the film until Mr Churchill himself had seen it ... Mr Churchill saw the picture a few days ago, and it is now passed for public exhibition ... No similar problem has ever confronted the British Board of Film Censors [BBFC]. Neither on the screen nor on the stage are living characters allowed to be portrayed.[35]

In fact, Churchill had not seen *Mission to Moscow*, minuting Bracken: 'I am told it is very bad. Please issue a contradiction, as I do not wish to be associated with it'.[36] The BBFC had encountered a previous reference to Churchill in feature films earlier that year, with the British production, *Warn that Man*, which depicted the attempted kidnap of the Prime Minister by enemy agents. This scenario was passed by the BBFC without reservation as 'the "important person" [in the plot] is never mentioned by name',[37] despite the character's identity being clear to cinema audiences. The British press book noted that the main protagonist impersonated the VIP as he 'swaggers out, smoking a huge cigar and talking airily of "blood, toil and sweat"'.[38]

Despite his reluctance to be portrayed in feature films, Churchill perceived, like many of his contemporaries, that he was living through historic times. For Churchill, film was the modern historical document and could be used to preserve the memory of the epic struggle. This was illustrated by his attempt to ensure the distribution of two US military films, *Divide and Conquer* and *The Battle of Britain*. He noted in 1943 that the films taught 'people about what happened in 1940, which very few people realized completely at the time and which is already beginning to fade in memory'. Churchill was so impressed by the films that he instructed the MoI to contact him directly should distribution prove impossible, noting that he 'would ask for legislation if necessary' to facilitate national release.[39] *The Times* confirmed, just one month later, in August 1943, that the films would be commercially released in Britain, reporting that 'the Prime Minister is taking a personal interest' in the films and that he 'is recording a foreword to be used on each of the films in the series',[40] such was Churchill's commitment to the project.

Representations of contemporary leaders, and of Churchill in particular, were popular with newsreel audiences.[41] However, this cinematic popularity sat uncomfortably with the Prime Minister. In 1944, he stated that 'tributes if deserved come better after a man's death than in his lifetime',[42] and for Churchill a clear distinction had to be made between 'reportage' and historical filmic documentation and glorification through semi-fictional, biographical or fictional feature length movies. Churchill, like the film producers and indeed the audiences, preferred to view the representation of his leadership during the war through historical parallel. As an historian, he was acutely aware of the past as a means of representing the present. One of his favourite wartime films, *That Hamilton Woman*, depicted the epic struggle of Nelson against the Continental aggressor at the Battle of Trafalgar.[43] H.V. Morton observed Churchill's reactions on viewing the film in 1941:

The story he watched was one that touched his heart: the story of a man who gave everything he had to give so that England might live in freedom and peace. Winston Churchill was completely absorbed in the story, and for the first time spoke no longer to those near him, but seemed to retreat into himself, as if he were sitting alone in the dark, his face, his body even, expressing an attention so complete that it seemed one might look and find him no longer there, but taken up, merged and absorbed by the screen … as the last scene came, and Nelson lay dying in the cock-pit of the Victory, and they bent above him and told him that the day was his, the man who was watching so intently took a handkerchief from his pocket and wiped his eyes without shame.[44]

Such was the impact of the film on the Prime Minister that he was still referring to it in letters to Stalin three years later.[45]

Like Churchill, contemporary filmmakers also saw the past as a feasible way of depicting the present. Historical parallel proved to be an effective means of conveying contemporary issues to the public. Audiences could be convinced that the past could be repeated, often reminded that, in desperate times in British history, the people had prevailed when coordinated by strong and effective leadership. More importantly for the industry, contemporary messages could be disguised under the veil of 'escapist' historical costume drama, Mass Observation frequently reporting that audiences were growing increasingly tired of contemporary themes and obvious propaganda.[46] In 1940, they noted that the public enjoyed a 'form of escape' into the past, in particular into 'Edwardian and Victorian days'.[47] By combining a topical theme with an historical storyline, the propagandist could aid the receptiveness of the audience to the message, and at the same time, the studios would not jeopardize profits for the sake of propaganda.

Two films in particular characterized the use of historical parallel to depict contemporary leadership and specifically the role of the Prime Minister: *The Prime Minister,* and *The Young Mr. Pitt.* Both films presented images of heroic leaders dealing with the continental aggressor, and were promoted as being parallel to contemporary events. However, their representation did not simply reproduce the past, rather it recast contemporary leadership roles in the mould of past trends and events. Furthermore, it was not merely a static reproduction. The image of leadership was reborn in the modern age, and fitted its particular circumstances and challenges. In addition, the representation of leadership in these three films corresponded to popular opinion regarding Churchill. If the historic leaders depicted in the films could be related to Britain's wartime Prime Minister, and that this depiction could reflect pre-existing public opinion regarding leadership and Churchill's role as wartime leader, the propagandists would have a greater chance of success. This connection was to be primarily generated by the publicity surrounding the release of the film. However, this was achieved by the creation of a complex web of psychological connections, established through the use of press books, publicity placement and reporting in the trade press and publicity within individual cinemas exhibiting the films. From these sources it is possible to tie the images of leadership in the films to specific observations about the character of Churchill in the popular mind.

In the aftermath of the political events of May and June of 1940, it was essential to restore the image of leadership in Britain. Mass Observation noted that:

> In recent years, this country's leaders have cleverly lulled the citizens into a land of wishful dreams so that the party can stay in power and carry on its own way. The events of May and June awoke the mass of citizens from this lethargy. Such an awakening was essential for the survival of democracy. Now people ... are determined to see that they are not deceived again.[48]

In addition, Mass Observation commented, in the same year, that the British public had demonstrated 'a low interest in politics'. 'People' they noted 'do not, for the most part, feel themselves personally involved in political problems'.[49] Mass Observation reports claimed that the public had very little specific conceptions of political values and issues and awareness was 'certainly not focused on Parliament [or] on the House of Commons', which seemed 'too remote'.[50] Where public interest and politics coincided, however, was in their fascination with personality.[51] The British public found a distinctive, iconic personality in Churchill and, in comparison to his predecessor, he had attained a high level of popularity among the British public. The Mass Observers recorded that Chamberlain had never reached the eighty per cent popularity favour accorded to his successor.[52] In assessing Churchill's popularity, they noted that:

> The position of the Prime Minister in popular government, and much of what people think about the Government and the whole democratic machinery is tied up with what they think about the Prime Minister. The present Prime Minister's high popularity is associated with a high degree of confidence in our own way of Government ... The very fact of a strong and exciting personality tends, as things are at present, to heighten the prestige of this particular system to the minds of ordinary people who are not very interested in the details.[53]

Given this, it is unsurprising to find that feature films sought to concentrate on the personality as representative of democratic government, and the preserver of British democratic values in the face of the European dictatorships. Significantly, in November 1940, Mass Observation detected 'a genuine stepping up of political awareness'. One of the most important explanations for this increased interest was 'the great prestige of the present Prime Minister [which] ... tends to step up the political awareness of the nation'.[54] This was a theme that the studios could capitalize upon, whilst producing works fitting with the MoI's own agenda for political propaganda. Historical epics could exploit public interest in personality and leadership, and carefully constructing a film whose propaganda was disguised by the dislocation of time and by the escapism of costume drama. Wartime Prime Ministers and monarchs, therefore, provided an excellent opportunity for filmmakers in 1940, ensuring that these themes were fully exploited in the press and cinema publicity releases.

Such an approach also allowed both propagandists and studios to exploit the US film markets. Promoting the concepts of democracy set against the backdrop of costume drama was appealing to both political promoters and audiences alike. Some filmmakers, such as John Grierson, the then Film Commissioner of Canada, were aware that 'the Americans do not feel "on intimate terms with British democracy"'.[55] The United States, he contended, needed more action: 'the demand for "bold utterance", "more about active people", "fewer qualifications" and for a language understood by the people, seems to be fairly constant'. He advised that the '"traditional England" angle should be somewhat tempered' and that filmmakers should avoid making the British look 'nervous'.[56] Grierson recognized the need to combine the elements of bold action and tradition, using leadership as a vehicle to deliver an image of a powerful, modern power, still focused on its heritage. Grierson observed that British propagandist should emphasize that 'England's international reputation and England's leadership in the deeper matters of human progress are complimentary'.[57] Moreover, by May 1940, Britain had the most appropriate leader for the times who could not only understand the modern condition but could also be aligned with the past. As Grierson noted in 1941:

[L]ooking at England ... I have been concerned with conceptions like bringing "a country alive to itself" and "projecting it" ... In propaganda, internal and external, it is the image that counts. In the beginning was the Image. One might say it is the basis of all comprehension, the crystallizer of sentiment, and the determiner of will ... For the propagandist, Churchill ... is simply the dramatic form in which the drums of Drake have been brought out from the English subconscious and beaten again.[58]

For Grierson, as the propagandist, and the studios as the entertainers, this mystical connection between past and present could be embodied in the depiction of leadership. It presented them with the golden opportunity to attain that elusive combination of propaganda and entertainment film, so precious to propagandists because it provided the veil with which to disguise the propaganda content, exacerbating its effect, and to the studios, who were not keen to jeopardize profits. Film was, after all, a business, as well as a tool in the battle for hearts and minds.

An analysis of two of the major feature films to depict leadership through historical parallel and the role of the Prime Minister produced in wartime Britain, *The Prime Minister* and *The Young Mr. Pitt*, demonstrates how closely the past was connected to the present. In discussing the films, of particular importance was studio promotional activity - press releases, features in the press, press books and instructions to exhibitors – that sought to create the image of past leadership in the Churchillian mould. Textual references within the film obviously reflected the specific construction of the image of leadership. However, promotional activities sought to reinforce the cinematic portrayal either by planting the idea before audiences entered the cinema or by reflecting upon the film in retrospect. In this way, studios, and indeed propagandists, could ensure that the central connection to the present was not lost. Moreover, it provides an indication that the studios were actively promoting parallels between past and present in a variety of ways. This form of promotion had the potential of a dualistic impact on audiences, either by playing upon the popular desire to apply personal meaning to events in the past, making them more relevant to today, or by drawing on the escapist appeal of historical costume drama.

In addition, these films, although perhaps not intentionally, tapped into public perceptions of the Churchillian premiership. It is interesting to note that they were both set within a wartime context, with Britain fighting against an autocratic continental aggressor determined to ensure territorial expansion. Each figure, whether Benjamin Disraeli or William Pitt the Younger although not warmongers, did not shy away from war. As Churchill, they were war leaders. Indeed, Mass Observation reported, as early as November 1942, that Churchill was viewed by the public as predominantly a wartime, and not a peacetime, leader.[59] Moreover, the image of the 'men of destiny' depicted in the films also corresponded to public perceptions of Churchill's qualities. In April 1941, Mass Observation asked the public to describe the Prime Minister in one word. The responses could be easily mapped onto past wartime leaders. In the popular mind, Churchill represented 'hope', 'genius', greatness, versatility, Britishness; he possessed tactical brilliance and nobility. He was Britain's 'bulldoggish' wartime leader, who was 'alright for a war', but 'not in peacetime'. Significantly, Churchill was also described as 'historic'[60], an image born out of the times in which he lived, but also deliberately cultivated by the propagandists. The promotional film poster for David Macdonald's 1941 production *This England*, in which the Prime Minister is portrayed as the most recent chapter in Britain's victorious history, provides a clear example that Churchill had inherited the mantle of British wartime leadership, displayed alongside other British wartime leaders: Elizabeth I, Francis Drake and Nelson.[61]

The first major feature film to depict these themes was Thorold Dickinson's 1941 production, *The Prime Minister*, starring John Gielgud as Disraeli. The publicity generated by Warner Bros ensured that the link to the political and military situation in Britain was clear. The studio press book, which recommended press releases, general advertising and exhibitor displays, placed a particular emphasis on Disraeli's role as 'England's man of destiny'. Drawing a parallel to recent events in Britain, the studio announced that 'in Disraeli's time too ... England's Empire was threatened by appeasers within and strong men without.'[62] As Mass Observation demonstrated, the public were quite aware of the 'hawk' and 'dove' camps in the lead-up to the Second World War, and as such this parallel to Britain's two wartime leaders, Neville Chamberlain and his successor Churchill, would not have been lost on audiences. This element of the film was reinforced to audiences in Disraeli's speech to Cabinet.[63] The debates of pre-war Britain were relived through the cinematic depiction of Cabinet discussion, with Disraeli fitting the model of Churchillian leadership. Historical parallel was occasionally attained by reference to contemporary events, as demonstrated by the following excerpt from the US press book, which raises, once again, the issue of appeasement:

> Disraeli, more than any other statesman, is well aware of the subterranean moves in German diplomacy and is determined to make his country recognise the dangers of the German Chancellor Bismarck's purposes. Then, as so recently, there were many who could not believe that there was anything but good intentions behind the assurances of the European dictator.[64]

Specific reference was made to the link between Churchill and Disraeli, *The Cinema* observing that the film was 'timely ... in that the political outlook of Disraeli is mirrored in the European upheaval of today. Then, as now, we had a Prime Minister entirely motivated by his devotion to his country and his high regard for her honour'.[65]

Repeating the themes outlined in the Press Book, *Today's Cinema* commented that the film was 'a comprehensive survey of the career of Benjamin Disraeli, England's astute Prime Minister of over a century ago, when the political upheaval in Europe was ... a mirror of events today'.[66] This was made all the more poignant during the filming because, as the press book commented, Gielgud's speeches were seen as 'mighty portentous words to utter the while the RAF kept watch over the Teddington England studios, where the enthralling drama was shot'.[67] This device was used by the studios to stress not just the thematic proximity of the film to wartime events, but also its literal proximity. It was also a device used by Gaumont British two years later when advertising Carol Reed's 1942 production *The Young Mr. Pitt*. In this way, the gap between entertainment and propaganda, whilst perilously close, was maintained, shrouded by the similarity of events and leaders.

In addition, the studio was keen to promote the cult of the personality and the centrality of the Prime Minister to British identity and democracy. In their advice to exhibitors, Warner Bros encouraged theatres to run essay-writing contests in schools, and run Disraeli quizzes in local newspapers. Extravagantly, the studio suggested that exhibitors mount lobby displays of a full-size blow up portrait of Disraeli, with a theatre attendant reading the 'Wit and Wisdom of Disraeli' via a PA system behind the display.[68]

However, despite the publicity, the film did not meet with a particularly favourable response[69] and even those involved in production were not satisfied with the final product. Dickinson, the director, recalled that the film was 'just a hack-job ... thoroughly commercial',[70] while Gielgud noted that it 'could have been exploited a good deal more than it has been from a wartime propaganda standpoint'.[71]

Far more popular was Robert Donat's portrayal of William Pitt the Younger in Carol Reed's 1942 production, *The Young Mr. Pitt*, which owed some of its success to the popularity of the film's star, voted second most popular British star in 1940, behind George Formby.[72] The film details the story of the Georgian Prime Minister, his great rivalry with Charles James Fox, the successes and failures of his career and the two military campaigns of his premiership against France in 1793 and during the Napoleonic wars of 1803-5.[73] Reportedly, the idea for the storyline came from Viscount Castlerosse, who invited Reed to dinner. Reed was said to have been 'struck by the parallel with the wartime situation ... and the relevance to Hitler's war'[74]. Castlerosse agreed to write the story and additional dialogue, for later adaptation by the script-writing duo Launder and Gilliat.[75]

In keeping with the propaganda objectives of the film, Reed's production was to be a sanitized version of Pitt's life. *Today's Cinema* commented that *The Young Mr. Pitt* was 'an epic of what a brave man can do when supported by soldiers and sailors of British blood. England called for a man whom the spoils of office could not buy, a man who, possessed of a strong will and opinions ... loved honour and his country

above all'.[76] Such was the importance of the virtue of the leader in the
film that the scriptwriters found themselves in conflict with Reed and
Donat over the image of Pitt. Launder and Gilliat wanted to show Pitt's
'human imperfections',[77] including a scene where Pitt makes a drunken
speech in the House of Commons. Gilliat noted that he wanted to show
that 'under the stress of trying to run a war, people do not behave
impeccably, and that if somebody is pissed making a speech, this is a
moving thing'. While Reed and Donat would 'not have [this] at any
price',[78] the two writers completed the script according to the limitations
placed upon them,[79] still convinced that, as Launder put it, 'untainted
heroes, unless biblical, are bores'.[80] Pitt was to be a 'paragon of virtue'
and the film was to be a 'simple yet spectacular tale of one man's
unremitting labours in the cause of England … a present day parallel in
the threat of invasion, [underlining] the almost magical resilience of an
unflagging courage … a film of yesterday for today'.[81]

Exhibitors too were encouraged by the studios to make clear
reference to the historical parallel in their publicity for the film in
theatres. Billed as 'a story of a generation like ours' and 'a thrilling drama
of a great nation, challenged by a power-mad dictator', the press book
encouraged exhibitors to 'sell its amazing timelessness'. The press book
specifically quoted Pitt's speeches in an attempt to stress the historical
parallel. Speeches were often used with tie-ins, serving to promote the
film and its message. One example was the use of the following speech
in the publicity campaign for the 1942 film:

> We are called to struggle for the destiny not only of this country
> alone, but of the civilized world … our highest exultation ought to
> be that we hold out a prospect to nations, now bending under the
> iron yoke of tyranny, of what exertions of a free people can effect.
> I trust that we shall at last see that wicked fabric destroyed which
> brought with it more miseries, more horrors than are to be
> paralleled in any part of the annals of mankind.

The speech was used to prompt a number of promotional activities in
theatres and local communities, appealing to a wide variety of
cinemagoers from adults to children. The studio advised exhibitors and
the press to:

> use this stirring and timely speech as an incentive for editorial
> comment in your paper. Blow it up for inclusion in your lobby
> displays, and use it on handouts, book-marks, and school and
> library bulletin board posters. It might serve as the basis of a
> school essay contest, with history teachers cooperating in asking
> their students to compare the situation in Pitt's time with that of
> today.[82]

The film was certainly intended to establish a link not just of the problems of the past and present, and the difficulties of leadership, but more specifically to Winston Churchill, personally. In the promotion of the film, as with Warner Bros publicity for *The Prime Minister*, Gaumont British did not disguise its intention to depict Churchill as the Pitt of his day. Under the heading 'amazing parallel with to-day's events' the press book for the film stated:

> What is happening to England now has happened to England before. Where Hitler stands now, Napoleon stood one hundred and fifty years ago. The grim threat of invasion was as strong then as it is now. The British Fleet was the bulwark against aggression even as it is to-day. And where Mr Churchill stands this day, four square against the hatred of the Hun, there stood in George III's time a similar man in No. 10 Downing Street, a bold earnest figure braced with the steadfast faith of the whole people of Britain. His name was William Pitt. And now, at a time when the spirit of Pitt is embodied in Winston Churchill, the great saga of a valiant statesman who in his time defied as brutal an aggressor, has been brought to the screen.[83]

That the press book provided a template for wider distribution of reports on the specific film is confirmed by the fact that this excerpt found its way, word for word, into the trade newspaper, *Kinematograph Weekly*.[84]

At every opportunity, trading on Churchill's iconic status, the studio sought to reinforce the parallel within the public consciousness. When filming scenes at Walmer Castle of the proposed invasion of Britain by Napoleon,[85] Gaumont British reminded the press, in October 1941, that, at the time of filming, Churchill had just become Warden of the Cinque Ports, of which Walmer Castle was a residence. *Kinematograph Weekly* reminded readers that 'it was from this retreat that Pitt was recalled to save the British from Napoleon – a strange coincidence with recent events in the life of our own Prime Minister'.[86] The film was reportedly seen by Churchill, who was said to have approved of the film,[87] giving the artistic directors of the film special permission to use his study in Downing Street.[88]

Such parallels, whilst popular with the executives at Gaumont British, also attracted criticism. The critical wartime magazine, *Truth*, objected to the link between Britain's wartime Prime Minister and Pitt the Younger. In July 1942, the editorial pointed out that 'before we raise Winston Churchill … to the pedestal occupied by William Pitt, the aspirant must prove his mettle. Britain is not yet saved, Hitler not yet defeated … Comparison between Pitt and Churchill can only serve a useful purpose if it stirs the latter to emulate the former',[89] a sentiment Churchill had previously espoused through his reticence to be portrayed in this way during his lifetime.

However, the link to the past could not only be defined through identification with the leader. Audiences could identify with the parallels between Pitt and Churchill but they also needed to feel a form of personal identification with the story and the times. Not only did the studios sell the historical similarities between Britain in 1793 and 1940 through the image of leadership, but they also sought to publicize the experience of the 'everyman'. The strap line for the film hinted at this inclusivity: 'The Story of a Generation like Ours - With a Job To Do'. Similarly, the press book drew on the contemporary experience of many men and women in wartime Britain, observing that:

> In this day, the famous William Pitt faced a situation parallel to that which confronts us today! Across the Channel was a ruthless dictator and an army waiting to invade England. Pitt's problem was much like that of millions of men today. He hears his country's call. Shall he give up the woman he loves and devote his life to fight for freedom? Pitt made his decision, and it is stirringly told in *The Young Mr. Pitt*.[90]

Here, Pitt's experience was similar to that of many men and women. This reinforced the link to the people, adding a new strand to the image of leadership. With this identification, the audience was led to believe that leaders were not unlike themselves - they are men of the people as well as men of destiny. Exhibitors were advised to 'get this timely, interest-catching situation across to your movie-goers'.[91]

In the film, one of the key vehicles for conveying personal identification, a powerful tool to the propagandist and entertainer alike, was the love story between Pitt and Eleanor Eden (Phyllis Calvert), stressing the theme of sacrifice, love and war. Exhibitors were encouraged to mount giant stills from the film in the foyer, one of which was to bear the caption 'Like a million lovers today, they waited their country's call, sacrificing love for duty!' In addition, local press tie-ins were encouraged, stressing the impact of war on relationships, and encouraging strength and patience in the face of adversity. Exhibitors could use this angle to gain additional publicity for their screenings. The press book offered the following suggestion:

> In "The Young Mr Pitt", Robert Donat, playing the title role, heeds the call of duty to his country and gives up the woman he loves. Similar problems face many a young man today going off to war. For an excellent "Inquiring Reporter" question or newspaper contest, you might offer this problem to moviegoers, asking for

the best letters giving arguments for an against marrying before entering the army. Newspapers have been running comments of their readers on this very subject, and your natural story tie-in should result in some extra publicity space for your playdate.[92]

Not only were the studios keen to stress the historical proximity of the film to contemporary events, but they also promoted the literal proximity to the actors and filmmakers to the war. As with the publicity for *The Prime Minister*, articles for placement in the press stressed the problems of wartime filming. It was, they stated, 'a race against the bombs'. The press book details that filming in London's Guildhall, the setting of the great banquet chamber in the film, was hampered by 'fallen masonry and fire-wrecked timbers'. The filming of the scenes in the House of Commons was thwarted by aerial bombardment, and the scene was eventually moved from the 'blitzed Parliament ... to the still-standing House of Lords'. The destruction of sites of national heritage and tradition tied in the propaganda image of the uncultured aggressor. Culture, artistry and creativity were pitted against the barbarous destruction of the enemy. This theme was stressed, not only in cinematic terms, but also in the promotional material. In detailing the work of the set designers, Gaumont British proclaimed that:

The weeks of designing and draughtsmanship on "The Young Mr Pitt" was a race against the Nazis, the three draughtsmen making their drawings of houses, streets and doors, Adam fireplaces, Georgian sidewalks, praying that they would get their old London replanned before further bombs obliterated the landmarks and the relics from which they were gaining their inspiration.[93]

As can be seen, both *The Prime Minister* and *The Young Mr. Pitt* not only depicted images of the role of the Prime Minister in leading the people in wartime, but they were also publicised similarly. Both were reflections on dogged-determination in the face of a continental aggressor and the nature of leadership in wartime, and both made a clear and unambiguous comparison to Churchill. Both films were promoted by Warner Bros and Gaumont British respectively in a similar way: stressing the timely nature of the story, the iconic status of the individual leader, enshrined in the Prime Minister and the historical parallel. However, one film, *The Young Mr. Pitt*, was more popular than the other. An analysis of the publicity reveals that there is one glaring difference between the promotional activity for both films - that of the importance of personal identification. Whereas the publicity for *The Prime Minister*, and to some extent the film too, stressed the historical importance of Disraeli and his work – in short, telling the story 'from above' - the advertising and promotional activity for *The Young Mr. Pitt* went further, building a bridge between the leader and the people. The filmic Pitt was promoted as a man with problems like the everyman. Audiences could identify with his dilemmas, simply because many were facing the exact same challenges themselves.

While *The Young Mr. Pitt* and *The Prime Minister* were both released in a similar period, 1940-1942,[94] this did not mean that depictions of wartime leadership were confined to those years. Laurence Olivier's *Henry V*, released in 1945, bore significant similarities to both films. In many ways, it was the last cinematic testament to inspired leadership produced in wartime Britain. As such, Olivier suggested that, before general release, the film should be screened to British and Allied troops prior to the official premiere.[95] Once again, veneration of contemporary wartime leadership was veiled by the historic setting. The promotion of the film in local cinemas also capitalized on the links to the past, with Two Cities, the film's producer's, advising cinema owners that 'there is an extraordinary comparison between Henry V's landing at Harfleur and the D-Day landing of the Allies'. They suggested that 'these might form the basis of an interesting display [in foyers] comparing the actual landing carried out by the Allies on D-Day'.[96] Stafford A. Brook, a scholar, in correspondence with Alan Dent, script advisor to Olivier on the film, also commented that the 'King is great minded [embodying] ... that which makes the heart of England great ... [his] words might almost have been written of the Battle of Britain in the autumn and winter of 1940'.[97] Dent expressed Henry V's style of leadership as 'appropriate to the times' in which the film was made.[98]

However, the time for drum beating had passed. In *Henry V*, war was depicted as 'a miracle of quiet, temperate, austere judgement',[99] and the subject matter 'a poem [of the] ... glorification of the dauntless spirit and invincible endurance of Englishmen'.[100] As Dent noted, it was the perfect example of the 'little man' being inspired by 'famous orations' into great words and deeds,[101] a film that would demonstrate that unity under a strong leader could 'defeat ... an enemy which was to all appearances ... stronger'.[102] Moreover, by now, as Sue Harper has observed, 'the lessons of history were less relevant as peace approached'.[103] The veil of escapism had slipped somewhat since the days of the Prime Ministerial roles of Gielgud and Donat. The obvious propaganda content in *Henry V*, which was promised to Jack Beddington, head of the films division of the MoI, by Two Cities,[104] was becoming apparent to critics; the *Boston Post* of April 1946 noting 'the voice is the voice of Shakespeare, but the hand is sometimes the hand of Brendan Bracken'.[105] The strength of personal leadership embodied in historical allegory and escapism could no longer disguise the propaganda that it had shrouded in the previous years.

Contemporary national leadership in British wartime feature film was represented through historical parallel. It offered the leadership the opportunity to enhance their own profile, through comparison to past successful leaders, and it offered the studio the opportunity to avoid producing an obvious propaganda picture, which would not necessarily maximize box-office receipts, either in British or in Allied cinemas, particularly given the public's desire to see more escapist films after winter 1941. In addition, film producers would not have to navigate the BBFC's complex rules concerning the representation of contemporary personalities. This trend was not only popular in British film, but was also used by the Axis Powers. Hitler was not often represented in German feature film, unless through historical parallel, compared to the great Prussian kings, such as Frederick the Great, and more recent political leaders, such as Bismarck. For both Britain and Germany, historical parallels fulfilled the same function: to disguise overt propaganda, capitalising on the public's desire for historical escapism and, most importantly, to demonstrate that, even under the most adverse conditions, the national leaders of the past had always led them to victory.

Moreover, in presenting the leaders of the present as an organic evolution of the past, Britain's image as a democratic force was projected both at home and abroad. But it was not a staid representation of history. As an analysis of the publicity campaigns of the studios has demonstrated, past leadership was recast in a modern mould. It was a renewed image of leadership, suggesting development, growth and innovation, as well as evolution. As S.C. Leslie, writing in *The Citizen*, aptly commented in July 1939:

> When one thinks of the "projection of England", one realises afresh the dangers inherent in any easy misuse of democratic phrases and symbols – any failure to express the essential spirit of democratic growth and purpose. But one realises too what a powerful leaven in the world's thought would be the spectacle, successfully conveyed, of Britain refreshing her own awareness of the historic roots of her social and political life, and remaking that life accordingly. The main problem, in any task, of communication is to determine and define the theme: we have the most perfect of all themes to present.[106]

As with all themes they had their half-life, but between the years 1940 and 1942, the 'Men of Destiny' were re-presented as Winston Churchill, the projection of a successful wartime Britain.

8

'Let us go forward together'
Clementine Churchill and the role of the personality in wartime Britain

Helen Jones

Two images of wartime women have dominated post-war public and popular history. The first image, from 1940-41, is that of the cowering, deathly, and passive women of Henry Moore's shelter drawings, on permanent display at London's Tate Britain art gallery. The second image, which relates to later in the war, is of active and determined women in the auxiliary forces and in civilian war work. Most photographs of women in collections that have been published in recent years depict working-class women, in groups, often at work but at least actively doing something, such as shopping, unless they are sheltering. Images of middle-class women usually depict them in voluntary work such as sorting clothes or running makeshift canteens. Photographs of individual women politicians are extremely rare. Despite their contrasts, the early images of women in the shelters and later ones of women at work, are of women collectively, and do not focus on specific women.[1] During the war, however, there were numerous individual women, from politicians to entertainers, who were familiar, and recognisable, to the public. As the Prime Minister's wife, Clementine Churchill (1885-1977) enjoyed a high profile for much of the war and has remained in the public eye. She is now represented chiefly in her domestic role as the wife of Winston in a range of media, most recently the film for television, *The Gathering Storm*, which is concerned with the 1930s, not the war period; and with their Kent country home, Chartwell, a National Trust property, where a homely image of Clementine is presented to the public on an almost daily basis.[2] Her image has thus gone full circle, for during the war the public representation of her personality shifted from an essentially domestic, wifely and private one, to a public one on the international stage. In this shift she also personifies the dominant post-war image of wartime women: initially passive and private and later active and public.

There are shelves of books on Churchill; biographies abound of varying lengths that cover every aspect of his life. Comments on the role of Clementine, however, tend to be either general or to refer to the period before the Second World War. Typically, biographers comment on her character, and note her dislike of his friends and of Chartwell. Passing comments about her during the war tend to refer to her criticism of the way he treated his subordinates in the early days of his premiership or her work for the Aid to Russia Fund. Richard Hough has written a joint biography of Winston and Clementine, but his whole thrust is so remorselessly hostile to Clementine, focusing on the flaws that he sees in her character, and lacking a nuanced analysis of her public role in wartime, that it is no more useful than the biographies of Churchill that pay her less attention.[3] It is perhaps surprising that more interest has not been shown in Winston and Clementine's wartime relationship, given that there seems to be a insatiable appetite for material on Churchill and that biographers are more likely than in the past to delve into the personal lives of their subjects. The most comprehensive and illuminating study of Clementine is a biography by her youngest daughter, Mary Soames. Soames also edited for publication the frequent correspondence between her parents.[4]

While Churchill's biographers have paid scant attention to the role of his wife during the war, there is evidence that she played an important role for Churchill at the personal and political level (and for him the two merged into one). The incessant correspondence between them is testimony to the close and affectionate relationship between the two of them.[5] Mary Soames later commented that, despite their dissimilar natures, Churchill's life and career might have been quite different without her.[6] During the war Clementine worked to enhance and strengthen Churchill, and in this effort she played a personal and political role that complemented her husband. For both of them, the war was a period when their images and roles changed and developed. They were both very conscious of their public images, and both worked to create the images they wanted; it was a joint operation in which they both played a part. It is in these ways that the title of this chapter is apposite.

Mary Soames sees Clementine playing two key roles during the war: first, in her role as a non-party figurehead of the Aid to Russia campaign, and thus a symbol of goodwill towards the Soviet Union and of the government being at one with the people; and second, as a bridge between the people and the government, which meant that on occasion she could force the government into action. Her role as a human bridge between government and people was symbolized, according to Soames, by her headgear, a working-class woman's turban scarf turned into high fashion on the head of the Prime Minister's wife.[7]

The symbolic role played by Clementine Churchill during the war has been eclipsed by the larger-than-life personality and influence of Winston, and by historians' focus on the institutions, such as Ministry of Information and BBC, of wartime persuasion. This chapter seeks to show that representations of Clementine's personality played a role in the government's persuasive techniques. On her own initiative, Clementine took part in trying to persuade international and domestic audiences that their interests and goals were the same as those of Churchill and the British government.

Photographs were ubiquitous in wartime and were used as an instrument of persuasion. The subjectivity of photographs makes photographic portraits especially suitable conveyors of messages. The press published a large number of photographs of Clementine during the course of the war of which three have been selected for discussion. Each was chosen because it was a means of Clementine developing and controlling her role during the war. The photographs are not used here merely to illustrate the argument but rather as evidence to develop it.

First, we will look at Clementine's role in 1940 in the early part of her husband's premiership, and show how she presented herself as a 'private' individual although at the same time playing a political role. Second, we will consider the more public role that she developed from 1941 onwards and discuss what she hoped to achieve.

Many politicians' wives performed an important public role in their husband's careers. During the Second World War, Stafford Cripps's wife, Isobel, played the closest role to that of Clementine. Between 1942 and 1945, when Cripps was Minister of Aircraft Production, his wife tirelessly toured aircraft factories with him. She was also president of the United Aid to China Fund, which between 1942 and 1945 attracted a good deal of publicity and raised over £1½ million for humanitarian aid.[8] During the First World War many upper-class women and wives of politicians had taken up some form of welfare work. Margaret Lloyd George, the wife of David Lloyd George, Prime Minister from December 1916, along with other Welsh women in London had raised money and packed off 'comforts' for the troops. After the war she continued to work for him in his constituency in Wales.[9] Dorothy, wife of Edward Wood, Lord Halifax, had run a hospital for Belgian refugees.[10] Clementine had undertaken welfare work in factories and Margot Asquith, wife of Herbert Asquith, Prime Minister 1908-16, had continued her role as political hostess. These are but a few of the numerous examples that could be cited.

Some politicians' wives, who were contemporaries of the Churchills, had pursued public issues independently of their husbands. In 1918 Stanley Baldwin's wife, Lucy, had received an OBE for her war work and between the wars, she was known for her welfare campaigns.[11] Sir John Simon's wife was a long-term campaigner against the continuation of slavery around the world.[12] Numerous women took up constituency work in order to support their husbands. Neville Chamberlain's wife, for example, was for many years involved with women active in the

Party. She acted as a hostess for her husband and undertook constituency work, which included making speeches.[13]

Many wives of leading politicians during the Second World War, however, played little or no part in their husband's public lives. Anthony Eden's wife, Beatrice, had no interest in politics; they pursued their own affairs and divorced after the war.[14] Ernest Bevin's wife, Florence, was not active in any of Ernest's trade union or political pursuits and stayed out of public view.[15] Clement Attlee's wife, Violet, was not interested in politics (although she did entertain visitors at 10 Downing Street and Chequers after the war when he was Prime Minister).[16] Hugh and Ruth Dalton lived apart for much of the war while she enjoyed a quite independent career. (She had earlier, however, supported him in his career, even standing in a by-election and winning a seat, which he then took over at the subsequent general election.)[17]

It was not a *sine qua non* for a successful politician during the Second World War to have a wife in the public eye. It was a matter of personal choice, and presumably agreement, whether or not the wife played a part outside the constituency. Clementine could have chosen a semi-private role confined to entertaining at Chequers and the rare public appearance at her husband's side. There is no evidence of pressure from Churchill himself or from the Conservative Party (which she disliked and tended to give a wide birth) for her to develop a public role.

Clementine, however, had always been active in supporting Churchill's career, both behind the scenes and in public. When they married in 1908 Churchill was already a successful politician; Clementine could never have been in any doubt about Churchill's passion for politics. In 1915, Churchill as the First Lord of the Admiralty was widely blamed for the disastrous Dardanelles campaign. Clementine, fearing that this could be the death of her husband's political career, took the audacious step of writing to the Prime Minister, HH Asquith, arguing that Churchill was irreplaceable and that few in the Cabinet had his power, imagination or deadliness to fight the Germans. (Churchill was sacked anyway, and she received no reply to her letter.)[18] This is an indication of the daring lengths to which Clementine would go to do what she thought was right for her husband. Even though she loathed the Conservative Party and many of her husband's closest associates she was active in constituency work, campaigning and speaking on his behalf. Clementine's public role was an extension of her private one, which was supporting Winston. Although heavily involved in welfare work during the First World War, and subsequently undertaking some charitable work in which she gained experience of heading fundraising campaigns, public speaking and broadcasting, she did far less of it than might have been expected. It was only ever an adjunct to Winston: 'Winston was to be Clementine's lifework'.[19] In private she offered him advice (which he often did not take) on crucial decisions. Her wartime

role was a natural extension of one in which she had experience that
stretched back thirty years.

When Winston Churchill became Prime Minister in May 1940 his wife
initially featured little in public life. Her role was seen as providing wifely
support to her husband at a time of immense pressure. This private role
was publicly reconstructed in a photographic essay that appeared in
Picture Post, a hugely popular yet serious documentary photographic
magazine.

Clementine Churchill is photographed in the drawing room of 10
Downing Street. She is sitting on the edge of a sofa, wearing a long,
elegant dress, with perfectly coiffured hair and a rather serious
expression. In the background are comfy chairs, a plain carpet, high
ceilings from which chandeliers hang down, and large windows at the
end of the room that let in plenty of light. The other images in the
photographic essay resonate with history and continuity: there is a statue
of William Pitt and a view from the Prime Minister's bedroom of Horse
Guards Parade and the Admiralty, but the text tells us that the Prime
Minister has the most modern telephone equipment next to his bed that
connects him with the government's main arteries.

The portrait of Clementine is heavy with symbolism. At the end of
1940 the government had not yet called-up women for war work or the
auxiliary services, although many were engaged in paid or voluntary
work, and many were looking after evacuee children in their homes. The
home-based role of women had not yet been eclipsed in the popular
image of wartime women, and a strong domestic representation of
Clementine Churchill did not jar with governmental or popular
expectations of an upper-class woman in late middle age. Although the
photograph was taken at a period when the German *Luftwaffe* was heavily
and continuously bombing London, there is not a hint of disruption: no
windows are blown out, there is no dust, no chandeliers have crashed to
the floor and Clementine looks serene. The materials and person in the
photograph are an oasis of calm.

The background enables anyone to peep inside 10 Downing Street:
the spacious rooms, opulent chandeliers and grand furniture all bear
testimony to the weight of the Prime Minister's office. The background
is a significant part of the picture; otherwise the photographer would not
have included it. (Most portrait photography is more focused on the
individual, for example, the famous photographic portraits of Churchill
taken in 1941 by Yousuf Karsh). Our eyes are drawn to the elegant
figure of Clementine, who perched cross-legged on the arm of a sofa,
gives a dash of informality to the otherwise formal setting. The
significance of such positioning can be best understood when it is
remembered that this is not a pose that the then Queen would have
struck for a photograph (or even the present Queen sixty years later).
The image shows a woman at ease with herself and her environment; she

is not lost in the grandeur of her surroundings. Although Winston is not in the photograph, the location implies that his presence is not far away. There are hints of their complementary functions. Clementine is strikingly youthful in comparison with him, and her evening dress suggests an upper class, entertaining and hostess role rather than a work role.

The photograph is not autonomous and is accompanied by a commentary that reinforces its messages. The reader is given Clementine's characteristics, which in essence amount to the ideal wartime leader's wife. She is shy of the limelight, but used to be a first-rate public speaker; she is a gifted hostess; she idolizes her children; she dresses simply (important in the austerity-rationed milieu of 1940); and she listens to Winston practicing his speeches and then makes suggestions.[20] The mention of this last role is hugely important, for his speeches are already part of people's sense of the historic moment in which they are living. Hers is a supportive, private, family role, but one with public and national significance.

The image of Clementine is a carefully constructed one. Clementine has controlled the image presented in this feature to the country. She allowed a *Picture Post* photographer into 10 Downing Street. This is not a snatched picture in the street, but a carefully composed one, and in fact quite an unnatural one. If she had not been posing for a photograph it is unlikely that she would have been sitting on the edge of a sofa, on her own, doing nothing and merely staring into space. Clementine chose at this point to present herself as private and elegant, although there is a contradiction here: by appearing in the photograph and magazine she was contributing to a more high profile, public role for herself. The readers of *Picture Post* may have thought that they were seeing something of the private Mrs Churchill, but in fact we learn very little. The rooms of 10 Downing Street were decorated by others and may or may not have been to her taste; it is not actually her permanent home that we see but an official residence. There are no direct quotations from her about life as the Prime Minister's wife. What we see is an expression of ideas that Clementine wanted to convey, not a 'record' of her private life as the wife of a public figure. In this sense she has kept her privacy. *Picture Post* and Clementine are complicit in the photograph and text that is presented. What we see is superficial; we learn more from the act of her being photographed.

For all its artfulness, from Clementine's point of view, the photograph does have two drawbacks. First, she is quite an isolated figure. There is no hint, for example, of other family members. Second, the image is of an upper class woman, unconnected to the lives of ordinary Londoners in a home that is untouched by bombing. Londoners, especially poorer ones, were undergoing the storm and stress of the blitz, and Churchill had just become leader of the Conservative Party (following Neville

Chamberlain's terminal illness), which many, including Clementine, considered an unwise move in that it weakened his claim to be the non-partisan leader of a united nation. There is no suggestion here of a gesture towards solidarity with the working class. She was, however, in other ways, publicly expressing her condolences to those suffering the worst ravages of the blitzes, for she often accompanied her husband on tours of bombed cities. She was also taking an interest, which was not publicised, in those suffering in air raids.

When Clementine first steps into a policy-related role as an advocate of safer, cleaner air raid shelters, it is still one that is an informal, behind the scenes one. Mary Soames suggests that her mother was able to influence government policy on air raid shelters because of her close and direct contact with the Prime Minister. Clementine visited shelters when she saw for herself some appalling conditions, and she subsequently wrote memoranda to her husband on the subject.[21] Churchill sent one of these memoranda to Herbert Morrison, the Home Secretary, and Malcolm MacDonald, the Minister of Health, and discussed the issue with them the following day.[22] This in itself is not evidence of influence over shelter policy. First, a memorandum from Clementine was only one of many crossing the Prime Minister's desk every day; second, shelter policy was to a large extent in the hands of local authorities; and third, by the time Clementine was writing a formal memorandum on the subject a great head of steam had built up around the problem of inadequate, unsafe and unhealthy shelters. Local councils across the country were bombarded with complaints, doctors were sounding Jeremiah warnings of the effects of public shelters on health, the Communist Party was calling for deep shelters, and a host of individuals and groups were making their dissatisfaction known. Although the public campaign could only worry not wound the government, Whitehall and local authorities made strenuous efforts to improve the safety and hygiene of shelters. Clementine's voice may have influenced the moment at which Churchill spoke to the Home Office about the problem, but the Home Office and local authorities' actions were the result of a complex series of events and situations. Clementine's next foray into policy would be a more public and substantial one.

In the autumn of 1941 the Red Cross launched a welfare campaign to help the Soviet Union. The campaign caught the public's imagination and aroused far more sympathy and support than any of the other wartime public fundraising efforts for aid to allied countries. Clementine Churchill headed the Aid to Russia Fund; she attended a press conference to launch the campaign and broadcast an appeal on the BBC.[23] Clementine launched herself on a public wartime role that was semi-detached from her husband and required a different image from that of wife and homemaker.

Mrs Churchill consults a chart of contributions to Aid to Russia Fund before her broadcast 23 May 1944. Photograph courtesy of the Imperial War Museum, London. IWM Photograph no. HU 60058.

This image is strikingly different from the one that appeared in *Picture Post*.[24] Here is a close-up image of Clementine looking at a chart of the money collected by the Aid to Russia Fund that is balanced on a mantelpiece. Clementine is not looking at the camera but at the chart, with just a hint of a smile. We see little of the room, apart from a bookcase that gives the room a functional air. Clementine is still immaculate, with manicured nails and not a hair out of place. She is an older woman, in a serious pose, who has lost none of her 'femininity'. Clementine is now dressed in a dark suit with hand on hip; she has a serious expression that is focused on the Fund's success, as demonstrated in the chart; and with bookshelves behind her, she and the message are more serious, formal and focused. The image also suggests an intellectual weight that is not present in the earlier image. Even so, she is still calm and unruffled by the job in hand.

Clementine became involved with the Aid to Russia Fund in part to bolster Churchill's image within Britain, particularly among the working class. In his history of the Second World War Churchill wrote: 'My wife felt deeply that our inability to give Russia any military help disturbed and distressed the nation'. Churchill went on to explain that he had told her that there was no chance of opening a second front, but that he and Anthony Eden had encouraged her to explore the possibility of raising voluntary donations for medical aid, which the Red Cross and St John's had already begun.[25] From this grew Clementine's involvement with the Aid to Russia Fund. Mary Soames offered an explanation that did not contradict Churchill's but was more explicit and carried it further. She wrote that when Chamberlain died in the autumn of 1940 Clementine had urged her husband not to accept the leadership of the Conservative Party. She feared that leading the Conservative Party alienated some of Churchill's working-class support, which he had gained as a result of his pre-war warnings about the threat from Nazi Germany and his record as war leader. In an effort to balance the harm that his leadership of the Party might have done to his support, and out of sympathy for the Russians, she took up the Aid to Russia Fund.[26] According to this version, her involvement was explicitly calculated to complement Churchill's image, which suggests that Clementine, self-consciously and with careful thought, took up a cause and moulded her public image in order to help her husband.

The combination of Clementine Churchill and the Red Cross provided the dream ticket for popular support. Clementine personified the concern and admiration felt by the British for the Russians, and she symbolized the importance that the British government attached to good Anglo-Soviet relations. Just as her husband symbolized Britain's unswerving, dogged and unyielding determination to win the war, so she personified the nation's caring, sharing respect for the Soviet Union and indeed the fund was often referred to as 'Mrs Churchill's Fund'. Clementine Churchill was an icon of individualized and personal, rather than inter-state, relations.

The Aid to Russia campaign gave civilians, including children, a feeling that they were positively contributing to the war effort beyond Britain's shores, and it enabled them to express in a practical fashion their admiration and support for the Soviet Union. Groups of adults at work and children at school regularly collected for the Russians; flag days and Anglo-Soviet weeks were held. (The Women's Institute collected and cured rabbit skins and made them up into coats and hats for Russian women.)[27]

Clementine Churchill's campaigning work for the fund brought her into contact with ordinary people, which was not a day-to-day, normal occurrence but an unusual one, with photo opportunities for publicity purposes.

Mrs Winston Churchill spends a day with shop girls now working in munitions factories. No date. Photograph courtesy of the Imperial War Museum, London. IWM Photograph no. P556

The photograph was taken when Clementine visited a munitions factory. She has just been presented with a cheque for the Aid to Russia Fund.[28] In this photograph we have a front view of Clementine, dressed in a fur coat and gloves with a turban on her head, smiling and talking to a young munitions worker, Irene Harper, who used to work in a shop. Irene Harper is wearing work overalls and scarf and has her back to the camera. Standing slightly back from them is a man, dressed in a suit, who could be a works manager. This photograph, like the other two discussed above, is staged. Clementine is continuing to reconstruct the image of herself presented to the public. It is not pure chance that she happens to be talking to a girl in a munitions factory; Clementine had to go out of her way and disrupt her usual routine to be in this situation. Clementine has made a clear choice about the way in which she will present herself and the image that will be recorded.

Despite Clementine's headgear, there could be no doubt that she was not one of the workers and that her arrival was a special event. The fact that a photograph was taken of the occasion denotes an instance worthy of recording. By stopping for the photograph they are slowing down the fleeting moment of their meeting, and by recording it they and the photographer are turning a transitory meeting into a more permanent moment, and one that may have been subsequently displayed in the factory or in the girl's home. A private individual female worker and a public female figure look each other in the eye, but the event is overseen by a man who comes between them in the picture. Clothes, age and work denote the class and status gulf between the women.

Yet, the Aid to Russia campaign did cut across class and party lines. Clementine Churchill's presence may have helped to bring those who were not natural sympathisers of the Soviet Union into the campaign. Women members of the Conservative Party expressed the view that when Conservative Associations supported and co-operated with the campaign they were able to counteract attempts to use Anglo-Soviet weeks for propaganda purposes.[29] Clementine Churchill's presence helped to depoliticise and take any potential radicalism out of the campaign. The range of the campaign's backers contributed to the image of cross-party unity in the country. Clementine Churchill acted as a symbol of a politically inclusive country, and her turban played a role in trying to persuade the country of this fact.

The sight of Clementine Churchill in her turban was a striking image that lent itself to widespread photographic reproduction. It was polysemic: it was a personal statement of confidence (any woman would need a degree of nerve to carry it off) and of thoughtful effort. It was also a social statement, of upper-class appropriation of a fashion accessory that was a working-class necessity. In addition, as Soames rightly stated, it was a political statement: it was part of the widespread effort by government to persuade the country that government and people were as one. It was an unusual and interesting attempt to personalise propaganda through a fashion statement. Its significance would not have been lost on wartime society. During the war what people wore denoted more than merely clothing for warmth and decency, or fashion. It sent out strong signals of one's relationship to the war effort; hence the popularity and status of a uniform.[30] People were well attuned to the political message of clothing. Clothing still carried, moreover, a strong message about class position, thus Clementine's gesture would have been quickly picked up, although its impact is unknown for it was part of a complex series of messages to persuade the people of the nation's common purpose and unity.

As the Prime Minister's wife, Clementine occupied a hybrid position, for she represented both the government and those not of the government. She was a symbol too of the forging of the traditional and modern in wartime society. She was an upper-class woman with a high profile because of her husband's position, taking on a traditional role of heading a welfare campaign, yet one that was supplying up-to-date medical equipment to a modern state, the Soviet Union.

The campaign's real value did not lie in the amount of relief provided for the Soviet Union, for this was paltry set against the need. By the end of the war over £7 million had been raised; nearly £5.5 million was spent through charities on surgical and medical items and clothes. The Government also gave a grant of £2.5 million for clothing. A great deal of the money was wasted, especially at the beginning when, for instance, the Russians did not provide adequate specifications for British manufacturers, and needles were sent which did not fit Russian syringes.[31] Such bungling not only undermined the aid Britain could provide to the Soviet Union, but it put British merchant seamen at unnecessary risk; the Russian convoy was notoriously dangerous. The fund also created its own tensions between the Soviet Union and Great Britain.[32]

For the Government the campaign's importance lay in the way that it was hoped that it could counter-balance strains in the alliance and so promote good Anglo-Soviet relations for the duration. By personalising the campaign, the human element in Anglo-Soviet relations was focused on, and this meant that the very real and intractable problems of Anglo-Soviet relations could be temporarily skirted around. During 1942 and 1943 the Soviet Union wanted the allies to invade occupied Northern Europe in order to divert German military attentions away from the Soviet Union. The British had repeatedly to resist such pressures because, as minor raids demonstrated, the allied forces were simply not ready for invasion and it would have resulted in needless deaths and humiliation. (Even though the allies waited until June 1944 there were still many casualties in the D-Day landings and in subsequent months.) The Aid to Russia Fund was used in high-level wartime diplomacy, as when Churchill informed Stalin in a telegram that special cargoes, including medicines and medical appliances purchased by the Aid to Russia Fund, would soon be on their way to the Persian Gulf.[33] On 14 April 1945 (only three weeks before VE Day) Churchill told Stalin that the money collected by the fund 'is perhaps not great, but it is a love offering not only of the rich but mainly of the pennies of the poor who have been proud to make their small weekly contributions', and he went on 'In the friendship of the masses of our peoples, in the comprehension of their governments and in the mutual respect of their armies, the future of the world resides.'[34]

In the dying stages of the war Clementine embarked on a five-week tour of the Soviet Union when she visited hospitals that the fund had supported. She made a broadcast on Soviet radio, which included a message from her husband to the Russian people. After Clementine had visited Russia in 1945 she contrasted the Russians favourably with the Germans, and although she emphasised that her visit was the beginning of friendly relations, in fact it was the climax. While she was unfavourably contrasting the Germans with the Russians who were 'heroic', 'brave' with a 'veneration for the cultural inheritance', and she referred to the 'great warrior leader of Russia, Marshall Stalin' such sentiments were already becoming dated. She even wrote of the Aid to Russia campaign as signalling friendship and comradeship, the latter an unusual term for a Conservative politician's wife to use. It certainly misled the Germans for a while: a Foreign Ministry memorandum in April 1945 stated: 'The fact that Mrs Churchill has gone to Moscow shows conclusively that these divergences [between the Soviet Union and Great Britain] are not very deep'.[35]

It is important to look at personalities when analysing persuasion because the messenger can have a significant impact on the way in which the message is received. The perceived qualities of the messenger are important in the persuasiveness of the message. Clementine Churchill benefited not only from her own perceived qualities but also, as the wife of Winston, from his perceived qualities too. As his stock rose in the public mind, so Clementine's stature would also have grown. Clementine always presented an attractive image to the public while Winston, having stood against appeasement and been proved right, as well as having led the country during the Battle of Britain, was now the most credible and popular politician in the land. Although in reality there was a chasm in the social class differences between Clementine and most of those to whom she appealed, she made a gesture of solidarity with her turban, and the country was bombarded with strong messages of the similar situation in which the war had now placed everyone. Her appeal for the Aid to Russia campaign went with the grain: there was much popular support for the Soviet Union after its switch to the allies' side when attacked by Germany. In her appeals for money she was pushing at an open door. The message was simple, it had a good deal of emotional appeal and there was an element of self-interest in supporting an ally. Thus, in this instance, there was a close relationship between an individual personality and persuasion.[36]

Clementine Churchill was a symbol, and an icon, but she was not a human bridge between people and government; that role was played collectively by groups of women, many of whose names have been almost forgotten now, and none of whom ever became iconic. While Clementine Churchill demonstrated the role of personality in wartime symbolism, there were numerous women in voluntary organisations, most notably the Women's Volunteer Service (WVS), and in politics who worked together as a bridge between government and the people. They were a bridge not only between the government and the mass of women in the country but also between war and peace in that they campaigned around issues that were not only of wartime relevance but also of longer-term peacetime significance.[37] Just as many saw Winston Churchill as a wartime, not a peacetime, leader so Clementine Churchill was a quintessentially wartime icon. Her role was a transitory one, a part of the culture of Second World War Britain.

Clementine was no passive player in the politics of wartime representation. She chose the role that she played, and carefully constructed the changing image of herself that was presented to the public by her clothes, by the activities with which she was involved and by the photographs in which she appeared. Photographic theory at this time assumed that photographs could reveal the essence of a person, that they could capture the true personality, and that the viewer learnt something about the personality of the subject. Now, in postmodernist photographic theory, the emphasis is on the superficial nature of the image, the way in which it can be manipulated, and the process of creating the image as much as the content of the image, and this has informed the way in which the photographs have been analysed in this chapter.

Clementine Churchill played a symbolic role, confined to the war. She symbolized the idea of non-party, apolitical, consensual public life in wartime. Despite her role being a short-term war-time one, her image has long outlasted the war. As a symbol, she is more in accord with the post-war public history and memory of the war than those women whose activities had longer-term policy significance. She has continued to receive attention as a spin-off from the insatiable interest in Winston Churchill.[38] Both of them are testimony to the power of personality in popular/public history.

9

The trials of a biographer
Roy Harrod's *Life of John Maynard Keynes* reconsidered[1]

Richard Toye

Roy Harrod's *Life of John Maynard Keynes* (1951) has, rather more than most biographies, become an object of historical curiosity in its own right. This is in part because it has been seen as a key factor in shaping Keynes's post-war reputation, which, arguably, had important repercussions for the acceptance by politicians of his economic ideas. But it is also because Harrod's book – which concealed Keynes's homosexuality and failed to tell the full story of the great economist's conscientious objection during WWI – appears, from some perspectives, to represent everything that was bad about pre-1960s British biography.[2] In the most extreme version of this view, it is not merely that the scholarship of Harrod's *Life* needs to be corrected, but its author is himself deserving of posthumous personal obloquy for his manipulation of the evidence undertaken in the interests of protecting Keynes's reputation and of promoting a distorted assessment of the great economist's ideas. Yet, whilst any attempt to mount a full-scale defence of the book would be merely quixotic, there has been insufficient appreciation of the constraints under which Harrod was working. By examining in detail Harrod's successful attempt to gain access to Keynes's Treasury papers, and British officialdom's consequent efforts to influence what he wrote, this chapter will illustrate some of the difficulties he faced, and will suggest that the condemnation he has received at the hands of some historians has not been fully deserved.

Roy Harrod (1900-1978) is best known as an economist rather than a biographer, although he also dabbled unsuccessfully with politics.[3] He is generally credited, along with Evsey D. Domar, as being one of the progenitors of modern growth theory. Having studied Greats and then Modern History at New College, Oxford between 1919 and 1922, he was elected to a studentship at Christ Church, Oxford. He then went to Cambridge for a term to study economics under Keynes, of whom he became a powerful admirer, in preparation for teaching the subject himself. After Keynes's death in 1946, Harrod's economic expertise made him a strong candidate to write a biography, although his literary gifts were not immense. He subsequently wrote another biographical work, a memoir of Churchill's scientific adviser Lord Cherwell, which was published in 1959. In both books, Harrod gave himself a place in the narrative that, arguably, was excessive.

Two authors have commented at length on the writing of Harrod's *Life of Keynes*. Robert Skidelsky, in his own landmark biography of Keynes, has provided a fairly substantial account of its genesis, and a thorough survey of its reception. Although critical of Harrod, Skidelsky is never less than judicious. He points out that Harrod, in persuading Geoffrey Keynes that he would be discreet about Maynard Keynes's homosexuality, was responsible for the preservation of the latter's scandalous correspondence with Lytton Strachey. Moreover, 'It would be absurd to blame Harrod for failing to write the kind of biography that would have been possible only thirty years later.'[4] Scott Newton, in a recent article, has taken a significantly harsher line: 'Writing in the style of Morley on Gladstone he [Harrod] had attempted to make his subject a model to be studied and admired by future generations'. Furthermore, 'In the process of writing Harrod dodged reality and invented a character who became a vehicle for his own brand of humane and patriotic, paternalistic Toryism – more J.M. Harrod than J.M. Keynes.' Newton goes further than Skidelsky in claiming, in fact somewhat misleadingly, that Harrod concealed the drift of Keynes's sympathies from the Liberal Party to Labour in the 1930s, and oversimplified the economist's vision with regard to international trade in the 1940s.[5] (These criticisms were to some degree anticipated by John Strachey in 1956 and by Michael Heilperin in 1960.)[6] The question of how far Harrod should be criticized can be illuminated by a key part of the tale of the book's origins, of which neither Skidelsky nor Newton have been aware. Both have noted that Harrod submitted his typescript to the Treasury for comment, but neither of them explains why. There exists in the British National Archives a substantial Treasury file on the book, which allows the story to be told.[7]

It has generally escaped notice that Harrod gained access to Keynes's Treasury files for the purposes of writing his biography.[8]   Given Whitehall's notorious obsession with official secrecy – and the rules were often interpreted extremely officiously[9] - how was it that he managed to see these confidential papers? The story began in May 1946, when Richard Kahn, Keynes's executor and trustee, wrote to Sir Edward Bridges, Permanent Secretary to the Treasury, expressing the hope that 'some of Maynard's Treasury memoranda may be allowed to see the light of day. I realise that some time will have to elapse before publication, even if acceptable in principle, can be permitted but if there is any possibility of that kind it is perhaps of some importance that the necessary material should be collected before it is forgotten and dispersed.'[10] It took some time before arrangements were made to gather the relevant material together for the sake of posterity; but by March 1948 it had all been collected in one place. On being informed of this, Kahn wrote to Dennis Proctor, the official responsible, to express his pleasure. He added: 'Under his Will he [Keynes] left to me his unpublished papers on economic subjects, and it follows that, in so far as any use can be made of the papers in the Treasury, it would be my concern. They will of course be of great interest to Roy Harrod and when I talk to him as I hope to do shortly, I will discuss with him the question of procedure.'[11] Proctor told Bridges: 'Kahn is not asking for any decision here and now on the question of granting access, either for him or Roy Harrod, but it looks as though one or the other of them may be making some such application before long.'[12] He then told Kahn that Bridges would await an approach from either Kahn himself or from Harrod on the question of giving access to selected papers.[13]

Thus, a few months later, Harrod made an official application to see the material in a letter to Bridges. He recognized that constraints were likely to be placed upon him as a consequence of seeing the material: 'It would, of course, be understood that anything I wrote which referred to or was in any way deduced from what I had seen, would be subject to vetting.'[14] Bridges felt that Harrod's was a request 'which deserves a great deal of anxious consideration' before it could be answered. He told his colleagues that the question raised two difficulties: 'the first is, if we make a concession in this matter to Harrod ... how can one refuse a like concession to other biographers who wish to write the lives of other distinguished men who toiled for a while in Government Offices? ... The other point is what limitation one can put on the use to which Harrod can put any material which he was allowed to see.' This second point was crucial because many of the episodes of Keynes's post-1940 Treasury career were still matters of current controversy. 'I should have thought it was extremely difficult to allow an account to be published now of the part which Keynes took in the [1945 Anglo-American] Loan Agreement without disclosing a great deal more than it would be decent to disclose at this moment.'[15]

The problems did not prove to be intractable, however. Given the nature of the files in question, it was not the case that anyone allowed to see the bulk of them would also have to have access to more general Treasury material; and Keynes's papers could be weeded in such a way that they would contain substantially only his own writings. Moreover, opined one official, Thomas Padmore, there was not much risk of having to do the same sort of thing in the case of other people who had worked for the government: 'Lord Keynes was something very much out of the ordinary. He was never quite a civil servant and that may be a technicality which may one day come in useful.' From the point of view of putting off future Keynes scholars who might want to see the same material, it was also convenient that Harrod was an official biographer: 'In the case of a public figure of the importance of Lord Keynes it would, I think, be defensible to make special and unusual arrangements for such an official biographer, while holding that anyone else must wait until the documents become public records.'[16]

The question was now referred to the Chancellor of the Exchequer, Sir Stafford Cripps, who agreed that it would difficult, if not impossible, to refuse Harrod's request in principle, and that the government should therefore accede to it with good grace. He referred the question to the Prime Minister, Clement Attlee, who approved of the course proposed.[17] On 25 January 1949, therefore, Bridges was able to write to Harrod telling him that 'your present project may be treated specially and quite exceptionally.' He would therefore be granted access to Keynes's Treasury writings on two conditions:

> First we must ask that whatever you may wish to publish as a result of your researches in the Treasury will be submitted to the Treasury in advance and that we shall have an absolute right of veto on any passage, reference or quotation which we prefer to have excluded. ...
> Secondly we must stipulate that no information acquired by you as a result of study of these papers shall be used in advance of publication of the biography for any other purpose, for example in connection with current economic or political controversy; and of course that any information so acquired which does not appear in the biography shall not be disclosed by you at any time without our permission.[18]

Harrod replied accepting the conditions, but, on the question of the government's right of veto, added: 'I assume that this is implicitly limited by the condition that the said passage contained reference to or implied some fact which I could only know by having had access to unpublished official papers.'[19] Bridges met with Harrod two days later, and assented to his interpretation on this point.[20] This series of events explains why Harrod was obliged to allow the Treasury to vet his work. Yet the fact that this situation arose is in itself surprising. After the publication of the biography, Harrod admitted that he had been astonished by the speed of the Treasury's co-operation in granting access to the papers.[21] That it was forthcoming at all, even with conditions, was testimony to Keynes's unique hold on the official imagination: even in death, he managed to bend the rules.

Harrod's researches gave him some difficulties. He encountered 'the most appalling conflict of evidence on simple points of fact'. Moreover, 'Close friends of Lord Keynes would remark how brilliant were his epigrams – and fail, when pressed, to remember a single one of them.'[22]

(Some of these friends, moreover, were sensitive about what might be written about them.)[23] Nevertheless, he wrote at considerable speed (much of the book was dictated).[24] By the end of 1948, he had finished the pre-World War I chapters, and by the summer of the following year had finished four chapters on the 1939-46 period, although he still had the inter-war section left to write.[25] On 1 August Harrod submitted the 1939-46 chapters of his typescript for consideration by the Treasury.[26] They could scarcely have arrived at a more sensitive time. The government was in the process of deciding to devalue sterling (a decision made public on 18 September). Wary of the potential US reaction to this development, Treasury civil servants were concerned that Harrod's account of recent history might have a bad effect on Anglo-American relations. This fear may, to modern eyes, appear almost absurd, but one should not forget the crisis conditions in which it developed.

The official deputed to deal with the typescript was Ernest Rowe-Dutton, Third Secretary to the Treasury. He had known Keynes, and in 1946, had travelled back with him from the inaugural meeting of the governors of the International Monetary Fund (IMF) and World Bank at Savannah in March 1946. (As will be seen, this fact proved to be of some significance.) Having read Harrod's draft, Rowe-Dutton informed Bridges that he had had a discussion with the economist Lionel Robbins, a war-time colleague of Keynes, who had read it too. Taking Robbins's comments into account, Rowe-Dutton wrote: 'I am uneasy about a certain tendency to represent Keynes as sincerely seeking Anglo-American co-operation, but frustrated by a section of opinion at home all the time trying to run out of existing obligations, especially Article VII ... ' (Article VII of the Mutual Aid Agreement provided 'for agreed action by the United States and the United Kingdom ... directed ... to the elimination of all forms of discriminatory treatment in international commerce, and to the reduction of tariffs and other trade barriers.') He conceded:

This may be true, but it is a bad time to encourage the permanent American suspicion on just this point. Strictly, we cannot "censor" on this, but I believe we should appeal to Harrod's good sense, and ask him to modify. The more so, since he *has* seen official papers, and writes in this way after doing so. The inference can be made that official papers at least do not contradict this view. All very awkward if a row were to start! [Emphasis in original.][27]

Rowe-Dutton then sent Harrod a set of interim comments on his chapters. He stressed that 'Maynard would not have wished to justify himself at the expense of good relations' with the USA, which certain passages might damage: 'Life continues, and many sections of American opinion eagerly seek justification for their perpetual suspicion of British good faith.'[28] At the end of August Harrod sent Bridges his 'record of compliance' with Rowe-Dutton's suggestions, but also pleaded to be allowed to retain a few of the points which had been found objectionable.[29] A few weeks later, Harrod wrote to Kahn, telling him that Rowe-Dutton had made 'a number of requests for changes or excisions' and that although he had agreed to 'practically everything' Rowe-Dutton had warned him that 'there were *other* points he will have to take up with Bridges and then probably with Ministers. I don't know what these are' (emphasis in original).[30] At the end of October, Bridges wrote to Harrod suggesting a meeting, which took place on 3 November.[31]

Bridges admitted to Harrod that 'virtually all the points on which we were entitled to exercise a censorship by virtue of the use of official documents' had already been settled. But, he said, he wanted to go outside this:

> All of us who had read his draft felt that in certain respects he had written things which would stir up unnecessary troubles and would be prejudicial to national interests, particularly the relationship between this country and the United States. After all, although Keynes was a very great man, he did express himself very pungently, and there was no reason to assume that he would wish all his most pungent criticism to be published so soon after the event. ...
> I realised that in taking this line I was going outside what we were entitled to comment on, but I thought that as a former colleague and as a friend he would not mind my taking the points.[32]

On 20 December Harrod sent Bridges revised versions of the four chapters that he had previously submitted. By this time, he had made many changes in the light of long talks with Lionel Robbins, Frank Lee and R.H. Brand – these, presumably, were the 'wise heads' that Rowe-Dutton had earlier anticipated would urge moderation on Harrod.[33] Moreover, he told Bridges,

> I have made all the corrections desired by Rowe-Dutton, save for two or three points ... I have also made very considerable revisions, especially in the chapter on the Loan Agreement, in the light of our talk. I have tried to soften criticisms in regard to that negotiation. I have felt it needful to retain a criticism of the Government's handling of events, because I think this is a necessary contribution as a vindication of what Maynard actually achieved in Washington. But I have made it quite clear that this is an expression of personal opinion.[34]

Rowe-Dutton read the revised version, and informed Bridges: 'I really think we can congratulate ourselves on the effect of the representations you made to Harrod, who has certainly done a great deal of revision in his book'.[35] Accordingly, Bridges wrote a minute to Cripps, advising that publication should be allowed to go ahead. Although the book contained 'some fairly forthright and direct criticism of ministerial policy ... I do not think that we are entitled, or indeed that we can or ought to do anything about it.' Regarding the question of Anglo-American relations, Harrod 'has paid a good deal of attention to what we said on this point and here again I do not think we can or need object to one or two passages in which a fairly forthright account is given of differences between Keynes and the Americans, e.g. at the Savannah Conference.' Cripps gave his approval, noting that criticism of ministers 'is perfectly legitimate and calls for no comment at all', and accepting Bridges's judgement that no harm would be done to Anglo-US relations. Indeed, 'I think myself it may be a good thing.'[36] Although Harrod now received the go-ahead for publication, his travails with the Treasury had clearly contributed to the 'crise de nerfs' that he was now experiencing. As he confessed to one of Keynes's close friends, 'I have now reached the end of my tether.'[37] He returned the Keynes papers to the Treasury (to Kahn's vexation).[38] The book was finally published in January 1951.[39]

What, then, were the alterations that the government requested, and which of them did Harrod agree to make? In his 'interim' letter of August 1949, Rowe-Dutton said that Bridges thought Harrod's version of the story of Bridges's own visit to Washington at the conclusion of the 1945 loan negotiations was inaccurate. Bridges had not merely been 'approached' by ministers to be asked to go to the USA, as Harrod had claimed: 'He was sent. He tells me he spoke very little throughout [the remaining loan negotiations], certainly did not "plead the livelong day". He was in Washington until the signing, there were no negotiations after he left, so that it is misleading to speak of "minor victories .... after his back was turned".'

Rowe-Dutton also added some further points. Harrod should not refer to the attitudes of individual government ministers and officials; in particular, reference to the concerns of Ernest Bevin (Minister of Labour 1940-5, Foreign Secretary 1945-51) about Keynes's Clearing Union plan and Bretton Woods should be deleted. There were some 'not very happy references to the Bank of England' that should be removed. Furthermore, a letter from Keynes to Lord Halifax (dated 1 January 1946) should be omitted. Rowe-Dutton gave specific details of these and other 'Major Points' in a list that he appended to his letter, together with a list of six 'Minor Points'. The most significant of the latter were: -

1. It seems unfortunate to refer by name to the part played [in Anglo-American negotiations] by individual Americans. To call

them "good friends to Britain" is a sure way to lose their
friendship. ...
2. The references to [Fred M.] Vinson [US Treasury Secretary,
1945-6] ... are only too likely to upset him.[40]

In his reply, Harrod agreed to make many of the adjustments asked for.
He would make the requisite corrections to the 'Bridges story'. He would
remove explicit references to Sir Wilfrid Eady (Second Secretary to the
Treasury, 1942-52), Cameron Cobbold (Deputy Governor of the Bank
of England, 1945-9, Governor, 1949-61), Lord Beaverbrook (Lord Privy
Seal, 1943-5) as well as some (but not all) references to Bevin.
References to the Bank of England would be deleted. American 'friends'
of Britain were to become 'those with the greatest knowledge of the
broader issues'. Harrod was also accommodating in relation to a passage
on the loan agreement, the original of which was apparently very critical
of the government's subsequent actions. However, Harrod found
himself in a quandary at the point where modifying his criticism of the
Labour government in the interests of Anglo-American relations
conflicted with his desire to preserve Keynes's reputation:

> To vindicate Maynard it is necessary to show – which I firmly
> believe – that those things were not subsequently done which
> ought to have been done to make the Loan Agreement a success.
> On the other hand I want to avoid, subject to the above, saying
> anything that is damaging to our present relations or to what they
> may be a year from now. ... In the new version I have sought some
> solution of the problem by making the text -- at the expense of
> seeming egotistic -- more a statement of my personal view.[41]

Nevertheless, on other issues Harrod put up a certain amount of
resistance. At the most trivial level, he pointed out that there could be
little harm in saying that the 1944 re-election of FDR was 'an event
which gave joy to British hearts' – something Rowe-Dutton had wanted
him to omit. He also wanted to retain the tale of how Bevin had
responded to Keynes's optimism in August 1945 that the Americans
would provide generous financial help: 'When I listen to Lord Keynes
talking, I see to hear those coins jingling in my pocket; but I am not so
sure that they are really there.' Furthermore, he wanted to keep the story
of how the final amount of the loan had been arrived at by the
Americans, President Truman splitting the difference between the two
figures with which he was presented. On these points, the Treasury's
caution was in due course overcome.[42]

At a more significant level, Harrod requested that not all of the letter
from Keynes to Halifax be excised from his text. The letter – which dealt
with the state of parliamentary opinion on the loan upon Keynes's return

from Washington in December 1945 – had not come from the Treasury files but from Keynes's private papers. Not only did it refer to 'a perfectly public, and non-confidential, matter', but Halifax had agreed to its publication.[43] From the government's perspective, it was an especially sensitive document because it suggested that both Hugh Dalton (Chancellor of the Exchequer, 1945-7) and Lord Catto (Governor of the Bank of England, 1944-9) had been ignorant about key points of the loan agreement, and needed to be disabused by Keynes upon his return from Washington. The fact that Harrod had initially wanted to publish the letter virtually in full is significant – given that he has so often been accused of a whitewash – as it showed Keynes at his anti-semitic worst. (It may also be noted here that Harrod himself found anti-semitism distasteful.)[44] Keynes had told Halifax that the Labour Party's 'Jewish economic advisers' were 'like so many Jews ... either Nazi or Communist at heart and have no notion how the British Commonwealth was founded or is sustained'.[45] Overcoming his original instincts, Harrod now told Bridges that 'I am proposing in the end – reluctantly! – to omit the passage on Jews'. He now asked the Treasury to indicate which parts of the letter they found objectionable, so that these could be removed in preference to the deletion of the whole. He pointed out:

> What I could *not* have said, if I had not seen the letter, was that Keynes thought that, in spite of everything, the Americans could be reassured that the policy was being accepted as something which must be loyally and sincerely carried out. ... This seems helpful to have in print from the point of view of Anglo/American relations [emphasis in original].[46]

Harrod in the end got his way, and the letter was printed in the biography, albeit with the most controversial and embarrassing parts omitted.[47]

Moreover, Harrod was reluctant to excise his criticisms of US actions at the inaugural meeting of the governors of the International Monetary Fund (IMF) and World Bank at Savannah in March 1946. This had been Keynes's final international conference, and had been marred by Anglo-American disputes over the location of the head offices (the USA successfully pressed for Washington DC) and the role of the institutions' executive directors (on which a measure of compromise was reached), leading to much bitterness on his part. Fred Vinson played the part of Keynes's nemesis. In September 1949, Harrod told Kahn that he had softened his account of Savannah in the interests of Anglo-American relations.[48] Yet Harrod's self censorship was apparently less severe than Newton has imagined; his criticisms of Vinson remained fairly harsh. He told Bridges:

I realise that this [the criticism of Vinson] is a serious matter, but it is unavoidable, and an essential element in the story. ... I have done my best to represent Vinson as honourable and well-intentioned in the whole matter, as a counter-weight to his bad treatment of Keynes. He cannot like the passage, but he knows quite well what is coming to him.[49]

Indeed, Harrod had interviewed Vinson, and, as he later recalled, the latter's first words had been 'I know they say I killed Keynes'; Vinson had then spent two hours vigorously defending himself.[50] Harrod also told Bridges that he had asked a number of Americans if they thought the story of Savannah could possibly injure Anglo-US relations, and they had all denied that it could do so. To boot, Vinson had now been appointed Chief Justice and it was unlikely that he would re-enter political life.[51]

So, on several significant points, Harrod's initial response to government pressure was reasonably robust. There followed Bridges's meeting with Harrod, in which the former showed, in terms of detail, two particular points of concern. First, he thought that publication of the first three paragraphs of Keynes's letter to Halifax 'would definitely do great harm'. Second, he took further exception to Harrod's account of the circumstances surrounding Bridges's own 1945 visit to Washington.[52] Harrod was prepared to meet his concerns. And, in response to Bridges's general concerns about Anglo-US relations, he did now undertake some further softening of tone. Rowe-Dutton reported to Bridges on the final version of the typescript: 'From the point of view of Anglo-American good relations, very much of the objectionable material has gone; in particular, there is scarcely anything remaining of what I might call strictures on the United Kingdom authorities for disloyalty to agreed Anglo-American objectives. Where this appears at all, it is confined to "a section of British opinion" or some similar phrase.'

Furthermore, whilst the story of American resentment at Bridges's Washington mission remained, it had been watered down. It was also made clear that criticisms of ministers reflected Harrod's views alone. Rowe-Dutton therefore thought it impossible to offer further objections on these points. It is possible that, in the newly revised version, Harrod had further moderated his tone in the section dealing with Savannah, but he nevertheless remained open in his criticism of Vinson. Rowe-Dutton – who had travelled with Keynes on the boat back from the conference – advised Bridges:

Harrod gives a forthright account of the differences between Keynes and Vinson, in which he says that the Americans rail-roaded their views through the Conference. The whole chapter is rather unpleasant reading, but it records an unpleasant incident in

Anglo-American relations. It in no way exaggerates the resentment and disappointment felt by Keynes himself (I can personally testify to this). ... In my view a full exposition of Keynes' own views and Harrod's comments is in no way out of order.[53]

Harrod's final published account of Savannah certainly did not pull its punches:

He [Keynes] regarded Anglo-American co-operation, with mutual give and take, as the only means of saving the world. Savannah seemed to show that this was an unattainable ideal. There he had seen power used, for irrelevant motives, to frustrate a good purpose, and he had been denied by the possibility of the defeat of the British Loan in Congress the weapons to which a combatant was entitled. "I went to Savannah expecting to meet the world, and all I met was a tyrant."[54]

Harrod went on to qualify this by saying that Keynes later felt 'more hopeful' about the US attitude: 'There was a nice balance between the possibilities of a good and of an evil outcome.'[55] Nevertheless, Newton's allegation that the former disguised the extent of Keynes's pessimism seems unfair. Neither is it true that it was the Savannah passages that were the Treasury's main concern. Civil servants were far more worried about criticisms of British ministers who were still in office (and indeed of themselves) than they were about attacks on US officials who had since passed from the political scene. Thus Harrod's comparatively forthright account of the IMF/Bank meeting passed relatively unchallenged; indeed, as seen above, Rowe-Dutton testified to its broad accuracy.

As has been seen, Harrod's decision to consult Keynes's Treasury files led him to concede the government's right to vet his typescript.[56] Arguably, any access to archives that is attended by such conditions is a form of devil's compact that biographers ought to avoid at all costs, even at the price of forfeiting consultation of key historical materials. Even more arguably, Harrod should have put up a more robust defence than in fact he did, when civil servants went beyond their legitimate area of concern and sought to influence the *tone* of his book. Nevertheless, it was not the case that – as Newton appears to suggest – Harrod allowed the government to read his draft for no good reason, nor that he was utterly supine in the face of the considerable Establishment onslaught with which he was confronted. He did not allow all the teeth to be drawn from his account of Anglo-US economic relations. This was partly because he was eager to defend Keynes, and this could not be achieved without some measure of criticism of both the British and American governments.

If this chapter has offered a cautious and limited defence of Harrod, this should by no means be taken as an endorsement of his view of Keynes. Even aside from his treatment (or non-treatment) of the homosexuality and conscription questions, there are clear problems with his account. For example, Robert Hall, the Director of the Economic Section of the Cabinet Secretariat, even though he admired Harrod's book, noted: 'Roy has no conception of the damage Keynes did us in the US by his arrogance.'[57] But it is one thing to argue that Harrod got things wrong, and quite another to attribute all his errors or doubtful interpretations to wilful distortion.

Moreover, to explain Harrod's book merely in terms of the personal proclivities of its author is to remove much of the fascination of the tale. What is most interesting about the story are the mechanisms by which the British state exercised its power to influence what he wrote. But this was not merely an exercise in naked censorship. Civil servants also used persuasion, in order to get Harrod to alter his manuscript in the interests of Anglo-US relations: they were eager to manage the government's public image, ostensibly in the interests of assuring the Americans that the British could be trusted over future international economic commitments, but to some degree for the purposes of protecting their own reputations.

The tale of Harrod's original intentions, and the official attempts to frustrate them, is thus illustrative of the relationship between political pressure and the historical record. It also illuminates the gradually shifting biographical conventions of the Twentieth Century. Harrod was caught between the conflicting demands of frankness and deference, when the former was not yet fully possible and the latter was on the verge of going out of fashion.

10

'Our Amazonian Colleague'
Edith Summerskill's problematic reputation[1]

Penny Summerfield

Edith Summerskill was described in 1954 as 'the most successful of contemporary women politicians'.[2] She was Labour MP for West Fulham from 1938 to 1955 and for Warrington from 1955 to 1961; she held a junior ministerial position as Parliamentary Secretary at the Ministry of Food from 1945 to 1950 and political office as Minister for National Insurance 1950– 1; she was made a Privy Councillor in 1949; she became Chairman of the Labour Party 1954– 5 (when the comment was made) and she was awarded a life peerage in 1961, playing an active role in the House of Lords until her death in 1980. Such achievements were indeed remarkable among women. By 1961, when Summerskill was promoted to the House of Lords, there had been only three other women ministers of state,[3] and Nancy Astor (who never held ministerial position) was the only other woman who had been an MP for longer than 23 years. Yet unlike other notable women politicians of her era (for example Ellen Wilkinson, Jennie Lee, Barbara Castle and Eleanor Rathbone) Summerskill has not been the subject of a biography.[4]

This was not because she was an insufficiently 'controversial' political figure to be interesting. Summerskill was an anti-appeaser, sceptical of the efficacy of the League of Nations, and won the West Fulham by-election that brought her into Parliament in 1938 on this platform, attacking her Conservative opponent on these grounds as well as defying the pacifists in her own party.[5] She supported Republican Spain against the uprising led by General Franco, visiting Spain during the Civil War in 1938 and touring the U.S.A. thereafter to advocate its cause.[6] She was unusual among Labour women in combining socialism and concern for women's and children's welfare with a robust commitment to equal rights. The latter was more often associated in the 1930s, '40s and '50s with Conservative than with Labour women, as a result of which Summerskill worked with political colleagues from across the political spectrum.[7] Her project was one of modernization, in which cause men as well as women must change if democracy and social justice were to be realized. The controversial issues with which she was involved included the advocacy of birth control, painless childbirth and abortion law reform; equal rights for women at work and in marriage; the provision of pure, nutritious and affordable food; and opposition to the sport of boxing. Within the Labour Party in the 1950s she opposed Bevan and the 'Keep Left' movement, was pro-Arab when most of her colleagues veered towards supporting Israel, and opposed the development and use of nuclear weapons. She presented herself as the embodiment of feminine modernity, fulfilling multiple private and public roles: the wife and mother; the medical doctor; the politician. On the political stage she manipulated these different identities to her advantage, using her status as both a doctor and a mother to heighten her political authority. In short, she constructed her own political personality persuasively, as the modern woman whose life's work was to dissolve social and political boundaries defended by traditionalists who sought to perpetuate class as well as gender disadvantage.

However, Summerskill's reputation was and is insecure. In spite of her political successes, historians and biographers have frequently either excluded her from their accounts or referred to her dismissively.[8] Politicians' reputations are inherently precarious because contest and rivalry are central to party politics and it is not unusual for women politicians to be ignored or belittled in personal and historical accounts. The silence of Herbert Morrison's autobiography on the subject of Ellen Wilkinson, who was an important political ally as well as a close friend and possibly lover, is an extreme case.[9] But one might suggest that since women were neither vying for leadership (until Thatcher) nor part of the 'old boy network' they were, in general, not considered worthy of a prominent place in the historical account. Indeed this has fed the relative historiographical neglect both of women and politics and of gendered studies of politics, to which Susan Pedersen has recently referred.[10] Nevertheless it is surprising that the woman who was Parliamentary Secretary at the Ministry of Food and Minister of National Insurance in the post-war Labour governments, who was a member of the Labour Party's National Executive Committee and Shadow Cabinet in the 1950s and who chaired the Party for a year, should be mentioned so infrequently. When Summerskill did attract attention it was often startlingly negative: 'Amazon', 'Gorgon' and 'numskull' are three of the hostile epithets applied to her.[11]

This chapter will explore Summerskill's political personality as she represented it herself and as it was represented by others. Its aim is not to seek to achieve for her identity the stable foundation that it has hitherto lacked. Any identity, as Liz Stanley points out, has a 'shaky ontological character'[12] because 'selves' are both unique in themselves and relational, in the sense that they develop and acquire meaning through interactions with other people. There is no end point to the process, which carries on for as long as the relationships that construct identity continue. The evaluative side of the interactive construction of identities is the formation of reputation, which occurs during a person's lifetime and, through the various ways in which they are remembered or forgotten, after their death. If identity and reputation are, as a result, inherently unstable, they are, in the case of public figures, relatively well documented: self-representation as well as construction by others constantly finds its way into a variety of texts. In addition to the books and articles Summerskill wrote herself, including an autobiography published in 1967,[13] her parliamentary speeches contributed many column-inches to Hansard,[14] she featured in newspapers and magazines, in cartoons and in newsreel film, she was the subject of a *Times* obituary, and, as indicated above, she occasionally appeared in the pages of diaries and memoirs written by fellow politicians. Drawing on such sources and focusing on a selection of the political causes for which she fought, this chapter will explore the fractures, contradictions and silences in the representation of Summerskill by herself and others, in pursuit of explanations of her particularly problematic reputation.

A dominant emphasis in representations of Summerskill was as a doctor. Her medical background was used to explain her socialism, which might otherwise have been surprising in a middle-class woman from a Liberal family.[15] An obituary explained that 'her father was a doctor and as a girl she frequently drove with him on his rounds and became familiar at an impressionable age with the squalor of many of the streets and homes in south-east London'.[16] Summerskill elaborated on this in her autobiography, demonstrating how these experiences led her to qualify as a doctor at the age of twenty-three, in 1924. Her experiences 'in the consulting room'[17] as a general practitioner informed her commitment to preventative medicine, birth control and the reform of the abortion laws, as well as to the improvement of social conditions generally. These concerns in turn shaped her political career. In 1933, as a young doctor, she was co-opted on to the Maternity and Child Welfare Committee of Wood Green Urban District Council in the area of London in which she was practising. This led her to stand for election to the Middlesex County Council the following year, and thence to her parliamentary candidatures, starting with a by-election in Putney in 1934 where she drastically reduced the Conservative majority, even though she did not win the seat.[18] She continued to work as a general medical practitioner throughout her political career.

Summerskill, as a local council committee member, a county councillor and a parliamentary candidate, worked not only as a politicized medical practitioner but also as a feminist doctor. She pulled no punches on reproductive issues and their relation to women's health and the home. She declared her admiration for Marie Stopes and her view that 'uncontrolled reproduction' was a prime contributor to the high rates of infant and maternal mortality in Britain and elsewhere. She wrote of herself in the 1930s, 'As a modern young doctor, I favoured the planned family on economic, social and humane grounds'.[19] But birth control was a controversial issue in the interwar Labour Party and abortion was practically taboo. As Pamela Graves discusses, Labour women's lengthy campaign for Labour Party support for freely available birth control was rebuffed in this period, both because of enduring suspicion of the advocacy of birth control, rather than of the removal of class inequality, as a remedy for poverty, and because the campaign for birth control was seen as potentially dividing the party. There was a strong Catholic lobby within the labour movement, located particularly in the North of England, Northern Ireland and parts of Scotland, which upheld papal pronouncements that the practice of birth control was contrary to Christian law. Birth control was therefore dismissed by the Labour leadership as a private matter for the exercise of personal conscience, and not, as it was to the women campaigners, a fundamental issue of social welfare.[20]

Thus, while Summerskill's views on reproductive issues were evidently acceptable in London, she suffered for them politically in Bury. She was invited to accept nomination as the Labour candidate for this Lancashire constituency in the general election of 1935. Birth control did not feature in her manifesto, but when asked about it at public meetings in Bury she gave characteristically forthright answers advocating planned pregnancies 'for the sake of the parents and the children', and demonstrating the link between large families, high rates of infant mortality and poverty. Her autobiography offers a remarkable account of an attempt by the local Catholic Church, five days before polling day, to silence her on the issue. Four priests met with Summerskill and local Labour officials and offered to use their influence in the pulpit to deliver some 5,000 votes for Labour if she promised never again to teach women to use birth control. Summerskill described how she robustly rebuffed the proposition. The confrontation was marked, in her account, by an exchange of insults characteristic of her dealings with men whose views she implacably opposed. She suggested to a priest with a long beard that his approach bore the hallmark of medieval torture methods. He responded that she deserved such treatment.[21]

Summerskill made sure that there would be no repetition of this attempt to silence her in the next candidacy for which she was selected, West Fulham, the constituency for which she was returned following a by-election in 1938. Her experience of just the sort of religio-political divisions that the Labour leadership feared, did not stop her from addressing controversial reproductive issues. According to Graves, she was the only leading Labour woman in the 1930s to speak publicly about abortion, which she referred to in the context of debate about the relationship between malnutrition and maternal mortality at the National Conference of Labour Women (NCLW) in 1936. Only a year after the Bury experience Summerskill argued that bungled abortion, as well as inadequate maternity services and careless medical practice, were the main causes of maternal mortality, and that malnutrition was, at most, contributory. She was thereby taking a number of political risks. She was challenging the leaders of the NCLW, who hoped to bring their concerns closer to mainstream Labour policy, at that time focused on the links between unemployment and malnutrition, and who would not discuss abortion. She was aligning herself with middle-class feminist groups like the National Council of Women and the National Union of Societies for Equal Citizenship, who urged abortion law reform and with whom Labour women's relations were strained. And her position was at odds with that of the Labour leadership, which, having refused to take up the cause of birth control, adamantly refused to listen to calls for abortion law reform.[22]

Why did Summerskill take a political stance that could be seen as risky? One reason is a general one relating to her career as a whole. She was, simply, committed to standing up for what she believed in. Her autobiography suggests that her determination and personal capacity to form and express her views forcefully stemmed from family influences. Her father features in her account as an advocate of women's rights and as a crucial supporter of Edith's medical training as well as her political awakening, and she quotes her mother saying of him: 'If you believe a thing is wrong then you should say so'. She also describes her Aunt Eleanor, who was 'highly regarded' by Edith's father. Eleanor had been denied a serious education and career, but was keenly intelligent, widely read, good looking and 'indulged in an astringent wit'.[23] Eleanor was evidently a role model. A second reason for Summerskill's political risk-taking specifically on reproductive matters related to her experience in London where women electors and members of the Labour Party supported her position. North London women, including patients from her Wood Green medical practice as well as members of the local Labour Party, came in bus loads to help her canvass first Putney and later West Fulham.[24] As Graves argues, family limitation was a popular issue with the rank-and-file women of the Labour Party, even if the leadership snubbed their attempts to have it included in the party's political programme, and in London in the 1930s women succeeded in persuading some local authorities to distribute birth control information, in defiance of the official ban.[25] Finally, Summerskill was facilitated in taking a forthright position on birth control because she spoke with the authority of a qualified doctor. She was able to arbitrate 'scientifically' on the causes of health and sickness and the medical solutions to them. She made the case for birth control not only or primarily in terms of women's rights, but in relation to public health more generally.

The centrality of Summerskill's medical background to her political formation was well established by her and others and dominated both her self-presentation and the way in which she was represented to the

public. Official film coverage of a visit of Canadian and British
representatives of the Empire Parliamentary Association to New Zealand
and Australia in June 1944 is indicative.[26] In this short newsreel film,
Summerskill is introduced as the only woman member of the delegation
and a doctor. The film cuts to shots of her in a New Zealand munitions
factory, taking an interest in a blind man working at a machine and in the
women workers. The film then closes up on her face, as she tells the
audience, in the manner of a sympathetic consultant, that she has come
to New Zealand because it is exemplary for its social services that enable
the country to achieve exceptionally low rates of infant mortality and
long life expectancy. She indicates that she will take back to Britain the
lessons she has learned from this dominion and ensure that they are
heeded in British post-war reconstruction. She enunciates a message that
derives its force from her position as a medical expert and that
simultaneously compliments her hosts and clarifies her political agenda
to the British public.[27]

Summerskill's medical background was seen as defining not only the
political causes she took up, but also the way she performed her role as
an MP. Use of 'medi-speak' and the deployment of the persona of the
doctor were characteristic of her style. Pamela Brookes, in her book
Women at Westminster, writes: 'A good platform speaker, she was apt to
deflate hecklers by finding clinical explanations for their obstructive
behaviour.'[28] In the House of Commons she was adept at humorously
implying that her opponents were ignorant of some matter concerning
human biology, on which she, as a doctor, could put them right. For
example, in the Adjournment Debate of 18 December 1941 she
protested that young boys were being allowed to join the Home Guard,
while women were not. The following exchange took place.

> Dr Summerskill 'If boys of 16 are now allowed to join the Home
> Guard, why not have mature women to help the Home Guard?'
> Mr Benjamin Smith (MP for Rotherhithe): What is a mature
> woman?
> Dr Summerskill: 'I am sorry the honourable member has never
> met one. I will take the opportunity of having a word with him
> after the Debate'.[29]

Summerskill regularly deployed the language of biological science to
counter arguments against social change. For example, in 1942 she
responded to fears that uniformed women would lose their femininity by
stating that 'certain ductless glands determine the degree of femininity
displayed by women and … it is scientifically impossible and quite
unsound to suggest that a uniform, however severely cut, can influence
the secretions of the hormones'.[30] Such arguments were, however, full
of tensions. As in this case, Summerskill often used essentialist medical

discourse that expressed gender as fixed and determined by biology. But she also drew on historical accounts in which gender relations and identities were determined by social and economic conditions that were changing under the pressure of modernization and enlightenment. In the article quoted above, Summerskill claimed that recruiting women to the armed services would not destabilize gender identities: 'femininity' was biologically determined and would remain as it had always been. But at the same time she argued that women's military participation was a step towards equality between the sexes, that gender relations were changing as a result of the Second World War and that femininity was in transition: a 'new woman' was emerging from the war, demanding an equal place at work and in civic life as well as a new style of marriage.[31] At the heart of Summerskill's formulations of the case for women's rights was the central feminist dilemma observed by Denise Riley, Nancy Cott and others: the tension between basing political claims on women's special, innate characteristics and simultaneously demanding a future free from gender distinctions.[32]

In spite of her essentialist view that women were motivated above all by the desire to have children,[33] Summerskill argued adamantly for equal rights for women, in marriage as well as at work. She was unusual among feminists of the 1930s and 40s for fighting simultaneously for both sets of goals: welfare and equality. We have reviewed above some aspects of her commitment to measures to improve maternal and child welfare. She was also a leading member of the successful campaign for equal compensation for war injuries in 1941-43 and the unsuccessful attempt in 1943 to pass a bill, known as the 'Equal Citizenship (Blanket) Bill', that would remove all existing sex discrimination embodied in law, and prevent future legislation discriminating on the grounds of sex.[34] She participated in the Equal Pay Campaign Committee, which worked for equal pay for teachers and civil servants from 1944 to 1955.[35] She helped to launch the 'Women for Westminster' campaign to increase the representation of women in Parliament and on all public bodies.[36] She also fought from the early 1950s to eventual success in 1963, for the right of women to half of the joint savings of a marriage on separation or divorce,[37] and for the Matrimonial Homes Act, passed in 1967, which gave separated or divorced wives the right to occupy the matrimonial home.[38]

Of the many campaigns that Summerskill fought in the name of women's equality, one that has been largely overlooked was for women's equal membership of the Home Guard in the Second World War. My own encounters with Summerskill in research have arisen principally from an engagement with this issue,[39] so I was surprised both by its omission from, for example, her obituary in The Times, and by the relative lack of attention she paid to it herself in her autobiography.

The Home Guard was a voluntary defence organisation (originally called the Local Defence Volunteers) set up in May 1940 to defend Britain against the invasion that at that time was imminently anticipated. Not only did Summerskill demand a place for women in the Home Guard, but she believed also that they should be taught to shoot, the better to contribute to home defence. She fought for three years, in and out of Parliament, for women to join the Home Guard, working with other women, including the Conservative MP Mavis Tate, to form an unofficial armed organisation, Women's Home Defence, which aimed to serve alongside the male Home Guard. She took on the intense opposition of the War Office. Its members justified their strong preference for an all-male home defence force in terms of shortages (of weapons, instructors, uniforms etc). But arguably their opposition to Summerskill's demands constituted a last-ditch resistance to the wartime pressures to bring women into the war effort in general and the military sphere in particular. These pressures led to considerable change: between 1940 and 1943 nearly half a million women were recruited to the armed forces as auxiliaries, including some who worked alongside men on anti-aircraft gun sites and were permitted to do everything but pull the trigger.[40] Nevertheless, spokesmen for the War Office repeatedly stated that there was no role for women in the Home Guard.

Summerskill made her case verbally by infusing the rhetoric of wartime citizenship with the meanings of gender equality. For example, in July 1940 referring to Churchill's 'never surrender' speech, in which he asserted 'we shall fight on the beaches, we shall fight on the landing grounds, we shall fight in the fields and in the streets, we shall fight in the hills',[41] she asked 'how we are to fight in the hills, in the streets and in the houses, as envisaged by the Lord President in Council on Sunday, if women are excluded from the LDVs?'.[42] She built up an effective pressure group, drawing on supporters from across the political spectrum, including the MPs Eleanor Rathbone, (Independent), and Mavis Tate and Sir Thomas More, (both Conservative), as well as such public figures as Dame Helen Gwynne Vaughan, Director of the Auxiliary Territorial Service from 1939 to 41. Her goal was for women to be trained to fight alongside men and not to be mere 'fetchers and carriers'.[43] Women's Home Defence gave women rifle practice, as well as teaching them the other military skills learned by men in basic training, (including, for example, signalling, military intelligence and the use of mines and hand grenades). Its badge, showing crossed rifles and a revolver, was a direct signifier of these objectives. However, the government's eventual concession in April 1943 fell far short of Summerskill's expectations. Women over 45 could help the Home Guard as drivers, cooks and clerks, without becoming full members of the force; they would have no uniforms or other organisational rights; and they certainly would not be taught to shoot. Women's Home

Defence was explicitly excluded from the official scheme, which stated that women should be nominated to the Home Guard by a quite different organization, the Women's Voluntary Service. Not satisfied, Summerskill and Women's Home Defence, claiming at its height 20,000 members,[44] continued to campaign throughout 1943 and 1944. Even though it was never officially recognized, there is evidence that Women's Home Defence continued to train and work with local Home Guard units across the country in some cases as equal 'combatants', and in others as 'fetchers and carriers'.[45]

This exciting story, however, is not to be found in the main sources that document Summerskill's life. Her *Times* obituary emphasises her achievements as a Labour MP and life peeress in the field of the social services, especially in relation to the health and welfare of women and children, but her three-year campaign for women's membership of the Home Guard is not mentioned.[46] This omission is repeated in other accounts of Summerskill.[47] Indeed in her own autobiography, published in 1967, Summerskill refers to it only in passing and inaccurately with respect to chronology and ministerial identities.[48]

There are three possible explanations for this omission. Firstly, the Home Guard had faded from popular memory by 1967, as both a wartime creation that was never needed as a counter-invasion force and as a less-well-known 1950s anti-communist force that never attracted popular support.[49] What is more, by the time of Summerskill's death in 1980 it was a joke, due to the creation of the immensely successful television sitcom 'Dad's Army' in 1968.[50] Secondly, the partial rather than total success of the campaign for women's membership may have contributed to the silence that fell across it. The absence of full official acceptance of women, and the liminal position of Women's Home Defence, did not constitute a victory that made a major contribution to Summerskill's political reputation. Thirdly, Summerskill received considerable abuse for her efforts on this front. Her alleged feminine aggression in asking for women to be combatant members of the Home Guard was the object of special derision. She was routinely ignored or rebuffed in formal parliamentary exchanges on the issue and was privately insulted. For example, in official correspondence between Sir James Grigg, Secretary of State for War, and Herbert Morrison, Minister of Home Security in 1942, Grigg referred to her as 'our Amazonian colleague', and Morrison replied sarcastically that she 'wants a gun not a dishcloth'. When Summerskill approached Grigg in the lobby about Women's Home Defence, he said to her 'I don't want to hear any more about your bloody women', an 'unparliamentary expression' that deeply offended Summerskill.[51]

There is evidence that Summerskill's feminism concerning women's employment and marital rights made her male opponents uneasy or awakened their misogyny.[52] But as the interchanges quoted above suggest, her feminism concerning the arming of women struck them as totally outrageous. She persuaded a range of male leaders and some journalists to back her campaign in the specific circumstances of the Second World War, which placed women closer to combat than usual and temporarily eroded gender boundaries. But in the post-war climate of the restoration of conventional gender relations, retrospective sympathy for this cause disappeared.

Was Summerskill's campaign for women's equal membership of the Home Guard consistent with other campaigns that she fought? She represented it as such at the time. For example, her speech at the Stand Down of the Home Guard, and with it Women's Home Defence, in December 1944, depicted the women's Home Guard campaign as one dimension of the long historical struggle of women for equal rights. A journalist reported that the speech included the following points: 'The W.H.D. had made a wonderful contribution to Britain. Some felt the organisation had not received the recognition it deserved. Women have still to establish themselves in the scheme of things. They had a long way to go before their merits are acknowledged. She urged them to keep on fighting, to establish once and for all that they can make a contribution to Society which is equal to that of any man.'[53] Women's Home Defence became the Women's Rifle Association at the end of the war, and Summerskill gave her blessing to this organisation for women to train and compete in shooting as a sport, seeing it as one among a number of new opportunities for women consequent upon the war.

Women's Home Defence may not have achieved all of its objectives, but its symbolic significance for Summerskill was that it demonstrated her capacity to mobilise popular support for a cause that was both controversial and, in gender terms, radical. Summerskill's charisma as a leader was not the only factor. She was also tapping into popular wartime feeling about resisting invasion, supporting the war effort and creating innovatory forms of organisation that ignored conventional class and gender divides. However, after the war Summerskill's promotion to government office marked a distinct shift in her rapport with the public. She remained a popular constituency MP, being returned for West Fulham in 1945, 1950 and 1951, and for Warrington in 1955 after boundary changes caused her old constituency to disappear. But her ascent to political office and committed approach to restrictive government policies considerably altered her political persona.

As Parliamentary Secretary at the Ministry of Food, Summerskill had responsibility for advocating the extension of rationing, notably to bread and potatoes, which had not been rationed in wartime. She also urged the acceptance of unpopular foods, such as snoek, a tinned fish from South Africa, and it fell to her to announce restrictions on imports of popular foods in favour of cheap and nutritious varieties. One case over which there were protests was French cheese, which was restricted in favour of types of cheese that were condemned as 'mousetrap' by her opponents.[54] Summerskill usually responded with patient explanations of the difficult import position and the government's responsibility to continue to ensure adequate food supplies for the health of the whole population. But provoked by the Camembert campaign, she snapped back with a counter-charge of snobbery: 'The function of the Ministry of Food is not to pander to an acquired taste but to ensure that the people who have never had time to acquire these tastes are suitably fed'.[55] In 1949 she declared to an Oxford University society that it was impossible to tell the difference between butter and margarine. She was lampooned for it for years, mainly for the implied arrogance of assuming that the public would not know any better.[56] But food was an issue that Summerskill, as a devotee of preventative medicine, took very seriously. She regarded as 'her finest hour' the achievement in 1949 of legislation requiring that all dairy herds must be tested for tuberculous infection and their milk pasteurized, to prevent the spread of bovine tuberculosis, a crippling disease affecting young children.[57]

However, far from leading a popular cross-party women's movement in the post-war years, Summerskill was subject to hostile questioning on the government's policy on food from many MPs, including Labour women elected in 1945,[58] and she also had to contend with pressure against government controls on food and clothing from the British Housewives' League, an organisation with a right-wing agenda critical not only of Summerskill but of Labour's post-war policies generally.[59] Her popularity with women from across the political and social spectrum, on which her success had previously been based, was placed under considerable strain, and an image of Summerskill as a middle-aged killjoy started to replace that of her as a lively young advocate of women's rights. This image was perpetuated later. In his popular account of the post-war years, Noel Annan described her as a 'progressive puritan' who took pleasure in imposing austerity on an unwilling population and denying them their desires.[60]

Summerskill's reputation as the functionary of a severe nanny state was strengthened by her opposition to the sport of boxing. She published an indictment of the sport in 1956, *The Ignoble Art*, and repeatedly attempted to introduce bills restricting it. Her main arguments were that there was medical evidence that punches to the head, the main target in boxing, caused permanent brain damage and that the sport debased spectators by appealing to what she called 'latent sadistic instincts'. Her statements linked boxing, the glamorisation of violence, and war, and she urged that boxing should be banned and young men should be taught to 'hate violence and control their aggressive instincts' in the interests of world peace.[61]

The contrast with her Women's Home Defence campaign is sharp. While Summerskill urged in 1943 that women's aggressive instincts should be developed, that they should be armed with rifles and that they should be taught to shoot to kill, she argued in 1953 that men's aggression should be constrained, that they should be prevented from hitting each other with their fists and that pugilism should not be regarded as suitable entertainment. The temporal context of each set of arguments perhaps explains the superficial contradiction. Summerskill saw the Second World War as a just war against a fascist enemy and was confident that women's participation could help to bring it to a successful end; whereas her anti-boxing campaign took place in the context of the Cold War threat of a nuclear war which, she believed, it was important that men did not start. (She was consistently anti-nuclear. She defied charges of covert communism when speaking at a Trafalgar Square rally against Nuclear Weapons Tests in 1957, and repeatedly advanced the argument that fall-out from nuclear tests contaminated the atmosphere and caused leukaemia.)[62] Summerskill achieved some successes in relation to boxing. For example in 1954 she prevented the lowering of Entertainment Tax on prizefights. (She hoped that high taxes would end their viability). But she suffered plenty of setbacks. Boxing was celebrated as a site not only of popular leisure but also of working-class aspirations and masculine aesthetics.[63] Her bills for the complete prohibition of boxing were defeated in parliament in 1960 and 1962 amidst derisive comment from both sides of the House to the effect that she was a spoilsport. Her critics included her fellow woman Labour MP Bessie Braddock who was a Vice-President of the Professional Boxing Association.[64] Summerskill's campaign lasted throughout the 1950s, 60s and 70s. These years devoted to anti-aggression were not ones in which to recall her campaign to arm women and teach them to kill.

Yet, ironically, in just the years in which she campaigned against male aggression, in the boxing ring as on the world stage, Summerskill was perceived by some of her male colleagues as an unattractively aggressive woman. Ian Mikardo, a left-wing member of the Labour Party's National Executive Committee in the early 1950s, referred to her and other women colleagues on the NEC as 'Amazons'[65] and to Summerskill specifically as 'Medusa the Gorgon'.[66] He was himself a controversial figure, seen by some as a communist fellow-traveller set on wrecking the Labour Party, while his allies (such as Aneurin Bevan, Barbara Castle and Richard Crossman) believed he was working with them against a right-wing leadership to maintain the commitment of the Party to its left-wing vision. As his use of the term 'Amazon' suggests, Mikardo's misogyny towards women who opposed him politically took a combative, embattled form. But his special venom towards Summerskill had more specific origins. It was prompted by her attitude to his support of Nye Bevan and by her behaviour on a particular occasion. In 1955 Bevan's opponents on the NEC tried to pass a motion of censure, which would

have led to Bevan's removal from the Executive. Numbers for and
against the motion were evenly divided, but in Mikardo's absence
abroad, and with Summerskill's casting vote as Chair of the NEC, the
motion would have been carried. Mikardo, however, received a tip-off
and returned just in time to defeat the motion. He compared
Summerskill's appearance on his arrival to that of 'Medusa the Gorgon',
the mythical female with snakes for hair, capable of turning men to
stone. Summerskill allegedly could not bring herself to say his name
when, as Chair, she had to allow him to speak later in the meeting, and
referred to him as 'the man in the brown suit', an epithet in which
Mikardo, Castle and others appear to have taken ironic delight.[67] It seems
mild compared with 'Medusa the Gorgon'.

Amazons and Gorgons are powerful figures. Even though the terms
were intended as insults, they attest to the political salience that
Summerskill had achieved. Possibly more serious for her reputation were
comments in the diaries of Hugh Gaitskell and Richard Crossman,
published in the 1980s, alleging that she was stupid. Gaitskell claimed in
1956 that she was emotional, did not listen and 'is not really intelligent'.[68]
Crossman, unable to secure for himself a place in the Shadow Cabinet,
referred to her as 'gaga' in a character-assassination of most of the
opposition front bench in November 1957, and as 'poor, old, effete,
numskull Edith Summerskill' in November 1958, when, in view of her
non-election to the NEC he had hoped that there would be place for
him in the Shadow Cabinet.[69] If Crossman's rudeness was prompted in
part by political rivalry, Gaitskell's was apparently provoked more by
Summerskill's manner, which could be patronising,[70] than by political
disagreements.[71] Both regarded her as emotional and inclined to
personalise issues. These were traits from which their male colleagues
(such as Bevan and George Brown) were by no means free, but when
attributed to Summerskill they became gender stereotypes that justified
dismissing her.

Summerskill herself emphasised her gender in the way she conducted
politics. In doing so, she constructed for herself a specific type of
feminine identity, that of the faithful wife and caring mother. This was in
sharp contrast to other women MPs, few of whom were married or had
children.[72] Summerskill's brand of uxorious and maternal femininity may
not have appealed to her male colleagues as much as the more sexually
daring personae of, for example, Barbara Castle or Jennie Lee.[73]
Summerskill drew repeatedly on her identity as a wife and mother for
authority, referring to her husband, her son and her daughter in speeches
in parliament when it suited her to do so. She publicly asserted that her
family came first. For example in her autobiography she told the story of
discovering on her appointment as Minister of National Insurance in
1950 that she would have no private telephone. 'The thought of not
speaking to my husband, the children and Nana ... dismayed me. As I

stood in that room for the first time as the new Minister I was only
conscious of a warm feeling of love for my family flooding my whole
being. I knew then that my family took precedence over any worldly
aspirations. "See that a phone is installed" I said. The telephone arrived
the next day.'[74] This account encapsulates the problem of sustaining the
dual role of a public career and a private family life. The striking
modernity of Summerskill's solution – the technology of the telephone –
and of her authority as a woman-at-the-top in ensuring that it was put at
her disposal, give the story its impact. But the claim is exaggerated: a
telephone could not and did not literally give the family 'precedence'
over ministerial responsibilities.

Elsewhere Summerskill indicated that technology alone was by no
means enough: her two careers as doctor and politician could only be
combined with motherhood due to a supportive husband, Jeffrey
Samuel, and a fulltime housekeeper, Agnes Wakeford, the 'Nana' of the
story of the phone. The employment of a housekeeper was not unusual
in well-off middle-class, professional households, including those in
which the wife did *not* work, in the period (although the Samuel-
Summerskill ménage was lucky to keep Nana through the war). But the
companionate marriage[75] with a co-professional in the 1920s to the
1950s, and Summerskill's use of her maiden name, were innovative. She
explained her decision not to change her name as a consequence of her
inclusion on the medical register as 'Summerskill' in 1924, before her
marriage. But she and her husband took the challenge to patriarchal
traditions further, by giving their two children the surname Summerskill.
Her daughter, Shirley, entered Parliament in this name as Labour MP for
Halifax in 1966.[76] Jeffrey Samuel was repeatedly questioned about these
transgressions, and responded robustly: 'A man doesn't change his name
when he marries, so why should a wife change hers? ... It's quite unfair
for the children always to take on the name of the father. I was glad to
make my small contribution to redress the balance.'[77] In spite of this
radicalism, Summerskill's marriage does not appear to have been read,
even retrospectively, as a model for the dual career family of the 1960s
and 70s and for the feminist challenge to marital conventions of the 70s
and 80s. Possibly as a counter to the self-assertion signified by her choice
of name, Summerskill was widely known in political circles as Dr Edith.

Sympathetic writers echoed Summerskill's declarations about the
balance between home and work, but used them to naturalize her by
restoring to the powerful professional and political woman her domestic
priorities. A film profile of 1945, entitled 'Mrs, Dr, M.P.' followed her
'tri-partite existence' through a typical day, walking the dog and
shopping, making medical visits, reading parliamentary papers en route
for the Commons and talking to a journalist there, and ended by
returning with her to the bosom of her warm and loving family.[78] The
Times obituary was explicit: 'Formidable feminist as she was, Edith

Summerskill was a devoted wife and mother and amid all the turmoil of the political life in which she later became involved she found her main happiness in her home and family'.[79] In the hands of less sympathetic commentators her combination of career and marriage was treated more critically. A *New Statesman* profile in 1954, for instance, suggested that her dual career robbed her of feminine charm: 'it is not enough to prove that some women without outside interests can succeed – it must also be proved that the wife and mother can succeed, and this Dr Edith sets out to do. She feels the responsibility heavily; and the strain of it has left its mark on her face and her demeanour, has robbed her of her beauty and left her sternly handsome'.[80] It was a re-run of 'our Amazonian colleague' – the woman who cut off a breast the better to fire her arrows, sacrificing femininity for the fight. The article concluded with a strong piece of normalization. 'Dr Summerskill may scare her colleagues: Dr Samuel's wife is a very likeable woman'.[81]

The *New Statesman* profile sought to open the lines of fracture in Summerskill's personality, by dividing the doctor and the politician from the wife and mother, and setting them against each other. There were, as we have seen, tensions between the identities she sought to hold together, as there were within her feminism and between some of her campaigns, notably before and after 1945. Nevertheless, Summerskill's self-representation emphasized the integration of the maternal, wifely, medical, political, feminist woman. She was throughout her career an authoritative medical practitioner. She was a faithful wife and a loving mother. She was steadfastly committed to the cause of women's rights and welfare. And she combined loyalty to her party with determination to stand up for what she believed in, however unpopular the cause.

But this consistency meant that in the 1960s, when Summerskill sat in the Lords, her political persona was dated: she was an Attlee rather than a Wilson woman, and the modernity of her feminist vision was soon to be over-shadowed by the new style of feminism that emerged at the end of the 60s, committed to libertarian experiment rather than constitutional procedures. Even though her combination of roles was innovatory, the way she conducted each of them was conventional. She was involved in no scandals. In the 1950s and 60s she placed herself outside the excitements and peccadilloes of her colleagues. While Barbara Castle was throwing hilarious parties in Highgate Village, Edith Summerskill was walking the dog and enjoying the company of her husband in Kenwood.[82]

It was, ultimately, less the contradictions in Summerskill's identity that made her reputation problematic, than the coherence and consistency that she strove to maintain and which provided the bedrock of her political influence and success. But she was, in consequence, constructed as 'an unattractive female';[83] her reputation was diminished; and the complex and fascinating task she set herself, of creating an identity for a public, professional and family woman in the twentieth century, was forgotten.

11

Michael Foot as Labour leader
The uses of the past

Paul Corthorn

Michael Foot led the Labour party through turbulent times. As leader of the opposition from November 1980 until October 1983, he had to face an on-going threat from the hard left – comprising not just high-profile parliamentary figures such as Tony Benn and Eric Heffer but also the Trotskyite Militant Tendency. He had to endure the secession from the party of a number of prominent right-wing figures to create the Social Democratic Party (SDP), which later joined forces with the Liberals to form the Alliance. Above all, Foot had to meet the challenge of Thatcherism - overseeing the Labour party's adjustment to a situation in which the Conservatives, since taking power in 1979 under Margaret Thatcher, were overturning the post-war consensus. Against the backdrop of these enormous difficulties, Foot's leadership is not widely considered to have been a success. The enduring image of Foot is of a man wedded to policies – such as unilateral disarmament – which were not popular with the wider public and who, after a lifetime in the Labour party, appeared at least as interested in the past as in the present.

There is no doubt that during Foot's tenure as Labour leader a large amount of attention was focused on the question of leadership. He was pitted against Thatcher whose personality, according to David Butler and Denis Kavanagh's Nuffield study of the 1983 general election, 'was central to British politics between 1979 and 1983'.[1] After a brief honeymoon period just after his election as leader, while Thatcher was being held responsible for rising unemployment, Foot consistently trailed her popularity – a trend that intensified after the Falklands' conflict of 1982.[2] As the 1983 general election approached, Thatcher 'came to be regarded by Conservative campaigners as their greatest electoral asset'. The public may not have considered her compassionate, but she was 'admired as a decisive, resolute and principled leader', qualities which 'seemed reinforced by comparison with Mr Foot'.[3] By this point Foot's standing was particularly low – markedly below that of the party as a whole. Very clearly he 'did not present himself as a Prime Minister in waiting'.[4] He was, moreover, the 'principal target' of Conservative and Alliance attacks.[5] Polls showed that Labour would be more widely appealing to the electorate if Denis Healey, the right-winger who Foot narrowly defeated in the party leadership contest in 1980, was leader.[6] In Australia a last minute change of leadership had seemingly played a part in the Australian Labour party's electoral success and this further encouraged press speculation that Foot should go. It was, in part, for these reasons that in the weeks before the election the Labour Campaign Committee decided to focus on the party's collective leadership. Nevertheless, Foot's personality, and its perceived weaknesses, continued to attract most of the attention.[7]

Popular views of Foot at this juncture were, of course, far from flattering. Foot, who was 70 years of age, was clearly unsuited to television campaigning.[8] Just weeks before the general election the Thatcherite *Sun* asked blatantly: 'Do you seriously want this old man to run Britain?'[9] Foot was seen as a 'nice, shambling, elderly and long-winded man', who had only hesitantly stood up to the hard left. Furthermore, Butler and Kavanagh noted how Foot's friends 'were dismayed by his propensity to fight past battles'. The most conspicuous example of this occurred in Oxford on 19 May 1983 when he criticized the Conservative Lord Hailsham, now Lord Chancellor, for his endorsement of Neville Chamberlain's policy of appeasement in 1938.[10]

On many other occasions throughout his time as Labour leader, Foot had invoked the memories of his early political life. Some of the more astute contemporary commentators noted his particular fondness for the 1930s, rightly recognising this as Foot's political childhood.[11] Others made broadly the same points, though in a less nuanced way. Discussing the speech he made upon becoming leader on 10 November 1980, *The Sun* criticized Foot's 'taste for nostalgia'. The leading article emphasized how readily he had mentioned '1934 - the year he joined the Labour party - the pre-war poverty on Merseyside ... and his romanticised hero, Aneurin Bevan, who died twenty years ago'.[12] Another contemporary commentator noted that:

> In every television and radio interview so far there has come a point at which the old boy's mind has started to drift back across the decades. Suddenly he is fighting, yet again, the epic battles of his youth and early manhood against altogether more glamorously evil foes than are on offer at present. Soon those foes become curiously subsumed in those of today.[13]

Perhaps one of the best-known occasions when Foot invoked the past, and was subsequently criticized for it, was over the Argentine invasion of the Falkland Islands in April 1982. Healey later aptly described how Foot saw it as 'an act of naked, unqualified aggression by a brutal military dictatorship' that was nothing less than 'a repetition of the Nazi challenge which Britain had failed to meet in the thirties'.[14] After initially favouring British action, Foot appeared to waver and at different points called for a negotiated settlement.[15] Overall, however, it is clear that Foot did see huge similarities between the Falklands and the Second World War.[16]

The principal political consequence of Foot's repeated invocation of the past is clear. It meant that, as Butler and Kavanagh rightly noted, Foot 'seemed out of date to many of the public', diminishing further his – and Labour's - electoral appeal.[17] The centrist MP, Austin Mitchell, wrote critically but perceptively of Foot's mistake in speaking 'to a young generation of Bevan, the health service [and] Neville Chamberlain, the great causes of yesterFoot'.[18] In any case, the Conservatives subsequently swept to victory in June 1983, increasing their majority from 44 to 150. This, in turn, strengthened Thatcher's position within the government, allowing her to fill the Cabinet with her own supporters and to push on with her radical agenda, which included privatization of many of the nationalized industries.

What this chapter investigates is the political uses Foot sought to make of his recollections of the past – an angle that has been largely unexplored. The early 'contemporary histories', mirroring press coverage, were almost all critical of Foot's ability, and damning of his achievements, as Labour leader.[19] More recent studies have, to an extent, succeeded in rehabilitating Foot. They have emphasized the difficult conditions in which he struggled to check threats from both the Labour right and left, and suggested that he did, in fact, exhibit a certain skill in managing the party.[20] Even so, few would go so far as Foot's biographer Mervyn Jones who has suggested that Foot 'was the man who saved the Labour party'.[21] This chapter seeks to add a further layer of understanding to Foot's time as leader by arguing that his use of the past was a central part of his broader political strategy. The chapter begins by giving an overview of Foot's career, demonstrating in particular how he came to political maturity in the 1930s. It then considers how Foot used memories of the 1930s, and to a lesser extent the 1940s, to criticize the Thatcherite attack on the post-war consensus. Finally it analyses how he also invoked memories of his early political life and connection with Aneurin Bevan as a means of discrediting the hard left. Throughout, the chapter draws extensively on reports of Foot's speeches, along with his contemporary writings.

Foot was born in 1913 into a politically active West Country family.[22] His father, Isaac Foot, was a staunch Liberal, and initially Foot followed his father's political inclinations. While he was an undergraduate at Wadham College, Oxford between 1931 and 1934 Foot was a prominent Liberal. Indeed, in 1934 he contributed a piece entitled 'Why I am a Liberal' to a collection of essays. At Oxford he befriended John Cripps - the son of Sir Stafford Cripps, the prominent left-wing Labour MP. Despite many visits to the Cripps family home, however, Foot remained a Liberal. It was not until after he had graduated from Oxford, and was working in a Liverpool firm owned by Cripps's brother, that he became a socialist. The unemployment and accompanying poverty that he saw in the North West now prompted him to move politically leftwards. He joined the Labour party, risking a rift with his family, and subsequently stood as a Labour parliamentary candidate for Monmouth - an unwinnable seat - in the general election of 1935.

Most of Foot's political energies were soon directed into the Socialist League, which he joined in 1936. The Socialist League, the organ of the Labour left between 1932 and 1937, had been formed from a merger between G.D.H. Cole's think-tank, the Society for Socialist Inquiry and Propaganda (SSIP), and the part of the Independent Labour Party (ILP) that chose not to disaffiliate from the Labour party in 1932. Foot quickly became very active in the Socialist League, getting himself elected onto its influential London Area Committee. Through the Socialist League Foot cemented his friendship with Cripps who was its chairman between 1933 and 1936 and funded a large part of its activities. He also met William Mellor, who Foot later described as 'the granite-like conscience of the Socialist League'[23] and who became its chairman in 1936. Furthermore, Foot's involvement with the League enabled him to become acquainted with the famous socialist writer H.N. Brailsford, and to establish a long-running political friendship with Barbara Betts (later Castle), another young Oxford graduate.[24]

Perhaps the most important influence on Foot at this stage was Bevan, a former South Wales miner and a renowned left-winger, who moved on the fringes of the Socialist League. For all their differences in social background, Foot quickly established a strong bond with Bevan, much stronger than that with Cripps. In early 1937 Foot, along with Bevan, was fully involved in the Unity Campaign - a proposed association or United Front between the three socialist parties - the Labour party, the ILP and the Communist Party of Great Britain (CPGB) - which sought to destabilize the National Government in order to bring to power a Labour government better able to meet the growing challenge of fascism in Europe. Foot also began work for *The Tribune*, the newspaper set up by Cripps in order to spearhead the Unity Campaign, co-writing a column on industrial matters with Betts. The Socialist League was soon compelled by the Labour party to shut itself down for its involvement with the CPGB, and the Unity Campaign fizzled out. However, Foot continued working on *The Tribune* until July 1938 when he resigned after an argument with Cripps over the merits of an extended Popular Front that would include Liberals as well as just socialists.

Next Foot began working for Lord Beaverbrook's *Daily Express* but retained his left-wing outlook. In summer 1940 he was one of the three authors (along with Peter Howard and Frank Owen) of *Guilty Men* - a fierce political polemic - published under the pseudonym of 'Cato'. This fiercely criticized the National government since 1931 for its failure to rearm in order to meet the threat from Hitler. Ramsay MacDonald, the former Labour leader who had defected to head the National government until 1935 was attacked, as was the Conservative leader Stanley Baldwin who succeeded him as prime minister in 1935. Particular vehemence, however, was reserved for the Conservative Neville Chamberlain who replaced Baldwin in May 1937 and carried the policy of appeasement to further lengths. Significantly, in taking this line, *Guilty Men* completely exonerated not only the Labour party but also the Conservative dissidents around Winston Churchill – the groups that had coalesced in May 1940.

Foot continued to work for the *Express* during the Second World War. In 1945 he won a seat for Plymouth Devonport and the following year became joint editor of *Tribune*. He established himself as a leading left-winger during the Attlee governments of 1945-51, and became the most prominent 'Bevanite' in the 1950s as the party divided between the followers of Bevan and those of the more moderate Hugh Gaitskell. Foot lost his seat in the 1955 election but returned to Parliament in 1960 as MP for Ebbw Vale, the seat held by Bevan until his death earlier that year. After Harold Wilson became Labour prime minister in 1964, Foot remained a backbencher, providing left-wing criticism of the government.

Following Labour's defeat in the 1970 general election, however, Foot's career changed direction: he accepted a place on Labour's frontbench, which allowed him easily to move into the Cabinet as Employment Secretary after Labour regained power in 1974. Following Wilson's resignation in 1976 he stood for the leadership but lost to Jim Callaghan. Nevertheless, he became Deputy Leader of the party and played a full part in ensuring the government's survival through the difficult years of the late 1970s. After defeat by the Conservatives in May 1979, Callaghan continued as party leader until October 1980. This prompted a leadership campaign, which Foot was initially reluctant to enter. However, after encouragement from several quarters, and believing he was best positioned to hold the party together, he put himself forward and eventually defeated Healey in the second stage.

Foot's career, then, had a number of distinct phases. However, it was undoubtedly during the 1930s that he had matured politically. Most obviously this was when he met his mentor, Bevan, whose two-volume biography he later wrote, and about whom he spoke with the utmost admiration at every opportunity.[25] It was also the era that most shaped his political beliefs. When Labour lost power in 1979 Foot contemplated writing an autobiography. He eventually rejected the idea and instead wrote *Debts of Honour*, which was published in 1980 and contained 14

essays. Some of the figures chosen were historical figures, ranging from
Daniel Defoe to Benjamin Disraeli. However, Foot also wrote about
eight people he had encountered during his lifetime and whom he greatly
admired. Interestingly, as Mervyn Jones notes, seven of these were
people he had met before 1940.[26] The collection, for instance, included
an essay on Brailsford, his former colleague in the Socialist League.[27]

Foot's habit of explicitly drawing lessons from his earlier political
experiences was an integral part of his criticism of Thatcherism and its
attack on the post-war consensus. This consensus – involving a
commitment to the welfare state, including the National Health Service,
Keynesian economics as a means of ensuring full employment, and the
mixed economy - had begun to develop during the Second World War.[28]
Most of the major legislative changes were, however, implemented by
the Labour governments after 1945. Significantly, although this was an
agenda largely set by the Labour party, it was one that the Conservatives
broadly accepted when they returned to power in 1951.[29]

During Thatcher's second term it was her privatization of nationalized
industries - such as gas and telecommunications - that most vividly
symbolised her destruction of the post-war consensus. However, in
1980, when Foot became leader, it was the Thatcherite attack on
Keynesian economics that was most prominent. Thatcher's government
argued that inflation, rather than unemployment, was the principal target
and that it could be controlled by the introduction of monetarism - an
economic theory asserting that the rate of inflation was directly related to
the rate of increase in the money supply. Since the Conservatives had
taken power in 1979 unemployment had risen continuously.

Predictably in his articles and speeches Foot drew attention to the
rising unemployment. Not only did this involve praising the
achievements since 1945, but also emphasising the horror of the 1930s.
In a perceptive recent article Philip Williamson has stressed that: 'In one
fundamental sense a British post-war consensus certainly existed:
repudiation and denigration of interwar governments and their leaders'.[30]
In particular, during the post-war years the 1930s were derided as an era
when the National government failed to deal with mass unemployment
as well as the threat from the dictators. This supposed link between
domestic economic policy and foreign and defence policies was
prefigured in Foot's own co-authored *Guilty Men* and firmly entrenched
in the years after 1945 by more literature and rhetoric in the
'Churchillian-Labour-Keynesian' mould.[31]

During the early 1980s parallels with the 1930s were readily made.[32]
On 29 November 1980, within three weeks of being elected as Labour
leader, Foot was speaking at a march in Liverpool to publicise the
number of unemployed in the area. Like many others, he stressed that
these levels of unemployment had not been seen since the 1930s.[33] Foot,

however, did more than simply make comparisons between the decades. In his account of the 1983 general election, *Another Heart and Other Pulses*, he retrospectively noted that after becoming Labour leader the development of an attack on the Thatcherite rejection of the post-war consensus, which he held directly responsible for the extent of mass unemployment, had 'become part of my Socialism'.[34]

Foot had made this clear from an early stage in his leadership. In his first article after becoming leader, which was published in the *Sunday Mirror* on 23 November 1980, he sketched out the nature of his criticisms of Thatcher's attitude to unemployment. He objected to the way that she treated it as 'temporary' on the basis that a certain amount of unemployment would have to be tolerated until the markets learnt to regulate themselves and inflation was brought under control. Foot argued that his own experience had showed him that 'every previous slump left ravages taking generations to repair'. He explained that in Liverpool in 1934 he had seen 'for the first time in my young life ... what poverty meant'. It was there he 'saw mass unemployment as the most fearful curse which could befall our people', and how 'long-term unemployment for more than a million of our citizens meant lives broken for ever'. Crucially, Foot argued that in the 1930s 'there was something even worse than the mass unemployment and its associated infamies'. What really stung Foot was being told that there was 'no alternative: nothing can be done', that it was 'not a question of compassion, not a matter of politics'. He recalled that in the 1930s the National Government said that unemployment was 'decreed by the laws of economics or, rather, the laws of arithmetic' – this was the assertion that money 'to help one industry in one place can be found only be robbing someone else'. Foot argued that this was 'strangely familiar'. He went on:

> Sometimes today in the House of Commons, when I'm listening to Mrs Thatcher, I can close my eyes and imagine I'm listening to that earlier Tory leader, Neville Chamberlain, reciting the Thatcher fairy tale (or demon-tale). Nothing can be done. The unemployed must wait in their dole queues until private enterprise, in God's own time, offers them 'a real job'.

Significantly for Foot, Thatcher's actions were more reprehensible than Chamberlain's. This was because experiences since the Second World War had 'proved in practice - contrary to all the nonsense preached by economic professors and Tory politicians in the 1930s - that something like full employment could be established and sustained in modern industrial communities, if the will was there'. Foot was passionate about 'our achievement, right from 1945 to just about the early 1970s', which 'Thatcher and her ministers ask us to cast aside'.[35]

Time and again throughout his leadership, Foot pushed the same themes in a number of different settings. He made his case when speaking in a debate at the Oxford Union - of which he had been President during his final year at Oxford - in late 1980.[36] He reiterated it to local parties on a number of occasions.[37] At the 1982 Labour party conference he memorably argued that 'what we are suffering from now is not so much the slump as the Tory measures of recovering from a slump'.[38] And he made such arguments absolutely central to his election campaign in 1983 - ensuring not only that they were placed prominently within his foreword to the manifesto[39] but also emphasising them constantly as he toured the country in May 1983.[40]

In criticising the abandonment of the post-war consensus, Foot made sure that earlier Conservative governments and leaders since 1945 were not attacked with the same intensity as Thatcher. Speaking in Ebbw Vale in the week before the 1983 general election, he argued:

> We are facing a new breed of Tory leadership. I am not saying that we never attacked the earlier manifestations. Of course we did, and rightly. When we attacked Churchill for what he did to the Labour movement in the 1920s and 1930s, we were right. When we attacked Churchill for what he tried to do after 1945, to destroy the Labour Government of that time, to block the introduction of the Health Service and the great measures which we introduced then, of course we were right to attack him. And when we attacked the Never-Had-It-So-Good Macmillan Government – even though it was vastly superior to the present one – we were right ... But I must say I think the present breed has an odious nature all its own. The Thatcher-Tebbit leadership of the party has a special streak of meanness in it. It is that Tebbit-Thatcher meanness which dictates that in a crisis they cut the pay of the unemployed, cut the benefits of those who are poorest, try to economize on the people who are suffering most sorely.[41]

The nature of Foot's attack on the 'curse of monetarism'[42] meant that he had to champion Keynesian policies. As a one-time 'socialist critic of Keynes'[43] he now had to portray himself as 'an unreconstructed Keynesian',[44] which was not an altogether easy transition. However, the potential difficulties were minimised because Foot kept discussion of his alternative economic policies deliberately vague. This was a strategy with an additional political advantage: it conveniently enabled him to shift attention away from Labour at a time when it was struggling to formulate new economic policies. This was why Foot often fell back on obliquely asserting that Labour would introduce 'first-aid measures' as well as 'more far-reaching measures'.[45] Similarly, on other occasions he contended simply that reflation was needed.[46]

In any case, Foot's use of the past to attack Thatcher involved more than just economics. He made it clear that, in his view, the Conservatives' failure to tackle unemployment in the 1930s was still related to their unwillingness to stand up to Hitler. In December 1981 the Conservative MP, Julian Critchley, began a campaign to erect a statue of Baldwin in the House of Commons. By March 1982 he had collected 103 MPs' signatures including those of the former Labour prime ministers Wilson and Callaghan. However, Foot adamantly refused to sign the petition. For him Baldwin epitomised everything about the 1930s that he despised (and which he argued Thatcher was trying to recreate). Unsurprisingly, Foot offered to send Critchley a copy of *Guilty Men* 'to make plain his view of Mr Baldwin'.[47] Of course, Foot's arguments may have carried less weight after Thatcher had recaptured the Falklands later in 1982 but they did strike a chord with other Labour MPs at the time. A quick poll in *The Times* showed that many of them identified Baldwin with unemployment and appeasement.[48]

Foot also used references to the past as a means of attacking Thatcher's emphasis on what she famously termed 'Victorian values'.[49] Speaking in Ebbw Vale in early June 1983, he expressed his hope that the 'whole might of these valleys will be mobilized to ensure that we are not going to be driven back to any Victorian darkness'.[50] Foot developed this point after the 1983 election defeat. Asking the party to re-evaluate its priorities, he nevertheless stressed that 'the Tories have brought about a return of spectres we thought had died in the thirties'. Linking unemployment with the wider Thatcherite attack on the public services, the trade unions and local government, Foot argued that the 1930s stood for 'the Victorian society so beloved by Mrs Thatcher which the Labour Party, beneath its veneer of democratic socialism, came into being to exorcise'.[51]

Foot's use of the past, and in particular the emphasis on his own 'Bevanite' inheritance, was also part of his strategy for controlling the rival factions within the Labour party. Existing work on Foot has emphasized just how deeply divided the party was when Foot became leader. Peter Shore, a Labour MP at the time, later acknowledged that 'no leader inherited so disastrous and bankrupt an estate as did Michael Foot in November 1980'.[52] The level of infighting clearly affected Tony Blair, who entered parliament in 1983. He has since stated emphatically that 'our party won't return to the factionalism … or feuding of the seventies and eighties'.[53] Certainly Foot faced tremendous pressure from both right and left. This meant that, as it has been aptly put by Eric Shaw, 'Foot's years as leader were dominated by problems of party management'.[54]

After Labour's defeat in 1979, parts of Labour's right wing became increasingly restless as the party appeared to move to the left.

Speculation mounted that David Owen, Shirley Williams and Bill Rodgers (and later Roy Jenkins) were about to defect from Labour altogether and form a new centre party as the left scored a number of important victories. Although the left failed to secure overall control of the party manifesto for the NEC (which had a left-wing majority), they succeeded in securing a party conference vote in favour of mandatory reselection of MPs, and at the 1980 conference they secured an agreement that the PLP should lose its exclusive right to choose the Labour leader - the details of the new electoral college were to be decided at a special conference the following January. When the special Labour conference duly voted in favour of an electoral college for choosing the Labour leader which gave the trade unions forty per cent of the votes, the Parliamentary Labour Party thirty per cent and the Constituency Labour Parties thirty per cent, this proved too much for the 'Gang of Four' who were already disgruntled by Foot's election to the party leadership (and the defeat of Healey). Shortly afterwards, in March 1981, they formally launched the SDP.[55]

The departure of the most restive right-wingers from the party did not end Labour's factional troubles. Foot tried to prevent further defections, which was a difficult task given that his election as leader was a major cause of discontent. He also worked to conciliate other right-wingers - such as those in Roy Hattersley's Labour Solidarity Group - who were committed to remaining in the party but were nevertheless deeply unhappy with the way in which Foot handled the threat from the left. Most of Foot's efforts between 1980 and 1983 were, however, directed towards meeting the challenge from the hard left (and thus also appeasing the right). It has been readily acknowledged that Foot had to tread carefully. Foot's background was on the left of the party, but since his support of the Wilson and Callaghan governments from 1974 the left had begun to see him as a compromiser, a man whose earlier radicalism had been moderated by the pragmatism of power. The hard left's criticism of Foot was that he had abandoned his earlier principles. Heffer's view was that Foot 'was rejecting his own record in freedom of speech and organization within the party. He was no longer the man I had grown to respect over the years'.[56] Similarly, Benn was certain that Foot was actually 'a leader of the right'.[57]

Foot was nonetheless certain that he had to act to discredit the hard left. Writing after the 1983 election defeat, Foot made clear his view that if Benn's ambitions had not been thwarted then 'one likely consequence would have been either a declaration of independence by the Parliamentary Party or a much larger defection of so-called SDP MPs'. Foot speculated that this would have meant 'a Parliament in which the mould of British politics truly had been broken, and a Liberal assortment of some kind constituted the official opposition'.[58]

Foot's first major challenge was to deal with Benn's decision, taken in April 1981, to contest the deputy leadership, which had been given to Healey in November of the previous year. Foot initially asked Benn not to stand. However, Benn not only refused to do so but also subsequently criticized Foot as undemocratic for asking him. Throughout his campaign Benn then developed further his call for greater democracy. He argued repeatedly in favour of yearly elections to the posts of leader and deputy leader, and suggested that the party conference should assert its supremacy over the parliamentary party in shaping the manifesto. These arguments clearly suited Benn who was at odds with the parliamentary leadership and in tune with the party conference over issues such as payment of compensation upon re-nationalization of parts of the oil industry.[59]

Foot was himself aware that parallels could be drawn between Benn and Cripps, which increased the need to exert his own historic left-wing credentials. Writing in 1986 he noted that Benn in the early 1980s 'reminded me of Stafford Cripps, and of course the young Stafford of the 1930s who had just discovered Marx, and not his statesmanlike post-1945 successor'.[60] In these circumstances Foot found the use of an appropriate type of rhetoric was a subtle (but potentially effective) weapon against the hard left. He, therefore, set out to show that he was still Bevan's heir by attacking the lack of democracy on the hard left.

Foot argued frankly that there was a 'considerable difference' between his and Benn's views on parliamentary democracy. Significantly, not only did he contend that his views were 'more likely to appeal to the British public and therefore to assist the Labour party in our common aim of destroying the Thatcher government', but also that 'my views accord more closely with those of all the great Labour party leaders in our history from Keir Hardie to Aneurin Bevan'. Powerfully he added that it 'might do Tony a little good if he stopped to think why they and many like them would not accept doctrines which he now tells us should be regarded as axiomatic'. Foot did not want party conference decisions to be regarded as absolute and binding on every Labour MP in all circumstances. He argued that it was actively desirable that MPs should sometimes be able to express their own views on subjects about which they felt passionately, noting that on occasion even 'Aneurin Bevan opposed party conference decisions'.[61]

At the Trades Union Congress meeting in September 1981, just before the crucial vote on the deputy leadership at the party conference, Foot made the same points, once again very powerfully evoking Bevan's memory. He said:

I happen to be the Member for Ebbw Vale, and being the member for Ebbw Vale it is not possible for me to agree with the doctrine sometimes preached that MPs must be reduced to a subordinate position. If you had said to Aneurin Bevan that he must, at critical moments on major great issues, suppress his own political judgment and his own conscience and keep quiet – if anybody had said that to him he would have begged to differ (laughter), and he would have begged to differ in language that would still be burning.[62]

It was indeed the case, as K. O. Morgan has noted, that 'Foot in the years from 1980 was engaged ... in demonstrating that he was simply a better democrat, as well as a better socialist, than Tony Benn'.[63] In the event, at the Labour party conference in 1981 Healey narrowly defeated Benn. Foot now attempted to be conciliatory, speaking of a future Labour Cabinet 'in which Denis Healey and Tony Benn [would] ... play leading and honourable parts'.[64] In early November Foot attempted to foster further reconciliation. He allowed Benn to speak during a debate in the House of Commons on North Sea oil. The Labour party conference had voted for re-nationalization of the privatized assets without compensation but Shadow Cabinet policy pragmatically did not, in fact, rule out compensation. Benn was aware of this and so when he argued publicly for no compensation, Foot was 'fuming'.[65]

In response Foot drew further lessons from the 1930s to attack the Bennites in *The Observer* in January 1982. He likened the swing to the left after 1979 with events after 1931, when many in the party had adopted a particularly radical left-wing stance and some had even questioned the efficacy of parliamentary democracy. Significantly, Foot argued that this was before the likes of R.H. Tawney 'had examined the full nature of Soviet totalitarianism'. By the 1950s, however, many Labour figures (including Foot) had begun to recognise the unsavoury 'accompaniments of the Soviet dictatorship'. They became, particularly in light of the revelations made in Khrushchev's secret speech of 1956, willing to criticize the Soviet Union and to denounce the Stalinist purges about which many of them had remained publicly silent in the late 1930s.[66] Foot's argument then was that if left-wing extremism was permissible in the aftermath of 1931, it certainly was not in the early 1980s. He argued that the Bennite dismissal of Parliament 'as at best a mere platform' and the desire for the left to exert a 'rigid dictation of the party' showed a worrying similarity to the totalitarian direction that the Soviet Union had taken. Furthermore, Foot stressed that the lessons of the Soviet Union applied not just 'to the greatest questions of peace and war, of totalitarian victory or defeat in the contest for state power' but also 'to the lesser but still inescapable question about the means whereby socialists should seek and carry through industrial change'.[67] This was clearly a pointed reference to Benn's stance on compensation for re-nationalized industries, a criticism of his proposed ends as well as his means.

By 1982, however, the threat from the Bennite left had begun to recede. Not only had Healey defeated Benn, but the hard left had also lost control of the NEC. From this point on, an alliance of centrist and soft left began to take control of the party.[68] This meant that by early 1982 the main problem for Foot came from Militant Tendency, an entryist, Trotskyite organization that aimed to radicalize the Labour party from within and to foster revolution in Britain. Militant had used these tactics since the 1960s, and by the early 1980s had managed to get some of its members adopted as parliamentary candidates. While it never looked likely to get its candidates elected onto the NEC, Militant did strike many as a 'party within a party' and thus as being totally at odds with the party constitution. Militant's membership had also been rising rapidly. In 1979 it had been 1,800 but by late 1982 it was 3,500. There had been a general reluctance to act against Militant, with many on the left fearing it would lead to a wider witch-hunt - a concern that Foot had initially shared. The new NEC elected in 1981, however, took action by setting up an inquiry, which eventually concluded that Militant was in breach of the party constitution and thereby began the slow process of eradicating it from the party.[69]

Foot's wider attempts to deal with Militant, and his very cautious attempts to expel some of its leading figures, have been documented elsewhere. Perhaps most famously Foot was forced to backtrack after initially refusing to accept Peter Tatchell, a Militant sympathiser, as Labour candidate for Bermondsey.[70] What is also clear, however, is that, given Foot's reluctance to meet the Militant threat directly, his use of rhetoric invoking his links with Bevan and Cripps provided a way of justifying the tolerant approach he was taking. It further enabled him to portray Militant as 'anti-democratic, opposed to our traditions'.[71] Foot brought out this point clearly at the Labour party conference in September 1982 when he explicitly rejected the idea that 'Militant Tendency are just like Stafford Cripps or Aneurin Bevan'. Referring to the United and Popular Front campaigns of the late 1930s as well as to the Bevanite agitation in the 1950s, he argued emphatically that there 'was no secret conspiracy with Stafford Cripps or Aneurin Bevan; they wanted everybody to know what they were doing. There were no false colours about the way in which they went about propagating their views'.[72]

Foot was certainly one of Labour's most literary and intellectual leaders. By the time he became leader he had also spent nearly 50 years in the Labour party. These factors alone make his repeated invocations of the past relatively unsurprising. What this chapter has sought to reveal, however, are the wider political purposes to which he put this rhetoric.

It has argued that Foot used references to the past as a means of attacking Thatcher's rejection (mainly through the implementation of monetarism) of the post-war consensus. In particular, he presented the 1930s as the type of society that would be recreated if Thatcher's experiment continued and unemployment rose further. He attempted to give these points added impact by stressing his own experiences of the 1930s when he was prompted – after witnessing the horrors of poverty caused by unemployment at first hand - to join the Labour party. It was all clearly part of his attempt to secure 'the exposure of the moral insufficiency and shoddiness of Thatcherism'.[73]

Foot also referred to his own past experiences, and particularly his connection with Bevan, as a means of discrediting the hard left. In the face of constant criticisms from Benn and Heffer that he had abandoned his left-wing convictions, Foot stressed that his view of socialist democracy was still more in line with that of Bevan. For these reasons he was obviously delighted when his fellow member of the soft left - Neil Kinnock - secured the party leadership in October 1983 following Foot's decision to resign after the general election defeat. Kinnock had grown up in South Wales and, as a result, was strongly influenced by the legacy of Bevan.[74] Moreover, from the mid 1960s Kinnock and Foot had established a significant rapport - not least through their shared admiration for Bevan.[75] This meant that Foot was now able to suggest that, despite his own departure and the best efforts of the hard left, the Bevanite tradition remained powerfully entrenched at the helm of the party. Indeed, it was with a sense of triumph that at the 1983 party conference Foot stated that 'he [Kinnock] has the true spirit of Aneurin Bevan in him'.[76]

The threat from Militant severely tested Foot. He was initially inclined not to persecute its members and when he did decide to do so he acted only hesitantly. In this context Foot condemned Militant as anti-democratic and completely at odds with the traditions of Cripps and Bevan. No doubt this served as a subtle way of attempting to discredit them but it was also potentially problematic because it highlighted Foot's ambivalent attitude to Cripps. Having talked dismissively of how Benn was emulating Cripps in the 1930s, Foot chastised Militant for being insufficiently like Cripps who - during the United and Popular Front campaigns - defied the party but did so in an open rather than a clandestine manner.[77]

Even so, on balance, Foot's use of the past does appear to have been useful in enhancing his power within the party - especially in allowing him to marginalize Benn. Jon Lawrence has written of how, given that the Labour party has undergone a series of incarnations and developed rapidly in the twentieth century, party activists have 'displayed a powerful need to believe in continuity ... and to place themselves within an unfolding, seamless history of political commitment'. This has meant that the 'myths' produced by different Labour leaders about their own past positions have often become very powerful (regardless of whether they were true or not) when they have chimed with popular understandings of the party's history held by the rank and file.[78] Foot's repeated, but at times simplistic, use of Bevan's identity is surely a prime example of this phenomenon.

Considering the broader public context, however, it is difficult to disagree with the conclusion of Butler and Kavanagh that Foot appeared hopelessly out of date to many people by the time of the 1983 general election. Together with his dress sense and apparent unease on television, his rhetoric sealed his image as a man from another era and undoubtedly contributed to the scale of the Labour defeat. But is an invocation of the past necessarily disastrous in this way? It appears that occasionally the same use of the past can be persuasive both to internal party and wider public audiences. During the late 1990s Blair found that his criticism of Labour's internecine feuding in the 1970s and early 1980s resonated with a public which had for so long judged Labour unfit to govern. He also found that it enabled him to attack left-wing critics within the party and to conciliate others who were keen for Labour to regain power.

Foot's use of the past then was a particularly pronounced example of a broader, and continuing, Labour tradition. He commented in *Another Heart and Other Pulses* that it was 'no crime ... to take instruction and inspiration from the past: the best Socialists have always done it'.[79] Indeed, in his own rhetorical manipulations of Labour's history, Blair, who hosted a ninetieth birthday celebration for Foot at 10 Downing Street in July 2003, has himself, almost literally, taken a leaf out of the former leader's book.

'I don't think of myself as the first woman Prime Minister'

Gender, Identity and Image in Margaret Thatcher's Career[1]

Anneke Ribberink

The 15 December 1999, issue of the Dutch weekly *De Groene Amsterdammer* ('The Green Amsterdammer') includes a 'hall of fame of strong women'. Alongside iconic women political figures such as the 18th-century Russian empress Catherine the Great, the former Dutch queen Wilhelmina, and the German revolutionaries Rosa Luxembourg and Ulrike Meinhof, stood the former British Prime Minister Margaret Thatcher.[2] The inclusion of Thatcher on this 'honour roll' of powerful women throughout European history suggests that she not only made a significant impression on the history of her own country, but also on the history of gender and power more generally.

Of course, Thatcher's legacy is not an entirely positive one. Indeed, many biographical studies of Thatcher's and critical examinations of her political record and legacy adopt, at best, an ironic or sarcastic tone, and even more are decisively negative in their appraisal of her contribution to British politics and society. Irony and sarcasm permeate the aforementioned article in *De Groene Amsterdammer*, which states that Thatcher presented herself as the 'nanny of the nation' and that her electoral success can mostly be explained by the 'boarding-school subconscious of the average Brit who yearns for a firm hand,'[3] expressing both common European stereotypes of Englishness, and the notion that Thatcher represented a strident but rear-guard version of female power that does not conform with feminist aspirations towards women's empowerment *qua* women.

On the other hand, political commentators and historians have also voiced more positive assessments of the 'iron lady'. The American political scientist Michael Genovese, for instance, points to the fact that Margaret Thatcher differs in two respects from other female world leaders to have emerged since 1945: she was not high-born, and her achievement was more impressive as a result. Although Thatcher's origins were not proletarian, with her respectable lower-middle-class origins, she did not have the support of a rich and powerful family to pave the way to her political success. In contrast, most other female national leaders were born 'with a silver spoon in their mouth', and, by dint of birthright, they were members of the ruling elites of their respective nations. Even among women leaders who were not born to privilege, such as Cory Aquino (Philippines), their access to leadership was due to a male 'power behind the throne', and their period of leadership was often colourless. (There is also, of course, the slightly different case of Eva Perón of Argentina, who, although holding no official position in her husband's government, wielded enormous personal power.) The slight achievement of women leaders of this type tends to be accounted for by their sex, and the sexism they encountered.[4] In contrast to the aforementioned 'great women' of the twentieth century, interpretations of Thatcher are noteworthy for their diversity and the decidedness of their judgement, both applauding and condemnatory. Therefore the looming figure of Margaret Thatcher begs a number of questions that will be examined in this chapter: what are the features of Thatcher's biography that account for her course in politics and for the deep feelings of love or animosity that she excited in her contemporaries? Where does Thatcher's story fit in the history of twentieth century European women's history, especially as she herself rejected the feminist heritage as such? Was Thatcher a feminist in practice if not in ideology and belief, and what does her 'practical feminism' tell us about the gender order within the Conservative Party more specifically, and about British sexual politics more generally?

Thatcher was the longest serving incumbent British Prime Minister in the twentieth century, and she was in office for eleven and a half years (May 1979 to November 1990). She won three successive general elections, two with a large majority – a success unequalled by any other party leader in the twentieth century. Even if she had been a man, this would still have been a remarkable achievement for a leader of the Conservative Party, even during this notional 'Conservative century' of British history. But Margaret Thatcher is a woman, the first female British party leader, the first woman Prime Minister, and, in fact, the first female premier in a Western country. Gro Harlem Brundtland, who occupied a comparable position in Norway only took up office in 1981, and then only for a short period, and it was not until 1986 that she was to begin her second term of office.[5]

Does Thatcher deserve the accolade of 'great' because she was a woman who managed to rise to the top in a male-dominated society; because, born to the lower-middle-class, she was able to transcend her class origins in a class-bound society; or because she was an outstanding success as a politician and as Prime Minister? Thatcher herself, when commenting on her own performance during her three successive cabinets, has been far from modest. She is proud of having wrought fundamental change in British society and elsewhere in the world, which she is convinced have been for the good. Her self-image, self-righteousness, conviction and undiminished national pride are all expressed in her autobiography. Of her government's achievements she says that they 'pioneered the new wave of economic freedom that was transforming countries from Eastern Europe to Australasia, which had restored Britain's reputation as a force to be reckoned with in the world.'[6]

Thatcher has actively contributed to the creation of her political image first, while in office, through attempts to control her media representations, and since by contributing to a burgeoning market in political apologia with her two-volume autobiography. This self-construction and controlled image runs along the following narrative lines: born in 1925, she was a dutiful daughter, who always had to work hard but could nonetheless look back on a happy childhood and youth. This was, above all, thanks to her father, Alfred Roberts, the owner of two grocer's shops in Grantham, Lincolnshire, and later the mayor of that town. Her father was the source of her interest in politics. The family was neither poor nor particularly prosperous. But Margaret was an apt pupil, did well at school, and was admitted to Somerville College at Oxford University to study chemistry, before turning to law. Through her marriage to the rich businessman Denis Thatcher, she gained financial freedom and could thus devote herself to politics, her great passion. Margaret and Denis had twins, a boy and a girl. Despite her career as a Conservative Party MP, Margaret was a good mother, and she has consistently maintained that family life was balanced, functional and happy.

During her political career, Margaret Thatcher became increasingly convinced that the Keynesian policy of consensus conducted by post-war governments was ruinous for the British economy and for British society. This policy was especially supported by Labour, but it was also supported by many Tories up to and including Ted Heath's administration. Going against party orthodoxy and the tradition of Conservative 'one nationism', in the 1970s Thatcher became an adherent of monetarism, as advocated by the American economist Milton Friedman, and she became part of the group around the most prominent and vocal New Right intellectual, Keith Joseph. This group propagated ideas that would later be brought together under the umbrella term of 'Thatcherism', ideas that were very familiar to Margaret due to paternal influence and to her father's right-wing conservative inclinations. On the basis of this new direction, initially in a minority but gaining ever more supporters among the Conservatives, Thatcher was able to push through the necessary fundamental changes as Prime Minister and to save the country from disaster. An important principle for Thatcher throughout her career has always been her father's adage that she should rely on her own judgment and not be afraid to adopt the position of an outsider.

All of these images emphasize that Thatcher was able to combine femininity with ruthlessness. Nor was this image uncultivated or accidental. Prefiguring the spin and image politics of the present day, on becoming Conservative Party leader Thatcher put herself in the hands of Gordon Reece, a former television producer, who engineered the manufacture of her image.

> The hair was wrong, too suburban; it was restyled. The clothes were wrong, too fussy; they were replaced. The voice was wrong, too shrill; it was lowered in pitch through lessons from an expert in breathing. With singular dedication, Thatcher made herself into 'Maggie', the leader who is remembered, and she did so knowingly full well that she was not born to it, that it did not come naturally or easily. [7]

Her love of clothes is also legendary and she paid close attention to her wardrobe. To emphasize that she was one of the people, in an interview with the BBC she showed her favourite clothes, going as far to announce that she had bought her underwear at Marks & Spencer. There was a similar attention to detail and developing a media-friendly image in terms of speech writing, and Thatcher turned to others for expert help, employing the playwright Ronnie Millar as one of her chief speechwriters. Thus, alongside the transformation in political and economic thinking, we can see a shift in image and a careful responsiveness to the politics of celebrity. Essentially, the distinctiveness of Thatcherism was not only in terms of ideas and ideology, but also in terms of political technology and the manipulation of the media as the vehicle for Thatcher's populist messages. As Peter Clarke argues: 'Her purposeful projection of herself, moreover, was part of her populism - not to distance herself from those whom she often referred to as "our own people", but to represent them more effectively.'[8]

The above picture has been propagated, with variations, by Margaret Thatcher in her two volumes of autobiography, through many interviews with the media, and also in the – not entirely uncritical – biography of her husband written by her daughter Carol Thatcher. Carol quotes her father, who was proud of being married to 'one of the greatest women the world has ever produced.'[9]

To what extent is the self-created life narrative reflective of reality? And what is the meaning of this self-image? One can find an answer to these questions in the extensive historiography on Margaret Thatcher. Most of the literature has been produced by her compatriots, and a number of different approaches can be discerned. First there are the accounts written by male authors who mostly analyse her period in office from a gender-neutral perspective. In other words, the fact that this was a female and not a male Prime Minister is hardly considered as fundamental to their analytical framework. However, this does not apply to the two best-known biographies, written by Hugo Young and John Campbell, who do apply a gender perspective.[10] Overall, the aforementioned political analyses do not present a uniformly negative picture. This is in contrast, however, to another body of literature, mostly written by (British) women, which is based on a gender perspective. Here it is generally concluded that Thatcher took an indifferent attitude to those of her own sex and that she was downright hostile to the feminist movement, which she regarded as part of the left-wing community that she so detested. Despite this, one can usually detect a degree of admiration for the way that Margaret Thatcher was able to use her sex appeal in politics, which strongly influenced her leadership style.[11]

John Campbell's biography draws attention to the great emphasis that Margaret Thatcher placed on image building. From the beginning of her period as Leader of the Opposition (1975-79), she was concerned with the way that she appeared to the public at large.[12] Moreover, according to Campbell, the way that she depicted her childhood and youth as warm and happy 'is in fact a supremely successful exercise in image management.'[13] It is indisputable that, in line with modern advertising models, a happy childhood was certainly beneficial to Thatcher's image and added lustre to her status as Prime Minister. Nonetheless, this part of Campbell's biography is not totally convincing. He may be correct when he notes that Margaret's upbringing was indeed very strict and ascetic, but this is exactly what she herself also recounted later: 'There wasn't a lot of fun and sparkle in my life.'[14] And it is certainly questionable whether she was as unhappy about this as Campbell suggests. He gives too little credit to the compensatory power of a father who gave her great encouragement and did everything to provide his youngest daughter with the education he had never enjoyed himself.[15]

Although having had a good childhood was important for the image of a successful Prime Minister, it was arguably even more important to have a good marriage and to be a good parent. Modern American presidents have good reason for devoting so much attention to the presentation of their family life in the media.[16] In this respect one should also consider Thatcher's political background as a member of the Conservative Party. Although until the 1980s Great Britain did not differ from other Western countries regarding the low number of female parliamentarians and the Conservative Party had always produced few female members of parliament, the party did have a long tradition of politically active women.[17] Since the Primrose League, the conservative organization formed at the end of the 19th century in order to mobilize popular support, women had been busy canvassing votes for the

Conservative Party and also helping the male party leadership in other ways, without, however, contesting its dominance. Following the attainment of women's suffrage at the end of the First World War,[18] the activities also included support for female parliamentary candidates. It is no coincidence that the first woman to take her seat as an MP in 1919, Lady Astor, was from the Tory Party. A Conservative female candidate for parliament did well to keep in mind this rank-and-file of politically aware women. In the 1950s and 1960s the Conservative women's association, the British Housewives League, had a strong voice in forming the part of the New Right ideology – later to become known as Thatcherism – that focussed on family and personal life. The core of these ideas was to be found in the idealization of the traditional family, accompanied in the 1960s by a rejection of the rising youth revolution and permissive society with its characteristic loose sexual morals. A happy full-time housewife and mother and a happy, harmonious childhood for the children completed the picture. Throughout her political career and her time as Prime Minister, Thatcher presented this model as an ideal – although it was at odds with her own reality as a paid working mother – and realized it in part by modelling her own family on a 'desirable conservative' pattern.

To what extent is Thatcher's harmonious image of her marriage and family based on reality? Regarding her marriage to Denis Thatcher, there is little reason to suppose that the truth has been distorted. There is enough 'objective' evidence that supports the subjective autobiographical sources, or at least does not disprove them. For one thing, the marriage enabled Margaret Thatcher to undertake law studies and to devote herself to a political career. Even more eloquent is the fact that Denis Thatcher, by then retired, was convincingly willing to take on the public role of male political consort once Margaret Thatcher was Prime Minister. In her biography of her father, Carol Thatcher does, however, suggest that he was not always happy about his wife being away from home so much due to her ministerial duties, but that can hardly be interpreted as a sign of a poor marriage – in fact on the contrary.[19]

Thatcher's relationship with her children is a different story. The twins grew up in the 1950s and 60s, the period before the women's liberation movement took flight and challenged the convention in sexual and gender politics and the myopia of the patriarchal state. As in the rest of the Western world, the traditional nuclear family was the desirable mode of living, with a male breadwinner and a woman whose primary responsibility was to keep the household and to raise the children.[20] And Denis Thatcher had a demanding job. Since the traditional breadwinner/housewife model formed an inalienable part of Thatcherism, Margaret Thatcher never completely managed to 'sell' her political career in combination with her role as mother. She continued to trumpet traditional full-time motherhood as the ideal – even when this

was increasingly at odds with the reality of British society in the 1980s –
but always portrayed herself as an exception and as someone with an
urge to 'greatness'.[21] In her autobiography Thatcher writes about her
emotional bond with her children, but also that she was nonetheless sure
that she wanted a career in politics. The children were partly brought up
by nannies and educated at boarding schools. According to Thatcher
herself, the children wanted for nothing and they each had good
relationships with their parents. As Thatcher put it:

> I was especially fortunate in being able to rely on Denis's income
> to hire a nanny to look after the children in my absences. I could
> combine being a good mother with being an effective professional
> woman, as long as I organized everything intelligently down to the
> last detail. It was not enough to have someone in to mind the
> children; I had to arrange my own time to ensure that I could
> spend a good deal of it with them.[22]

But this positive picture can be easily contested. Her daughter Carol is, in
fact, rather critical, especially regarding the expenditure of family time
when the twins were small. Both her parents, but above all her father,
were often away from home. And there were hardly any family holidays
in this period either, although this changed later. 'Neither of my parents
could be described as being natural or comfortable with young
children.'[23] John Campbell goes a step further by claiming that Margaret
Thatcher always put her career before her family. 'What the young
Thatchers missed was "normal" family life in the sense of the continuous
presence of one or both parents […] there was not much spontaneity or
warmth in their upbringing.'[24]

There would be little point in condemning Thatcher for the way that
she tried to combine her children with a political career. By now there is
more than enough sociological and feminist literature to suggest that the
pervasiveness of the 'double burden' experienced by modern women was
not a mean thing. Not only were there few female MPs in the 1950s and
60s, in the United Kingdom as elsewhere in the Western world; but
besides this, a large number of these women remained unmarried or only
began a political career in later life when family obligations receded in
importance. For most of them, the combination of parliamentary work
and raising children was simply too difficult.[25] In this respect Thatcher
was thus one of the exceptions, but she was in part able to take this
position because she received support from other quarters.

One can, however, ask why Thatcher did not admit how difficult this
combination of work and private life must have been for her too, even
though others helped her. It is not enough to say that she preferred to
avoid the subject because it was a sensitive one in right-wing
conservative circles. An explanation can also be found in the importance

she attached to a good presentation of herself in the media. A toiling housewife and mother seemed less sound and reliable than someone who created the impression that it was easy to juggle the demands of work inside and outside the home: better to be a 'superwoman' than a household drudge. Carol Thatcher had good reason for using the description 'superwoman' for her mother, and she writes: 'Somehow she juggled working, studying, organizing the household, shopping, cooking, sewing, ironing and liaising with nanny.'[26]

It is not the most insignificant of the authors surveying Thatcher's period as Prime Minister who concludes his account with the following words: 'Her impact while in office was less only than that of Lloyd George and Churchill. Perhaps she was even their equal in this.'[27] This is at least close to a description of a 'great' politician. Peter Hennessy points to several elements of Margaret Thatcher's enduring legacy that are also mentioned in other examinations of her period in power. He cites the fact that she broke the power of the trade union movement and that the boundary between the public and private realms was fundamentally shifted. Furthermore, Hennessy mentions the increase in the number of shareholders from three million in 1979 to nine million in 1989 and also the sale of a million council flats to private persons on favourable conditions, 'a substantial shift towards that long-standing Conservative ideal of a "property owning democracy."'[28]

Is it thus true that Thatcher saved the country from ruin in the 1980s, as she herself claims? This is certainly debatable. To begin with, one can qualify this legacy in various ways. Thatcher indisputably gave the trade union movement the *coup de grace* with her restrictive legislation against the right to strike and the principle of the closed shop, and certainly with the successful end to the miners' strike of 1984-85. She was supported in her victory, however, by the fact that the trade union movement already had been on the defensive since the early 1980s, due to the blows it received from the economic crisis.[29] Further, the ideal of the 'property owning democracy' is less impressive on closer examination. This brought benefits mainly to a specific group in British society, the social layer of skilled workers, petit bourgeois and higher up the social ladder. In this context one should also point to 'Thatcher's children', the yuppies who were able to undertake successful careers in the 1980s thanks in part to the stimulation of the services sector and of new 'creative' industries such as pop music, fashion, hi-tech and software.[30] Old industries, such as the textiles sector, disappeared as a result of the strict monetary policies applied during Thatcher's first cabinet period (1979-83). This led to high unemployment – in the mid-1980s there were 3.5 million unemployed in Britain – and a widening of the gulf between rich and poor. The ghettos in the large cities were a sad monument to a policy that claimed many victims, especially in the lower social levels of society.[31]

This does not detract from the fact that Thatcher managed to halt, at least for a while, the economic decline of the 1970s and above all the feared spectre of inflation – even though there were signs of a new recession during her last cabinet (1987-1990). The literature devotes a great deal of attention to the socio-economic dimension of Thatcherism, and in this context the word 'revolution' is frequently used to describe the enormity of socio-economic change.[32] This term seems incorrect insofar as 'revolution' refers to a unique event. The policies applied under Thatcher were part of an international trend, and one that included Reagonomics in the United States and Lubberism in the Netherlands.[33] One can, however, claim that Thatcher was among the pioneers of monetarism and privatization. With the reference to privatization, Kenneth Morgan writes: 'It chimed in with a mood of *anti-étatisme* in many countries, notably in France where the Chirac government used the Thatcher policy as a model in its privatization of state banks and other enterprises in 1984-6.'[34]

The effects of these policies were more spectacular in Great Britain than elsewhere because in the 1970s Britain was experiencing an acute socio-economic crisis in comparison to other European countries. As Hennessy comments: no 'other Prime Minister (except perhaps Nigel Lawson had he made it to No. 10) would have pushed these policies so far, so firmly or so swiftly.'[35] Perhaps 'revolution' is too strong a term, but Thatcher's policies did leave a lasting mark in the socio-economic sphere. The legacy of Margaret Thatcher can be recognized, for instance, in the introduction of the 'Third Way' by the Labour Prime Minister Tony Blair on taking up office in 1997. This partnership between the private and public sector forms a radical break with the Labour Party's past, and it was catalysed by Thatcher's 'conviction' politics, if not by her 'revolutionary' policies.[36]

Thatcherite policies are also much discussed by feminist critics, and an important aspect here is Thatcher's own gender identity. The verdict is far from positive: Thatcher showed no solidarity or sorority whatsoever with other women who shared political aspirations. An important element of Thatcherism was family policy. The traditional breadwinner/housewife family was propagated as the ideal and used as a bastion against the moral degeneracy that was, supposedly, a consequence of innovations in the fields of sexuality and modes of cohabitation since the 1960s.[37] In the process, Thatcher ignored every criticism made by the modern feminist movement of the traditional family as a repressive institution that maintained women's dependence on men.

Moreover, this imperative norm was now completely out of step with reality. Aside from the fact that Thatcher herself had always been a paid working mother, the number of paid working mothers in general had consistently risen since World War II. This process continued in the

1980s as well: while in 1983 around 23 per cent of mothers with children aged under five in Great Britain carried out paid work, by 1990 this percentage had already increased to 41 per cent.[38] Under Thatcher the traditional family also served as a mechanism against excessive state influence and was thus an instrument in the policies of privatization and deregulation and in austerity policies. The increasing number of families with a single parent (most often mothers) was hit particularly hard by the freezing of child benefits by the government and cuts in child-care facilities. This latter development was conducted under the motto that the decision to do paid work was a private matter, which did not need to be subsidized by the state. While in 1945 some 62,000 child-care places were funded by the state, by 1983 this figure had fallen to just 29,000.[39]

Furthermore, as Prime Minister, Thatcher made no attempt to promote the careers of other women. On the contrary, she sometimes even worked against the interests of women. Thatcher owes her successful career in part to the achievements of the women's movement, which pressed for an increase in the number of female politicians, but she never acknowledged this. She always claimed that she owed her success to her own performance and personal qualities, and, correspondingly, adopted the position of the infamous 'queen bee' who denies that women are faced with discriminatory practices when climbing the social and political ladder.[40]

Nonetheless, one can qualify this justified criticism by feminist writers. Was Thatcher's lack of solidarity with her own sex and her refusal to acknowledge that her gender either produced advantages for her or stood in the way of her career, not also prompted by the fear of seeming weak? Thatcher needed to hold her own in a male world and female politicians were in danger of not being taken seriously by their male counterparts.[41] The Henigs, a British couple who have written a book on women and political power, comment as follows on how a British female member of parliament needed to behave in the 1960s: 'To be successful, and to make their mark in such a male-dominated environment, women had to compete with men on their terms and be tough.'[42] Being tough meant, among other things, that one had no wish to be identified with 'women's subjects,' such as health, social work and legislative emancipation. In the course of her political career, Thatcher always sought to concentrate on 'hard men's subjects' such as finance and the economy.[43] As Prime Minister she increasingly became her 'own' Foreign Secretary. And few disputed her knowledge in these areas. Her fear of being understood as a woman in a man's world was also revealed in her remark, made when taking up office as Prime Minister: 'I don't think of myself as the first woman Prime Minister'.[44] Someone who expresses herself in this way cannot immediately be expected to act as a 'feminist' by promoting the careers of other women.

Significantly, this is actually what happened, however unintentionally. Martin Pugh points out that Margaret Thatcher functioned as a role model. Through her political achievements she put a definitive end to the widely held view that women could not be skilled politicians. In the Britain of the 1990s a number of women were appointed to high positions, amongst others in the sphere of justice, the House of Commons and at newspaper publishers, profiting from Thatcher's shattering of the 'glass ceiling'. Another unintentional effect of Thatcher's position as Prime Minister was that the stimulation of the services sector under her administration created a large number of jobs for women, not least because these were often part-time jobs that were particularly attractive to women.[45]

Much has been written about Margaret Thatcher's demeanour and actions, from both gender-neutral and gender-specific perspectives. The term Thatcherism is also taken to include her militant, aggressive and authoritarian bearing as Prime Minister.[46] According to Peter Hennessy this 'very personal style of government', in which an 'over-mighty Prime Minister' dominated the cabinet, really took shape after the victory in the Falklands War in early 1982 when her popularity increased dramatically.[47] He objects to the way that Thatcher's ministers are often depicted as simply being victims of her dictatorial tendencies and refers to a comment by the Chancellor of the Exchequer Nigel Lawson. According to Lawson, the longer-serving ministers often found it easier not to participate in endless consultations with fellow ministers and instead to make a private deal with the Prime Minister.[48] However, ultimately, her leadership style, in combination with her resistance to further European unification, proved to be her undoing. But it is typical that this only happened towards the end of her third term of office (1987-90) when things were already going less well, especially in economic terms. In particular the resignation of two of her most loyal ministers, Nigel Lawson and Geoffrey Howe, heralded the beginning of the end for Thatcher and the last days of her premiership came within sight.

There is much debate as to whether Margaret Thatcher really was a political outsider, or whether she exploited this status as part of her media image. John Campbell and Peter Hennessy believe the latter. In Campbell's view, the way that Thatcher used her lower-middle-class origins to underline her position as an outsider amid the upper-class aristocrats who made up a large part of the Tory Party was rather exaggerated. Before becoming leader of the Conservatives in 1975 she had already been married to a rich husband for twenty-four years, and had thus long ago transcended her humble birth.[49] Hugo Young and Kenneth Morgan, in contrast, believe that her social background did indeed make a difference. Young regards Thatcher's aggressive leadership style as a way of disguising her insecurity due to her origins and her sex. Morgan sees her provincial bourgeois background as decisive for her later espousal of the ideology of neo-liberalism and her focus on successful business people – whose careers she liked to promote – instead of intellectuals, whom she described collectively as the 'chattering classes'.[50]

In my view the truth lies in the middle - both perspectives are useful. There is no doubt that the media image of the underdog further amplifying her status as a self-made woman, and it suited Margaret Thatcher well. On the other hand, there are enough indications that, as *nouveau-riche*, she was not in fact fully accepted by the members of the true upper class in her party. In the early 1980s, Defence Secretary Francis Pym spoke not only for himself when he argued 'that the real problem for the Tories was that 'we've got a corporal at the top, not a cavalry officer."[51] One can assume, however, that the confronting, uncompromising way Margaret Thatcher behaved added to her isolated position. Her predecessor as Leader of the Party and Prime Minister, Ted Heath, who was from a similar social background to Thatcher, had less difficulty being accepted by the Tories, but was much more prepared to compromise than she was.[52] And he was a man.

There is no doubt that Thatcher's gender made her an outsider in high politics, as underlined by Hugo Young. And it was precisely here that she gave the least ground to others, probably due to the aforementioned fear of being seen as 'weak' and 'feminist', the latter a term of abuse in Right-wing circles. All her cabinets had exclusively male ministers, thus even further emphasising the gender of the Prime Minister.[53] The fact that Thatcher did not openly cite her gender as a determining factor in the political game does not mean that she did not exploit her status as a woman: this is just what she did, but in a much more round-about fashion. Her leadership style was marked not only by aggressiveness and dominance but also by a high degree of skill in switching between male and female roles: Thatcher was an expert 'gender-bender'. She could seem masculine and instil fear through her aggressive and iron-ladylike behaviour. In this way she confounded her (male) colleagues, who were not sure how to react to this precisely because she was a woman. Nor did Thatcher hesitate to make use of their confusion. On the other hand, she also played the female card by using her charms when necessary. Eric Evans quotes one of Thatcher's advisors, a Hungarian emigrant, on her personality as a woman: 'He believes that her "perplexing charm" enabled her to be "getting away with" political ploys and stratagems which a man would not.'[54]

John Campbell writes that Thatcher used her gender in an extremely clever way in the political game:

> She was able to tap into a range of female types: established role models of women in positions of authority whom men were used

to obeying. Thus she was the Teacher, patiently but with absolute certainty explaining the answers to the nation's problems: and the Headmistress exhorting the electorate to pull its socks up. She was Doctor Thatcher, or sometimes Nurse Thatcher, prescribing nasty medicine or a strict diet that the voters knew in their hearts would be good for them. Or she was the nation's Nanny, with overtones of discipline, fresh air and regular bowel movements to get the country going [...] Finally she was Britannia, the feminine embodiment of patriotism, wrapping herself unselfconsciously in the Union Jack. No politician since Churchill had appealed so emotionally to British nationalism.'[55]

Campbell also points to the way that Margaret Thatcher used the role of housewife and a domesticated language in her political and media campaigns. This is a theme much discussed by feminist authors. One of Thatcher's favourite ploys was to compare the national economy with a household purse that needed to be managed through sensible policies, i.e. by 'Thatcher the housewife'. Moreover she was often depicted standing in the kitchen or with a shopping bag in her hand.[56] Beatrix Campbell notes that this housewife act was transparent – partly because Thatcher herself was not a real housewife – but Campbell can also admit that this self-created image functioned as an effective ploy. It is pointed out that Thatcher was supreme in her ability to set out complex matters in simple words. [57]

The successes and failures of the gendered image that Thatcher attempted to project can be seen in her popularity with the electorate, and especially with women voters. In the mid-1980s Margaret Thatcher was at the peak of her popularity with the electorate, although the Conservatives never gained more than 43.9 per cent of the popular vote under her leadership and thus failed to equal Labour in its golden period around 1950. Moreover, the Tory victories of 1983 and 1987 certainly owed much to the weakness of the opposition.[58] Under Thatcher there was a halt to the post-war trend of more women than men voting for the Conservatives. Thatcher scored low with young women especially, whereas middle-aged women were relatively well represented among Conservative voters. This could indicate that Thatcherite family policies and the promotion of a conservative view of women were quite popular with this category of older women, but in fact failed to impress younger women.[59]

A desire to appear as a 'superwoman', and to be someone who had things under control no matter what, was the winning formula of Margaret Thatcher's leadership style. Both Hugo Young and Peter Hennessy[60] have pointed out that under her aggressive and seemingly tough exterior Margaret Thatcher was actually an insecure and hypersensitive woman. She refused to label herself as the 'first woman

Prime Minister' but she was clearly very aware of her sex, as demonstrated by the way that she used her feminine status in the media and in political practice. The way that she tried to maintain her perfect image can be explained by her strong awareness that she, as the first woman in such a position, was in great danger of being shot down. She was a much more vulnerable outsider due to her gender than due to her origins in the provincial bourgeoisie, even though this latter aspect is important too. Her 'queen bee' behaviour and lack of solidarity with other women can be explained in this light.

What is the reality of Margaret Thatcher? The image she created of her childhood and marriage are reasonably faithful to the truth. As a mother, however, she 'failed' much more than she was later prepared to admit. Her children paid a high price for her career, in the form of a mother who had little time for them. But one should ask whether anything else was possible under the circumstances. Thatcher was not a 'great' Prime Minister if we understand 'great' as an unconditionally positive adjective: her policies brought too many disadvantages, in particular the increase of social inequality and the creation, in rhetoric as much as in reality, of an 'underclass'.

The supposed uniqueness of Thatcherism can be strongly qualified by pointing to the international and time-bound nature of Thatcher's socio-economic policy. She was, however, a Prime Minister of vision and conviction, and one who was also prepared to take responsibility for the less pleasant consequences of the indisputably major changes that she brought about. The paradox is that the woman who above all did not want to be seen as a *female* Prime Minister is important precisely in this respect. Through her impressive, albeit controversial, performance Margaret Thatcher showed what women are able to achieve in politics and thus unintentionally caused a major breakthrough in women's political history. There are many who leave a less impressive legacy.

13

New Labour and *The Sun*, 1994-97

Sam Gallagher

'We detest the Labour Party. The Labour Party detests us. Because of convenience, they've got into bed with us and we've got into bed with them. But it's not natural. It's all because of Tony Blair.' *George Pascoe-Watson, Deputy Political Editor of* The Sun.[1]

'Old friends are passing them by on the other side of the street'.[2] Robin Oakley, BBC Political Editor, on the day *The Sun* announced its support for Tony Blair.

The general election of 1997 was a landmark in the political history of Great Britain. The Conservatives' dominance of the polls was broken for the first time in eighteen years and broken emphatically. The Labour majority of 179 seats was the largest two-party shift since 1935, and the 10 per cent swing from Conservative to Labour was the largest since 1945.[3] This was the first election that 'New Labour' had contested and it won it decisively. 1997 was also an important year for *The Sun*, marking the first time since 1970 that the newspaper had supported the Labour Party in a British general election.[4] A natural enemy of the Labour Party in their years of opposition to Margaret Thatcher, *The Sun*'s switch of support was of huge importance to New Labour and symbolic of a wider trend within other Fleet Street publications. In 1992 *The Sun* dedicated its coverage of the election campaign to the vilification of the Labour leader Neil Kinnock, urging its readers to vote Tory and keep the Welshman out of power. It was this election and, especially, *The Sun*'s damaging coverage of it, which can be identified as the genesis of New Labour's policy of getting the principal tabloids 'on board'. Tony Blair and his associates, like Galileo, believed an awful lot revolved around *The Sun*.

This chapter is based on a detailed analysis of *The Sun*'s coverage of the Labour Party throughout the period 1992-97. By using *The Sun*'s library (based at the News International Archives in Wapping) and its extensive electronic and cuttings catalogues, every article, editorial, opinion, front page and cartoon featuring New Labour or Tony Blair was tracked down. In addition, interviews were conducted with influential figures from the newspaper's political and editorial staff. These interviews produced a unique insight into the internal machinations of *The Sun*'s political decision-making process, and yielded quite revelatory attitudes towards New Labour and Tony Blair. Although certain principal figures were approached to give a Labour perspective on the party's media relations, none agreed to be interviewed. Instead, a Labour perspective on these years was garnered from the wealth of accounts written by, or about, those central Labour players. Philip Gould's account of the Labour 'revolution' and Peter Oborne's biography of Alastair Campbell, for example, present a highly interesting backdrop to Labour's metamorphosis at this time, while Peter Mandelson is unusual in being both the subject and author of some very informative literature on this period. Of the further, very extensive, secondary literature, of particular note are Nicholas Jones' excellent series of books on press and party relations in Blair's years of opposition and first term of office[5] and an important volume edited by Anthony King: *Leaders' personalities and the outcome of democratic elections* (2002). This latter work offers a strong challenge to the assumption that leaders' personalities have an important bearing on the outcome of election results - an assumption that underlay New Labour's media strategy in the run-up to the 1997 election.

It is a truth universally acknowledged that New Labour before and after the 1997 general election showed an intense interest and belief in the political power of the media. As yet, however, there has been no specific and detailed evaluation of how the party's new approach to the media was implemented with respect to the nation's biggest-selling daily newspaper. This chapter will examine how the newly media-aware Labour Party secured a turn-around in press relations with a newspaper that five years earlier had poured scorn on it and its leader. It will chart the evolution of *The Sun*'s attitudes toward its old political enemies throughout the period in question and ask whether *The Sun* was as politically potent as it had been in 1992. It will evaluate the importance of Blair and his spin-doctors, Campbell and Mandelson, in the party's improved press relations. Finally, it will ask the most important question: did it make a difference? That is to say, was the New Labour preoccupation with the media a prerequisite to achieving power in 1997, or an unnecessary obsession based on a deep mistrust of opinion polls and a fear of the tabloid press? Further, was it actually counter-productive?

This chapter will suggest that when considering *The Sun*'s treatment of, and impact on, the 1997 general election it is useful to make a comparison between the newspaper's performance and role in the previous general election of 1992. With the exception of *The Daily Star*, *The Sun*'s famous front-pages paid least attention of any national newspaper to the election of 1992. During the twenty-five day campaign, only nine of its page ones were concerned with the general election, with five of these coming in the last fifteen days of the campaign. Slack it may have been on front-page lead stories, but the election was the subject of a substantial 59 per cent of *The Sun*'s hard-hitting editorial column. Despite the tabloid's allegiance to the Conservative Party, its 'memorable' campaign focused largely on Labour and its leader Neil Kinnock.[6] Of the thirty-three politically related editorials in the campaign, Labour was the subject of nineteen and the Conservatives only ten. Correspondingly disproportionate was the share of *The Sun*'s front pages given up to its political opponent, with two-thirds written about Labour and not the Tories.

The Sun made a concerted and sustained effort to question Kinnock's credibility, to contrast his 'untrustworthiness' with 'honest' John Major. These themes of trust and political credibility which characterised *The Sun*'s venomous campaign reached their conclusion with an election day edition which has come to be seen as important in the election's outcome as well as memorable in its reporting. Constructed upon an all-blue background was a picture of Kinnock's head in a light bulb and next to it the headline read 'IF KINNOCK WINS TODAY WILL THE LAST PERSON IN BRITAIN PLEASE TURN OUT THE LIGHTS.'

Two days after the election, *The Sun* quoted David Amess, a Tory victor at the swing seat of Basildon, to the effect that the *Sun* had made a difference in its result. The story appeared under the headline 'IT'S THE SUN WOT WON IT.' The headline sparked a wealth of discussion and investigation. If *The Sun* had the power to win elections, as it claimed, then surely it was the greatest political weapon in any party's armoury?

There are some studies that suggest that the popular press have a very tangible impact on the outcome of elections.[7] However, for every piece of evidence to claim that the press, and *The Sun* in particular, had an important role in the 1992 election, there is also evidence to the contrary. For example, the swing towards the Conservatives over the long campaign for readers of *The Mirror* was around the national average despite the fact that *The Mirror*'s advocacy of the Labour cause was as potent as *The Sun*'s for its political opposition. Perhaps, as Margaret Scammell suggests, 'The late swing was a national, not newspaper phenomenon', and the Red Top's self-congratulatory front page was nothing more than 'a typical piece of *Sun* self-aggrandizement.'[8] Indeed, the validity of *The Sun*'s claim to have won the election is somewhat dented when one considers the reaction of Trevor Kavanagh, Political Editor at *The Sun*, when asked about the now famous headline. He said that he did not think the headline was right: 'I think it was what was described as an emotional spasm. We were so delighted Kinnock had not won ... I don't think that newspapers win or lose elections. I think that, again, we were going with the grain of public opinion.'[9]

This refutation of the impact of the press was not shared by all in the aftermath of Labour's surprise defeat in the polling booths. Neil

Kinnock clearly felt that the demolition he received at the hands of the more expressive popular press was decisive in the result of the election. In his resignation speech Kinnock, quoting Lord MacAlpine, claimed: 'The heroes of this campaign were Sir David English, Sir Nicholas Lloyd, Kelvin McKenzie and the other editors of the grander Tory press. Never in the past nine elections have they come out so strongly in favour of the Conservatives. Never has their attack on the Labour Party been so comprehensive ... This was how the election was won.'[10]

When Blair took the reins after the death of John Smith and Labour gained the prefix 'New', this belief in the power of the press was adopted and enhanced. Shortly after Blair was announced as leader, the political strategist Philip Gould, a member in the Shadow Communication Agency in the 1987 and 1992 general elections, developed a list of hindrances to the Labour Party's chances of electoral success. These included: a mistrust of Labour, including the fear of strife, strikes, unions and alteration, and the price of voting Labour, translated in terms of higher interest rates and more tax. But also, they included the effect of a partisan tabloid press, with its huge negating influence on the party image, its ability to hinder the Labour politicians and to set an anti-Labour agenda.[11] Blair, however, was not unduly surprised by Gould's findings; he personally had been shocked by both *The Sun*'s and The *Daily Mail*'s treatment of Kinnock in 1992 and 'joked privately in October 1996, that he would have had trouble voting Labour if he had been exposed to such coverage.'[12] Alastair Campbell noted it too, remarking years later that the virulent attacks on Kinnock were 'bound to have had an effect on the way politics was perceived during those years in which people are actually making up their minds'.[13] It was this awareness of the press and the adoption of a belief in its political importance that was an integral force in the shaping of the entire staff and strategy behind the New Labour campaign of 1997. The proximity of Alastair Campbell, Peter Mandelson and Charlie Whelan (press secretary to Gordon Brown) to the heart of the New Labour election machine, and the power vested in their positions is testament to this fact. And as 1997 was to prove, New Labour had clearly learnt this supposed lesson from 1992.

The decision for *The Sun* to back Blair in the 1997 general election was finally announced to its readership on 18 March that year. However, the route to this decision ran over several years and involved the personal work of Labour's biggest names and News International's most central executives. New Labour believed strongly in the importance of *The Sun*, the power of News International and especially the antipodean entrepreneur at the very top of it all. It was their belief also that the support of this man's mass-market tabloid was 'a necessary, and possibly a sufficient, precondition for Labour victory at the General Election.'[14] Therefore, in recognition of the importance of Rupert Murdoch, the

Australian was 'wooed like a beautiful woman',[15] with Blair and other
senior figures putting dinner with him at the top of their schedule
whenever he arrived in London. It was, according to Peter Oborne,
biographer of Alastair Campbell, 'Only President Clinton' who 'counted
for more with Blair in those three years of opposition'. As leader of the
Shadow Cabinet, Oborne claims, Blair ensured that 'Murdoch's needs
and wishes became New Labour's needs and wishes'.[16] The support of
The Sun was the ultimate prize and when it came these unprecedented
levels of 'wooing' seemed justified.

Peter Mandelson is often 'assumed to have been the chief architect of
this amazing volte-face'[17] because of his training in the media, his
undeniable charm and reputation, and exaggerated stories that he was a
close friend of Elizabeth Murdoch, Rupert's daughter. Mandelson (who
was MP for Hartlepool from 1992) did indeed lunch with Murdoch on
several occasions and was also aware of, and in agreement with, the New
Labour desire to court the tabloid press. Mandelson had been actively
involved in both Labour's election campaigns of 1987 and 1992, and had
witnessed first-hand what he saw as the devastating effects of a hostile
tabloid press. It was not until Blair's party leadership victory in 1994 and
the campaign of 1997, however, that Mandelson became widely regarded
as a core political figure. His training at London Weekend Television
(LWT) in the 1980s and his intuitive understanding of the industry,
allowed him to flourish and gain prominence in a political environment
that was now increasingly aware of the power of the media. Blair, indeed,
was a firm believer in Mandelson's talents claiming in reply to the latter's
resignation letter of 22 December 1998 that 'without your support and
advice we would never have built New Labour'.[18]

In reality, however, it was more Alastair Campbell and Blair himself
who were responsible for putting in the groundwork with the central
characters at News International. It is thought that around August 1994
Campbell began to instruct Blair to start courting the tabloid press,
conscious as he was of Kinnock's contempt for it.[19] It was Campbell, in
particular, who saw the benefit of getting *The Sun* 'on board', and it was
he who was instrumental in organising Blair's July 1995 trip to Hayman
Island. It was this trip to the annual general meeting of News
Corporation that can be seen as marking the genesis of the relationship
between New Labour and *The Sun*. As Trevor Kavanagh remembers:

> We were quite well aware of the attempts of Alastair Campbell and
> Tony Blair to win the support of News International and this first
> became evident when Tony Blair was invited to address the News
> International conference in the Hayman Islands in 1995. So a
> seduction process was underway from very early on.[20]

Piers Morgan (who at the time was editor of the *News of the World*) records that Blair 'went down an absolute storm' at the Hayman Island meeting. 'He spoke passionately of his "new moral purpose" – particularly with regard to family life – and vowed to set free media companies from "heavy regulation" and allow them to exploit their "enterprise". All just what Murdoch wanted to hear.' Murdoch, for his part, 'tried to make light of the mutual love-in that was going on by saying in his speech: "If our flirtation is ever consummated, Tony, then I suspect we will end up making love like two porcupines. Very, very carefully.'[21]

Between 1994 and 1996, *The Sun*'s approach to Blair and New Labour was somewhat ambivalent. This ambivalence – which from Labour's point of view was a significant improvement on the paper's previous hostility – may itself have been a result of the 'seduction process'. While *The Sun* and the late John Smith had what Trevor Kavanagh refers to as a 'modus vivendi', in 1994 Blair and New Labour were 'untried and untested'.[22] This initial scepticism was evident from the tone and nature of the pieces appearing in *The Sun* about both New Labour and its new leader in the two years after his appointment. Blair was elected leader in July 1994, but *The Sun* remained fairly muted on the subject of his electoral credibility until the latter stages of 1995. On 23 September of that year, *The Sun* ran an article on its second page that speculated upon whether Richard Branson, one of *The Sun*'s heroes, would vote Labour at the next election. The article was headlined 'FLY VIRGIN BLAIRWAYS' and sub-headed with the suggestion that 'Branson salutes "witty" Blair but scorns his shadow team'.[23] The article is of interest because Branson, as a staunch supporter of Margaret Thatcher and an advocate of *The Sun*'s ideal of enterprise, is naturally a figure with whom *The Sun* identifies and who may influence or reflect the sentiments of the newspaper and its readership. It is also of interest due to the fact that, even at this early stage in Blair's life as leader, he was being separated by *The Sun* from his less palatable party.

This separation did not always work to Blair's advantage, however, with *The Sun* often carrying stories of criticism of the leader from within the party. The paper enjoyed a quotation from Paul Flynn on the New Labour line on grant maintained schools. 'We may be a government of political eunuchs in a land of sterile prosperity', Flynn said; 'BLAIR THE EUNUCH', said *The Sun*.[24] Despite the nation's favourite tabloid printing plenty of these anti-Blair stories, it wasn't until 5 October 1995 and the Labour Party Conference that *The Sun* published a clear opinion of him and his policies. When it did, it was rather negative. 'WHO'LL PAY THE FARE FOR BLAIR'S HOT AIR?' the headline asked, followed by the damning subheading 'Most of his vision won't add up'. The author of this article shared the fear of many others at *The Sun* that New Labour would be, like its predecessor, 'the old tax and spend party'[25]. Despite being less than two years away from the general election, *The Sun* in 1995 was some way off placing its support behind Blair and his party.

In spite of a concerted Labour effort to improve press-party relations behind the scenes, and a growing realisation that they had a commanding lead in the opinion polls, *The Sun* was still not convincingly pro-Blair in 1996. A proliferation of articles appeared in the paper over the whole of that year which attacked the prominence of soundbite over substance in New Labour and led *The Sun* to conclude that 'The closer the election comes, the clearer it is that Labour will tell you anything to get your vote … Apart from the worrying truth about themselves'.[26] However, this damning conclusion on Blair's New Labour was nothing in comparison to the slaughter that Kinnock had received at the hands of *The Sun*. Indeed, by 1996 it was becoming clear that New Labour's intensive media strategy was bearing some fruit.

The executive and editorial ambiguity about whether or not to ally with Blair's New Labour was reflected in the manner in which *The Sun* dealt with an accusation from an old school friend of Tony Blair's that his education policy was hypocritical. The first account from Richard Gibbon, who studied at Fettes College, Edinburgh, with Blair, was printed by *The Sun* followed, days later, by a defence of Blair and his policies from another old school friend, Nick Ryden. The thought of an article appearing in defence of a criticism of Kinnock in the same paper five years earlier is totally unimaginable.

But before *The Sun* could ally itself with New Labour, it had to renege on a previous alliance with the Tory Party. The difference between *The Sun*'s treatment of the Conservatives in 1992 and in 1997 was marked, but by no means as different as its treatment of Labour at these two junctures. In 1992 the Tory Party were supported more implicitly than New Labour were in 1997, with John Major's Tories being billed as the only election possibility when compared with Kinnock's apocalyptical Labour Party. The years after 1992, however, saw an unenviable twist of fortune for the Tories' portrayal in the press.

Alongside the sexual and political scandal that plagued the Conservatives throughout their term in office came a cripplingly fateful day in September 1992. In the eyes of *The Sun*, 'The Tories were holed below the waterline by the Black Wednesday fiasco, which wrecked the government's financial policy and destroyed the reputations of the Prime Minister John Major and his Chancellor Norman Lamont.'[27] Britain had joined the European Exchange Rate Mechanism (ERM) in October 1990, at what proved to be an unrealistically high rate, and when economic crisis resulted it was the '*The Sun*'s people' who felt the strain.

It was very difficult for *The Sun* to continue to support the Tories in light of the fact that their front pages had been dominated by portrayals of Tory misdeeds. If the withdrawal from the ERM created a divide between the party and *The Sun*, then the misdemeanours of Jonathan Aitken, Neil Hamilton, David Mellor *et al* burnt the remaining bridges. Many of *The Sun*'s readers had been personally hit by the economic 'pain and suffering', leading up to Black Wednesday.[28] This unenviable position was damaged further by political infighting and a crisis of confidence in leader John Major. As Trevor Kavanagh recalls, 'They were divided, they were split over Europe, they couldn't seem to make their minds up about anything.'[29] In support of this, Fergus Shanahan (Night Editor in 1997 and current Deputy Editor) succinctly summarises the situation when he states that 'It did not take much insight to realise the Tories were making themselves unbackable, and it was clear by early 1997 that the country had had enough and wanted a change.'[30] Perhaps then, the assumption that *The Sun* had 'jumped ship' is somewhat misguided. Since 1992, the Tories had committed a series of political offences that were making *The Sun*'s former bedfellows unelectable. Instead of jumping ship, *The Sun* was being forced to walk the Tory plank straight into the open arms of New Labour and, most importantly, Tony Blair.

On 18 March 1997, the paper carried a banner headline: 'THE SUN BACKS BLAIR'[31]. This endorsement for the would-be Prime Minister was exactly that – an acceptance of the leader but not of the Party he represented. As Stuart Higgins (editor of *The Sun* at the time) recalls: 'The lines of communication before the election were strictly with Blair and Campbell. That's why our headline was "The Sun Backs Blair" because we had reservations about the rest of his party'.[32] George Pascoe-Watson, one of Higgins's key subordinates, also shared this view as the quotation at the beginning of this chapter makes clear.

Blair's personality, his youth and his family life were central to *The Sun*'s decision and ability to back him. As Pascoe-Watson points out, the role of a *Sun* political journalist often involves selling politics to a naturally unwilling audience and the notion of an easily marketable image is an essential aid to the job. 'Sometimes, the image itself is enough to get *Sun* readers interested in a subject which ordinarily they wouldn't find interesting', he asserts.[33] The image presented of the New Labour leader was a gift to the tabloid journalists. In Pascoe-Watson's words: 'A new millennium, a new man. Youngish, fresh-faced with a family – a normal family (or so it seemed at the time). He was very much in tune with *Sun* readers. Or so it seemed. The point is this: the perception allowed us to support him. It was very important. Very important'.[34]

The idea of Blair as a family man with young children was certainly an aspect of the leader's image onto which *The Sun* latched. On 28 April 1997 an interview with Blair conducted by Chris Roycroft-Davis and Trevor Kavanagh appeared in the paper under the headline 'Family side of the man set to be our next PM'. It was a long and rather sycophantic piece that addressed the youthful family aspect of Blair's campaign, and how the former has influenced the latter. Blair's answers claimed that because of his family life he was better equipped to understand the ills of society than any of his opponents. Blair used the interview to announce that he knew 'about the way *Sun* readers live. I've [Blair] been burgled, my mother-in-law's been mugged and had to give up work afterwards, my kids all go to state schools, so I think I'm probably more in touch than the average Conservative minister.'[35] This successful aspect of Blair's image was bolstered by the dissemination of other connected images in *The Sun*. Trust was an important facet of Blair's campaign that contrasted sharply with the Tories while his youth and vigour allowed him to be presented as a strong man holding up national interests and 'fighting the dragons of Europe'[36] - a terribly important image for *The Sun*. The importance of Blair as a personality was certainly crucial in *The Sun*'s switch to New Labour, and it was his personality, and the themes that his image encapsulated, that was embraced by *The Sun* and distributed upon its pages. For *The Sun*, Blair was a leader who 'wasn't going to scare the children'.[37]

Even a casual glance at *The Sun*'s treatment of New Labour and Tony Blair between 1994 and 1997 would reveal a marked difference between its approach to the party and its approach to the leader. When *The Sun* dealt with areas of ambiguity in relation to Labour's policy - such as the unions or Europe - there was little or no mention of the leader. When, however, there was an article or editorial dealing with the positive aspects of Labour they were almost always intrinsically linked with, or solely about, Tony Blair. In the run-up to the 1997 election there was little mention of the Shadow Cabinet, or the roles its members would play in the formation of a New Labour government. Indeed, in *The Sun* between 17 March and the 1 May 1997, 76% of references made to named Labour politicians were about Blair.[38] Asked whether this was a conscious decision, George Pascoe-Watson, suggests 'Conscious decisions don't happen like that in newspapers. Especially not in ours'. This is not to say that the prominence of Blair above all others was an accident, but that it was a manifestation 'based on the premise that we support Tony Blair and not the Labour Party'.[39] There was no conscious decision because, as the Deputy Political Editor says, 'we do genuinely believe what we write, so it was obvious that we supported him and we'd write positive things about what he said and did'. He continues: 'The rest of the guys in this Shadow Cabinet were pretty much third-rate politicians. Two or three of whom have matured in government', but most importantly, 'They were certainly not *Sun* people in any way, shape or form. They, again, had the wrong image.'[40] Pascoe-Watson's remarks highlight again the importance of image in selling politics to *The Sun*'s audience. It might be natural to assume that by largely ignoring the Labour Party in *The Sun*, Blair's chances of electoral success could have been hindered. According to Pascoe-Watson this was not the case: 'You would write positive things about Tony Blair because ultimately punters don't vote for a political party they vote for a Prime Minister'[41].

This last assertion, however, is open to doubt. A challenging study, *Leaders' Personalities and the Outcome of Democratic Elections,* edited by Anthony King, sets out to quash the popular belief that leaders' and candidates' personalities are enormously important in determining electoral outcomes. Labour did not win in 1997 and 2001 because Tony Blair was leader, the work suggests. He happened to be leader in a year when the Labour Party were almost certainly going to win the election anyway. John Bartle and Ivor Crewe's contribution to King's book echoes the overall message by proposing that 'Blair's personal ascendancy over Major (which undoubtedly existed) made only a modest net contribution to Labour's victory'. Had Major and Blair been evaluated equally favourably, their research indicates, Labour's majority 'would have been cut from 11.9 to 11.0 points, altering the outcome in just four seats'.[42] Bartle and Crewe argue: 'Winners look good. Losers look bad. But winning or losing seldom has anything to do with their looks'.[43]

Further, they believe that the media's preoccupation with the primacy of the personality is detrimental to the true understanding of what wins and loses elections: 'The media further encourage the personalization of politics by focusing on the leaders, especially during election campaigns. Newspapers and television alike report elections if they were gladiatorial combats between two generals rather than battles between two armies'.[44]

The view that leaders are relatively unimportant in deciding electoral outcomes was certainly not shared by New Labour's own moving spirits as it entered into the election of 1997. It was their belief that in order to defeat the Tories they needed the support of *The Sun,* and that the image of their youthful leader was a means to achieve this. His image married well with the paper's natural inclination to translate politics to its readership through personalities, imagery and human-interest stories. As the comments from Pascoe-Watson above illustrate, image and personality were central to *The Sun*'s packaging of their support for New Labour.

Clearly it would be wrong to suggest that it is the personality of the leader that solely wins or loses the election for their political party. Perhaps what is most important for this study is that *The Sun* believed personality to be important. Not only did Blair's image and personality make the *Sun*'s change of allegiance possible but also, in fact, it was all that the paper became allied to. *The Sun* was not a natural friend of Labour, and personality took precedent over policy in terms of what *The Sun* supported. One cannot help but speculate as to how *The Sun* would have behaved in the run-up to the 1997 general election without the allure of Blair.

The 1997 general election was the first campaign in political history in
which the Labour Party secured the support of the majority of national
daily newspapers. This was a real coup for New Labour with a massive
21.6 million people reading newspapers supporting Labour, compared to
only 10.6 million for those newspapers supporting a Conservative victory
at the election. For *The Sun*, however, the 1997 general election was far
from its own finest hour. If the paper's reporting of the 1992 election
was minimal, in 1997 it was negligible. Despite a longer election
campaign of twenty-seven days, *The Sun*'s front page coverage had
dropped by a third to just six page ones dedicated to election related
stories,[45] while the percentage of editorial content dedicated to the
election had fallen by eight per cent to fifty-one per cent, twenty-five per
cent less than *The Mirror*.[46] There was also a marked transition away from
politics translated in the number of political photographs appearing in
not just *The Sun* but all national daily newspapers. In 1992 John Major
appeared in 334 photographs across all national dailies, and in 1997 he
appeared in only 195. The Labour leader fared better, proportionally.
Even so, Kinnock - the enemy of the tabloids - had featured in 277
photographs in 1992, while Blair, the ally of the majority of Fleet Street,
was only the focus of 263 photos five years later. As well as there being a
decrease in the number of photographs of the protagonists of the
campaign, there were also fewer images of the supporting cast of all
parties. In the election of 1992, the relatively minor Conservative
politicians Kenneth Baker and Sebastian Coe appeared in thirty
photographs between them. In 1997 Gordon Brown, key member of the
New Labour political framework and future Chancellor of the
Exchequer, was the subject of only twenty-seven.[47] For *The Sun*, as
much as any other newspaper, the campaign of 1997 featured less on its
pages than 1992 had.

Like its 1992 coverage, *The Sun* was almost muted on the subject of
the election on its front pages until the final stages of the campaign. The
one fundamental difference between the two campaigns, however, was
that this time the Labour leader was being praised, the Labour Party
tolerated and the Conservatives almost ignored. The first front page
dedicated to New Labour in the month prior to the election was that
which greeted roughly ten million readers on 4 April 1997. 'TONY'S
TRUST WHAT WE ALL NEED'. Despite *The Sun*'s endorsement for
'honest' Blair, the latter stages of the article returned to the paper's long-
standing reservations on the subject of unions and the prospect of closer
European integration. These subjects were treated with a mix of
admiration, hope and apprehension as the editorial moved to inform its
readers of Blair's Euro position: 'Blair has struck a more Eurosceptic
stance in recent weeks, but once again he's going to have to back it up
with action.[48] Later on in the month, in the 30 April edition, *The Sun* led

with an endorsement of Tony Blair just as it was to do the day after. 'WHO BLAIRS WINS', it suggested, and went on to propose that 'At 43, with three youngsters of his own, Blair understands why parents make education their main priority'. Indeed, it was Tony Blair's youth and fresh-faced vigour that *The Sun* claimed was a decisive factor in its switch of allegiance, declaring 'Tony Blair offers a fresh new approach that will take away the sour taste of the Tories'.

The Sun's final front page of the election campaign comprised a picture of the National Lottery hand resting its extended index finger on the head of a grinning Tony Blair. The headline shouted 'IT MUST BE YOU', adapting the Lottery's advertising slogan. The analogy was continued on the inside of the paper with readers being told that 'TODAY you have a unique opportunity to join the greatest jackpot syndicate ever'. The election-day analysis concluded with a bizarre mix of reservations about New Labour and a reminder to its readers why *The Sun* had come out in support for the party. A vote for Labour, *The Sun* suggested, would be a vote for Britain precisely because of Blair. Alluding to the cartoon that dominated the page,[49] the polling day piece suggested that by putting faith in Blair 'we'll have the strong man instead of the wrong man in No 10'. The 1 May edition of *The Sun* deviated no further from the line that it had established in the preceding year, namely that it felt comfortable with Blair but not with Labour, and although it may have admired Blair's qualities as a leader and a politician, it still harboured fears about the party he represented. It issued a warning to Blair on the perils facing a New Labour government: 'He must take on Europe, he must face down unions who wrongly reckon they are owed a pay-off, he must stamp on any in his Cabinet whose natural instinct might be to solve a problem by throwing taxpayers' money at it'.

The Sun's coverage of the election of 1992 had been characterised by the attacks on Kinnock and Labour, their contemporary political enemy. However, by the time of the campaign of 1997 when News International and New Labour had reached détente, *The Sun* was not quite prepared to push its old Tory allies into the mould of hated political opposition. The political pieces that featured in *The Sun* during the short campaign were, in the main, articles on Tony Blair and his personal appeal. There was little castigation of the Conservatives and especially not of their leader John Major. The contrast with the coverage of the election of 1992 could not be more profound. Scammell and Harrop have observed that 'The *Sun* in 1992 was aggressive, outrageous and memorable; in 1997 it was almost moderate, mainly positive and eminently forgettable, save for its switch to Labour. The *Sun*, in a word, was tame'.[50] However, it was precisely because of this switch that *The Sun*'s coverage was 'tamed'. Trevor Kavanagh who had overseen the crucifixion of Kinnock was still in the same position at the paper. He was well aware of the effect that had been wrought by the change in party allegiance: 'We didn't attack the

Tories very vehemently. We didn't really attack the Tories. We simply supported Labour. So that's not very interesting is it?'[51]

What is of interest, however - assuming that 1997 was a 'tamed' campaign - is to ask whether or not its effects on the result of the election were correspondingly weakened. Trevor Kavanagh was asked whether it could, or should be claimed that it was 'The Sun wot won it' in 1997?

> No, and I don't think the original headline was correct either ... If we'd said in 1997 'vote Tory' we would have been utterly wrong and in 1992 we had said 'go vote Kinnock' we would have been left high and dry because no-one would have taken any notice of it.[52]

It is worth comparing this remark with something else Kavanagh said on the subject of the power of the newspaper on which he works: 'they realised in the Labour Party, Mandelson in particular realised, that it was The Sun readership which was the core, the key to a potential Labour victory. As long as they had the Sun against them, they couldn't win'.[53] An interesting thing to claim, if Kavanagh believes, as he professes, that newspapers cannot win or lose elections. Fergus Shanahan delivers a more even-handed account when he proposes that 'it is facile to suggest that we just print stuff and don't have any impact on events. With ten million daily readers, our voice is bound to be heard'. But, he proposes, 'it depends very much on the nature of the particular election'. 1992, it can be argued, was an election that was susceptible to press influence, but in 1997, 'it is much more doubtful whether it had any more than a negligible effect on voting behaviour, despite Blair's fulsome message to Stuart Higgins after the election that it had "really made the difference"'.[54]

The political staff at The Sun concede that support for Blair in 1997 translated into a less memorable campaign than 1992. Hampered by their equivocal support for New Labour, The Sun's election coverage faltered. It was clear to The Sun that the Tories could no longer be backed. But what was it that The Sun gained from its uneasy alliance with New Labour? This point will be returned to below.

The benefits to New Labour itself from a more cordial relationship seemed fairly obvious. Nullifying what was conceived as one of the greatest single threats to it gaining power was clearly a remarkable achievement. But it didn't stop there. New Labour used the improved relationship with The Sun to the greatest possible advantage by plying Fleet Street with press releases and encouraging their newfound friends to print articles that, ostensibly, were written by Blair. The Labour Party media machine based at Millbank Tower was responsible for producing a plethora of articles with the Blair by-line that appeared in the British printed media both before and after May 1997. And, true to their special relationship, *The Sun* was a favoured platform for these stories. Joy Johnson calculated for the *British Journalism Review* that fifteen of the twenty-three articles with a Blair by-line published in the first eight months of the government were printed in *The Sun*. Three were also printed in its Sunday sister paper, *The News of The World*.[55] It was this plethora of articles, supposedly penned by Blair, that Nicholas Jones has described as the 'most visible manifestation of what I believe has developed into an unprecedented level of collaboration'.[56] This level of interaction between Prime Minister and media was indeed a new stage for British politics, although it should not be assumed that Tony Blair made much of a contribution, if any, to the articles that bore his name. Trevor Kavanagh recalls:

> one of the people who was writing them was a fellow named David Bradshaw who was on *The Mirror* as a political correspondent until he went over to Downing Street and one day a piece came through with his name on it. He rang me and said 'Have you got the piece?', I said 'Yes. You wrote it'. He said 'I know, I've had more page eights in your paper than you have Trevor'.[57]

These articles again highlight the importance attached to the individual in politics. It is difficult imagine *The Sun* carrying articles penned by David Blunkett or John Prescott. The fact that they were supposedly written by Blair allowed *The Sun* to distance itself somewhat from publishing what were essentially Labour Party press releases. However, not everyone at Wapping was happy at the extent of 'Blair's' contribution in *The Sun*. Trevor Kavanagh is reported to have been sceptical of the value of such pieces, a reaction which he does not deny today. 'I don't think that we should be fed stories and I don't think that that's a good thing for any newspaper', he says, describing the articles from Millbank as 'stories which are press releases dressed up as news'.[58]

> I don't suppose many people read Tony Blair's articles in *The Sun*. Readers don't do that. A small proportion will have been interested by a picture of Tony Blair above a by-line saying 'by Tony Blair'. But I'd be very surprised if many readers [pauses] I didn't read them anyway. I thought they were a load of rubbish.[59]

This indifference on the part of the newspaper's Political Editor leads one to ask who it was who decided that articles attributed to Blair should appear in such numbers in *The Sun*. Ultimately, it was the editor at the time, Stuart Higgins, who would set the precedent for the amount of newspaper space dedicated to these releases from Millbank.[60] The timing of the appearance of these articles, however, was entirely determined by when the Labour Party communications office released them. Each article acted as an accompaniment to a specific item on each day's news agenda. For example, a Blair article appeared in *The Sun* in April 1998 with the heading 'Britain will lead way in computer revolution' which was directly related to the announcement that New Labour planned to launch a £600 million investment programme aimed at improving information technology within the National Health Service and the education system.[61]

There is no doubt that in the year prior to Blair's election and the immediate months following it, *The Sun*'s political stance was watered down. The vitriolic and vigorous reporting that had existed in the political lives of Michael Foot and Neil Kinnock appeared a distant memory. Not until the notorious 'Most Dangerous Man in Britain' headline did the *Sun* return to its political strength of old.[62] So why did *The Sun* support Blair? It would be naïve to imagine that it was just Blair and his party who gained benefits in the détente with News International. Clearly, backing the winning horse makes better editorial, and therefore, commercial sense. Did, then, the massive potential Labour majority influence *The Sun*'s decision to support Labour? According to Fergus Shanahan the answer is not that clear cut. He claims that *The Sun* made an independent decision to support New Labour and was not influenced by the direction of its readership.

> The country clearly wanted to give Blair a chance to see what he could do, and so did we. And it is true that a newspaper - which is a business like any other - will sell better if it carries the mainstream of the public with it, rather than flog a dead horse. But the commercial perspective was not the first reason for changing. It was our conviction that the Tories were a spent force. But naturally we were pleased to know that the paper would be on what we were sure would be the winning side.[63]

Aside from the advantages of being seen to have both been on the winning side, and intimate with its leader, *The Sun* gained from more tangible benefits when it decided to back Blair in 1997. It is an incontrovertible fact that the Downing Street media machine will be more helpful to supportive papers than to opponents. This can express itself in fairly mundane ways, such as providing access to a minister for an interview, or in more potent ways, like making the ear of the Prime Minister available. For a man like Murdoch, who has a wide array of business interests, the ear of the Prime Minister is to be prized. This can lead, however, to interpretations being made on the exertion of Murdoch's influence on Blair's policy making. There remains suspicion in the industry, for example, that Labour's largely market-driven policy towards the concentration of media power might have been different had News International's two popular papers not backed the party in 1997.[64] Similarly, there have been reports, emphatically denied by Labour figures, that Blair had made promises to Murdoch that Britain would not enter a single currency in the next parliament.[65] There have also been allegations from, amongst others, Neil Kinnock, that Blair's U-turn on the referendum on the proposed European constitution in April 2004 came as a result of pressure from Murdoch.[66]

This is a relationship that George Pascoe-Watson sees as 'patronage',[67] while Trevor Kavanagh asserts that the relationship that *The Sun* enjoyed with New Labour prior to and after the election result was the same as it had enjoyed with the Tories.[68] Kavanagh's view was not that held by *The Sun*'s competitors in the years prior to, and after, the 1997 election. Rather, as Peter Oborne recounts in his unofficial biography of Alastair Campbell, it was

> swiftly noticed by correspondents from other papers that Sun journalists were the only ones spared Campbell's routine barbarism and scorn. When they asked questions, he listened politely and with an expression of lively interest, which contrasted with the sneer of contempt he held in reserve for ordinary jobbing hands.[69]

This accusation of professional favouritism is, understandably, denied by those alleged to have been the recipients of it. Kavanagh claims New Labour's awareness of his own reservations toward their party is testament to this fact. George Pascoe-Watson is also in a very good position to reject Oborne's claim that there are 'few journalists in the lobby whom Campbell has not attempted to abuse or humiliate at some stage. His only rule is that he leaves the *Sun* well alone'.[70] After an unhelpful piece on the Labour attitude to the single European currency, Campbell is alleged to have launched a vicious attack on Pascoe-Watson. This is not denied by the Deputy Political Editor who remembers 'him having me up against a wall, scruff of my neck, about to smash me in the face just down there in the corridor'.[71] Perhaps then, *The Sun* and its journalists were not treated with entire preference, although the conclusion to this anecdote rather betrays that assumption. It is alleged that Campbell thrust a written apology into the hands of Pascoe-Watson, who reportedly keeps it treasured in a drawer by his bed - so unusual is an apology from the former press secretary![72]

The perception of favouritism toward *The Sun* may also be seen to have caused later problems for New Labour's portrayal in other sections of the press. *The Mirror* certainly felt itself ill-treated by Labour's anxiety to court their largest competitor. It is no accident that *The Mirror* - the only newspaper to retain its support of Labour in every election since 1945 - pursued an independent line post-1997.[73] Even before the election, other sections of the left-leaning press were becoming disillusioned by Blair's pursuit of *The Sun* and its readers. Andrew Marr, furious with the Euro-sceptic tone that Blair had adopted in an article in *The Sun*, claimed that Blair's obsession with winning the press battle was resulting in confused policy presentation. 'One message for one group of readers on Europe, another for another' he announced, before suggesting damningly that 'Blair will have to choose between betraying the whole emotional tone of his *Sun* article, and betraying our nation's better future'.[74] It is clear, therefore, that although both *The Sun* and New Labour extracted mutual benefit from their newly forged association, it was not achieved without some degree of cost.

Despite the body of literature regarding or mentioning *The Sun*'s switch of support in 1997, none of it gives primacy to the question of why it had discarded the Tories. It is a common assumption that *The Sun* simply traded allegiance because they and New Labour had grown closer. The most prominent flaw in the theory that *The Sun* and Labour had converged politically is the simple fact that *The Sun* never supported the Labour Party. *The Sun* put its faith in Tony Blair as a personality, a leader and a future Prime Minister but never in the party that he led. The process was what Margaret Scammell has called 'dealignment'; in that *The Sun* was no longer aligned with the Tories but had not realigned itself wholly with New Labour - only with its leader. This lack of support for Tony Blair's party and the recentness of the 'dealignment' from the Tories were evident in the diluted reporting of the 1997 election campaign. In 1992 Britain's biggest-selling daily was vicious, ferocious and vehemently anti-Kinnock. In 1997 *The Sun* had no enemy and consequently its coverage suffered. The newspaper still harboured scepticism on Labour's attitude to the issues of Europe and union militancy - further proof that *The Sun* and the Labour Party were far from happy bedfellows - but this was somewhat submerged in the saturation coverage of Blair. By 18 March 1997, however, New Labour had achieved its goal of winning the electoral support of *The Sun* - or at least of preventing its enmity. It was the end result of a process that had begun in the wake of the 1992 general election, with those in the closest circles of Blair's entourage convinced that Labour's next prime ministerial candidate must not be pilloried by the tabloid press. Thus, spurred on by the excessive claim that it was '*The Sun* wot won' the 1992 election and a deep mistrust of opinion polls, the New Labour media campaign was born.

But it is doubtful whether the effort involved in wooing *The Sun* was proportionally effective - or even necessary. *The Sun* played little, if any part in influencing the voting patterns of 1997.[75] Therefore, it may at first seem difficult to understand why New Labour invested so much time and effort into courting *The Sun*, especially when one considers that at the end of the long campaign all that the paper produced was a relatively unconvincing endorsement for the Labour Party leader, and at a relatively late stage. However, it must also be remembered that as a result of their improved relations, both New Labour and *The Sun* benefited in other ways. *The Sun's* presentation of Blair as a one-man band allowed the would-be Prime Minister to distance himself from the less palatable elements of his party while strengthening his hand in it[76] and gave the newspaper a personality, if not policies, to present to their audience. Nevertheless, certainly by 1997 and probably even in 1996, New Labour was guaranteed electoral success and yet still their intensive media strategy continued.

Intoxicated with paranoia about the power of the tabloid press and a cautiousness over the validity of opinion polls, New Labour can be seen to have pursued a media strategy that was largely, if not wholly, unnecessary from the point of view of winning the election. Its preoccupation with ensuring *The Sun's* support at all costs may have blinkered it to the fact that by 1996 the old Tory-*Sun* alliance had been exhausted in the political scandals of the early nineties. The same preoccupation may well have produced a detrimental effect on the Party's relations with other newspapers and especially with the traditionally Labour-supporting *Mirror*. Although the pro-*Sun* strategy of the New Labour media campaign did nothing to harm Labour's election possibilities, it did not ensure its success. The misplaced belief in *The Sun's* ability to influence elections is testament to a wider trend in modern British politics. In an age of ever-weakening printed partisanship, increasingly pluralist opinion and issue-based editorialism, British newspapers are no longer as stringently aligned to political parties as they were in the previous century. It will be interesting to see whether *The Sun's* support for Labour – such as it is - will remain when Blair makes his inevitable departure. Or, as is more likely, whether its partisanship will wane further as support for Euro-sceptic candidates becomes a priority. Perhaps it is time for politicians to readdress the value placed in the political power of the British press - especially *The Sun*.

Notes

Introduction

[1] 'House of Commons', *The Times*, 29 March, 1945.
[2] King, Anthony, 'Do Leaders' Personalities Really Matter?', in Anthony King (ed), *Leaders' Personalities and the Outcomes of Democratic Elections* (Oxford, 2002), pp. 1-43, at pp. 29-30.
[3] Ibid, p. 6.
[4] Ibid, pp. 4-5.
[5] Ibid, p. 8.
[6] Williamson, P., 'Baldwin's Reputation: Politics and History, 1937-1967', *Historical Journal*, 47/1 (2004), pp. 127-168.

Chapter 1. Constructing Life Stories

[1] Byatt, A.S., *The Biographer's Tale* (London, 2000).
[2] Marsh, Peter, *Joseph Chamberlain: Entrepreneur in Politics* (New Haven & London, 1994).
[3] Churchill, Winston, *Great Contemporaries* (London, 1937), p. 57.
[4] Marsh, Peter, *The Discipline of Popular Government: Lord Salisbury's domestic statecraft, 1881-1902* (Hassocks, Sussex, 1978) reprinted in 1993 by Gregg Revivals.
[5] Roberts, Andrew, *Salisbury, Victorian Titan* (London, 1999)
[6] Steele, David , *Lord Salisbury: A political biography* (London, 1999).
[7] Bentley, Michael, *Lord Salisbury's World: Conservative environments in late-Victorian Britain* (Cambridge, 2001).

Chapter 2. Robert Lowe and Gladstonian Liberalism

[1] All dates are for 1868 unless otherwise specified. *Hansard*, third series, CLXXXII (13 March 1866), cols. 147-48.
[2] *Manchester Guardian*, 4 January 1867, p. 2. For Lowe's comments about himself, see *Hansard*, third series, CLXXXII (12 April 1866), col. 1151; and the House of Lords Record Office, Lowe papers, collection 383, item 34: Lowe to his brother, 25 July 1866. For Lowe's life at this time, see Winter, J.M., *Robert Lowe* (Toronto, 1976), Chapter 12.
[3] Winter: *Robert Lowe*, p. 230: Lowe to Delane, 9 December 1866.
[4] On the political press in this period, see for example Koss, Stephen, *Rise and Fall of the Political Press in Britain* (London, 1981), vol. I, Chapters 3, 4; and Lee, Alan J , *The Origins of the Popular Press in England, 1855-1914* (London, 1976), Chapters 3 to 5. For the rapid increase in politicians' speeches during the parliamentary recesses in the late 1850s and the 1860s see Zimmerman, K.,

'Speaking to the People: Liberal Crisis and Extraparliamentary Speech, 1850-1870' (Stanford University, Ph.D. diss., 2001).

5 Politicians' speeches outside parliament are cited here through newspaper reports, which are frequently the only surviving account of the speeches and which was the source through which most Victorians had access to them. Although such reports did not always perfectly represent what MPs said, they were fairly reliable as newspapers at the time took great pride in the accuracy of their reports and knew their reports could often be compared to those of their rivals.

6 White, William, *The Inner Life of the House of Commons* (Richmond, Surrey, 1973), part I, p. 167: 22 February 1862. White was a doorman at the House of Commons who wrote a regular column for the *Illustrated Times* describing parliamentary debates and personalities. This selection of his columns is based on an earlier edition edited by Justin McCarthy.

7 Winter: *Robert Lowe*, pp. 143-44; Patchett Martin, A., *The Life and Letters of the Rt. Hon. Robert Lowe, Viscount Sherbrooke* (London, 1893), vol. II, pp. 154-55. Lowe suffered a skull fracture, lacerated scalp wounds, two severe contusions, and severe bleeding. A police officer attempting to protect him died of related injuries.

8 *The History of The Times*, vol. II, p. 592: Lord John Russell to Dean Elliot, 28 April 1858. For the general view of MPs regarding Lowe's press role, see for example White: *Inner Life*, part I, p. 167: 22 February 1862.

9 *Daily Telegraph*, 14 March 1866, p. 6.

10 Bright, *The Times*, 28 August 1866, p. 4; Layard, *The Times*, 10 April 1866, p. 5; Forster and Childers, *The Times*, 4 April 1866, p. 12; Goschen, *The Times*, 6 April 1866, p. 10.

11 This aspect of the reform crisis is examined in more detail in Zimmerman, K., 'Liberal speech, Palmerstonian delay, and the passage of the Second Reform Act', *English Historical Review*, 118/479, (2003), pp. 1176-1207.

12 Henry Brand, *The Times*, 4 February 1867, p. 10; Collier, *The Times*, 1 November 1866, p. 4; Forster, *The Times*, 9 October 1866, p. 7.

13 This Adullamite was Samuel Laing, speaking at Wick: *Scotsman*, 27 August 1866, p. 2, 30 August 1866, p. 4.

14 *The Times*, 1 November 1866, p. 4.

15 *Scotsman*, 22 October 1868, p. 3.

16 *Scotsman*, 28 August 1868, p. 2.

17 Such as his toast to the Liberal party after the election: *The Times*, 28 January 1869, p. 8.

18 *Lloyd's Weekly News*, 13 December, p. 1; *Edinburgh Review*, January 1869, p. 270.

19 White: *Inner Life*, part II, p. 54: 2 March 1867. However, White's admiration of Lowe's oratorical skill was quite recent, as shown by his withering assessment of Lowe's speaking abilities in 1862: White: *Inner Life*, part I, pp. 164-66: 22 February 1862.

20 *Hansard*, third series, CXCII (10 June 1868), cols. 1364-67, and CXCI (2 April 1868), cols. 728-748.

21 Reported in *The Times*, 4 November 1867, pp. 8-9, 24 January 1868, p. 5, 25, January 1868, p. 6.

22 Winter: *Robert Lowe*, p. 244.

[23] Shannon, Richard, *Gladstone: Heroic Minister, 1865-98* (London, 1999), p. 59, and Winter: *Robert Lowe*, p. 245.

[24] For example, *Scotsman*, 7 December, p. 3, *Freeman's Journal*, 7 December, p. 2, *Illustrated London News*, 12 December, p. 562.

[25] *Scotsman*, 8 December, p. 2; *Dublin Evening News*, reprinted in the *Cork Examiner*, 9 December, p. 3; *Manchester Guardian*, 8 December, p. 4; *Leeds Mercury*, 8 December, p. 4; *Daily Telegraph*, 7 December, p. 4.

[26] *Examiner*, 19 December, p. 801; *Spectator*, 5 December, p. 1425; *Daily Telegraph*, 8 December, p. 4.

[27] The term 'triumvirate' was for example used by the *Daily News*, 9 December, p. 4, and the *Beehive*, 5 December, p. 4. Many journals that did not specifically use this term nonetheless singled out Gladstone, Lowe and Bright as the leading members of the new administration, including the *North British Review*, December 1868, p. 514 and *Saturday Review*, 12 December, pp. 761-64.

[28] For especially lyrical praise of Bright's character see the *Westminster Review*, January 1869, p. 107, and for an extended comparison of Bright and Lowe see the *Daily News*, 9 December, p. 4.

[29] *Daily News*, 9 December, p. 4; *The Times*, 7 December, p. 8 and 14 December, p. 6; *Dublin Evening News*, reprinted in the *Cork Examiner*, 9 December, p. 3.

[30] E.g. *Spectator*, 12 December, p. 1453.

[31] *Daily News*, 9 December, p. 4; *Illustrated London News*, 12 December, p. 562; *Daily Telegraph*, 9 December, p. 4; *Spectator*, 12 December, p. 1456; *Examiner*, 12 December, p. 785.

[32] Matthew, H.C.G., *Gladstone, 1809-98* (Oxford, 1997), p. 180.

[33] Winter: *Robert Lowe*, p. 248.

[34] For example, *The Times*, 14 December, p. 6 and the *Spectator*, 5 December, p. 1425.

[35] This was entitled 'The Happy Land'. Winter: *Robert Lowe*, pp. 254-55.

[36] These include Parry, Jonathan, *The Rise and Fall of Liberal Government in Victorian Britain* (New Haven, 1993) and Steele, E.D., *Palmerston and Liberalism, 1855-65* (Cambridge, 1991).

[37] *Leeds Mercury*, 5 December, p. 5.

Chapter 3. The Politics of Personality in the Asquith Coalition

The following abbreviations have been adopted: AMSD: Alexander MacCallum Scott diary (Alexander MacCallum Scott papers, University of Glasgow Library); BL: British Library additional manuscripts; CPSD: C. P. Scott diary (C. P. Scott papers, British Library); EM: Edwin Montagu; FS: Frances Stevenson; FSD: Frances Stevenson diary (Taylor, A. J. P. (ed), *Lloyd George – A Diary by Frances Stevenson*, 1971); GRD: George Riddell diary (George Riddell papers, British Library); HHA: H.H. Asquith; HHA-VS: H. H. Asquith to Venetia Stanley (Brock, Michael and Brock, Eleanor (eds) *H.H. Asquith Letters to Venetia Stanley*, Oxford 1982); MA: Margot Asquith; JAS: J.A. Spender; LG: David Lloyd George; McK: Reginald McKenna; McKP: Reginald McKenna papers, Churchill College Cambridge; PMcK: Pamela McKenna; WR: Walter Runciman; WRP: Walter Runciman papers, University of Newcastle Library; WSC: Winston Churchill.

Unless otherwise stated documents are currently in the possession of the author, who wishes to acknowledge the help and encouragement of David McKenna, CBE, 1910-2003.

1 HHA to PMcK, 11 November 1915.

2 HHA-VS, 16 April 1915.

3 FSD, 31 January 1916.

4 WSC to Clementine Churchill, 27 November 1915, Gilbert, Martin (ed), *Winston S. Churchill*, vol. III, Companion volume II (London, 1972), p. 1290.

5 Space precludes a comprehensive listing, but the most significant are: Cassar, George, *Asquith as War Leader* (London, 1994); Turner, John, *British Politics and the Great War* (New Haven, 1992); Fry, Michael, 'Political Change in Britain, August 1914 to December 1916: Lloyd George Replaces Asquith: The Issues Underlying the Drama', *Historical Journal*, xxxl/3 (1988), pp. 609-627; French, David, *British Strategy and War Aims* (London, 1986); Murphy, Richard, 'Walter Long, The Unionist Ministers, and the Formation of Lloyd George's Government in December 1916', *Historical Journal*, xxix/ 3 (1986), pp. 736-745; McEwen, J. M., 'The Press and the Fall of Asquith', *The Historical Journal*, xxi/4 (1978), pp. 863-883; McEwen, J. M., 'The Struggle for Mastery in Britain: Lloyd George versus Asquith, December 1916', *Journal of British Studies*, xviii (1978), pp. 131-156; Pugh, Martin, 'Asquith, Bonar Law, and the First Coalition', *Historical Journal*, xvii/4 (1974), pp. 813-836. The author's forthcoming biography of McKenna is intended to complete the picture.

6 LG to GR, GRD 20 August 1915.

7 Brock and Brock, *Letters to Venetia Stanley.*

8 CPSD, 13 November 1915.

9 CPSD, and, especially, GRD, *passim.* No sense of this can be gleaned from the published editions.

10 MA to Reading, 23 May 1932, Reading papers F118/63b.

11 Sir Walter Runciman to WR, 15 November 1918, WRP359.

12 FSD, 31 October 1916.

13 FSD, 21 November 1916.

14 McK to C.A.C. Repington 1918, Kettle, Michael, *Salomé's Last Veil* (1977), 47.

15 GRD, 14 January 1915.

16 Esher diary , 3 September 1910, Esher papers 2/15.

17 MA to Violet Tree, n.d., BL59895.

18 The phrase is that of McKenna's nephew, Stephen McKenna in his full, unpublished, life written for the *Dictionary of National Biography*, 1946.

19 McK to Repington, 13 August 1918.

20 Fisher to Esher, 5 May 1908, Esher papers 10/42.

21 LG to GR, GRD 5 January 1916.

22 JAS, *Herbert Henry Asquith* (London, 1915), p. 86.

23 McK to David Davies, 21 May 1918.

24 WR to Hilda Runciman, 25 January 1914, WRP303/2.

25 McK to C.A.C. Repington 13 August 1918.

26 Clementine Churchill to WSC, 28 November 1915, Soames, Mary (ed), *Speaking for Themselves* (London, 1998), p. 121.

27 The traditional notion that McKenna was a temporary appointment is unconvincing. Farr, 'Reginald McKenna', pp. 58-61.

28 HHA-VS, 7 March 1915.

[29] HHA-VS, 28 November 1914.
[30] HHA to Violet Asquith, 17 February 1908, Bonham Carter, Mark and Pottle, Mark (eds), *Lantern Slides: the diaries and letters of Violet Bonham Carter, 1904-1914* (London, 1996), p. 143; McK to Dilke, 28 April 1908, BL43920.
[31] HHA-VS, 24 October 1914; HHA to WR 1 October 1907, WRP131/302.
[32] HHA-VS, 16 April 1915.
[33] HHA to Kathleen Scott, 18 April 1916, HHA papers 152.
[34] HHA to Crewe, 4 July 1915, Crewe papers C40.
[35] HHA to PMcK, 20 September 1915.
[36] HHA to PMcK, 10 September 1915.
[37] Sir Henry Wilson to Leo Amery 19 August 1915, Barnes, John and Nicholson, David (eds), *Leo Amery Diaries* vol. I (London, 1980), p. 124.
[38] HHA to PMcK, 28 May 1915.
[39] HHA to PMcK, 17 June 1915; HHA to PMcK 25 May 1915.
[40] HHA to PMcK, 21 July 1915.
[41] LG to GR, GRD 14 November 1915; GRD 3 February 1915, 28-29 September 1913.
[42] GRD, 1 May 1915.
[43] GRD, 14 January 1915.
[44] GRD, 1 May 1915.
[45] GRD, 22 August 1915.
[46] CPSD, 8 May 1916.
[47] VS to Violet Asquith, 16 August 1908, *Lantern Slides*, p. 162.
[48] HHA to PMcK, 4 October 1915.
[49] HHA to PMcK, 3 October 1915.
[50] McK to WR, 22 May 1917, WRP161/1.
[51] AMSD, 27 November 1916.
[52] McK to Burns, 26 October 1914, BL46382.
[53] McK to J. L. Garvin, 28 May 1908, McKP3/13.
[54] Hugh Spender to WR, 18 December 1916, WRP153.
[55] GRD, 10 June 1915.
[56] Marcosson, I. F., *War after the War* (New York, 1917), 133.
[57] LG to GR, GRD 15 September 1915.
[58] LG to GR, GRD 19 February 1916.
[59] GRD, 4 September 1915.
[60] GRD, 14 November 1915.
[61] GRD, 14 November 1915.
[62] MA to PMcK, 28 December 1915.
[63] GRD, 28 November 1915.
[64] HHA to PMcK, 16 December 1915.
[65] HHA to PMcK, 1 January 1916.
[66] HHA to PMcK , 28 December 1915; MA to McK, 28 December 1915, McKP5/9.
[67] HHA to Violet Tree, 30 December 1915, BL59895.
[68] WR to Hilda Runciman, 28 December 1915, WRP303/2.
[69] MA to PMcK, 28 December 1915.
[70] HHA to PMcK, 5 January 1916.
[71] MA to PMcK, 28 December 1915.
[72] 'An even temperament in adversity'; MA to PMcK, 28 December 1915.

73 FSD, 31 January 1916.
74 GRD, 16 July 1916; 22 June 1916.
75 McK to WR, 19 June 1916, WRP149/1.
76 McK to WR, 26 June 1916, WRP149/1; McK to HHA, 16 June 1916, McKP5/8.
77 McK to WR, 26 June 1916, WRP149/1.
78 Robertson to Haig, 8 November 1916, Haig papers 3155/109.
79 FSD, 21 November 1916, GRD 10 December 1916.
80 McK to CPS, CPSD, 2-3 October 1916
81 HHA to George V, 30 November 1916, cabinet papers 41/37.
82 HHA to PMcK, 20 September 1916; HHA to Ettie Desborough, 25 October 1916, Desborough papers D/ERv/272. HHA's growing disenchantment: HHA to PMcK, 10 September 1915, 6 October 1915, 12 October 1915, 16 October 1915, 24 October 1915, 2 November 1915, 29 November 1915, 11 February 1916, 19 February 1916, 17 June 1916, 27 June 1916, 24 October 1916.
83 CPSD, 2-3 October 1916.
84 HHA to PMcK, 13 November 1916.
85 Memorandum, 25 November 1916, Bonar Law papers 63/A/3.
86 HHA to PMcK, 27 November 1916.
87 HHA to PMcK, 1 December 1916.
88 FSD, 20-22 November 1916; GRD 8 December 1916.
89 A.J. Balfour memorandum, 7 December 1916, BL49692.
90 GRD, 3 December 1916.
91 HHA to LG, 4 December 1916, [copy] BL49692; Balfour to HHA, 5 December 1916, BL49692; Samuel to JAS, 5 December 1916, BL46392.
92 EM, memorandum, 9 December 1916, Charles Roberts papers F170/10; EM to HHA, 5 December 1916, HHA papers AS1/12; Arthur Murray diary, 6 December 1916, Elibank papers 8815; GRD, 10 December 1916; AMSD, 4 February 1917.
93 HHA to McK, 17 December 1916.
94 JAS, *Life, Journalism and Politics* vol. I (London, 1937), p. 166.

Chapter 4. Charismatic leadership

1 Weber, Max, *Economy and Society. An Outline of Interpretive Sociology*, (edited by Guenther Roth and Claus Wittich) (Berkeley, 1978), especially Part One chapter III and Part Two chapter XIV.
2 Robert Michels conducted Weberian analyses of Mussolini's leadership, and Rauschning, Hermann, *Die Revolution des Nihilismus* (Zurich & New York, 1938) used the concept of charisma in his characterization of Nazi leadership.
3 Both mentioned by Weber, Max, *Politics as a Vocation* (Philadelphia, 1965), pp. 31, 38, as examples of leadership, though Gladstone is certainly his prime example of charismatic leadership.
4 For more material about some of these cases, in particular the Dutch ones, see te Velde, Henk, *Stijlen van leiderschap: Persoon en politiek van Thorbecke tot Den Uyl* (Amsterdam, 2002), Chapter 2.
5 Biagini, Eugenio F., *Gladstone* (London , 2000) p. 60.
6 Cf. Junco, José Alvarez, *El Emperador del Paralelo: Lerroux y la demagogia populista* (Madrid, 1990), p. 465, who says that Lerroux's movement was a movement of

transition from rural clientelist politics to institutionalized party politics and a
politics of interest groups.
[7] Cited in Biagini, Eugenio F., *Liberty, Retrenchment and Reform: Popular Liberalism in
the Age of Gladstone, 1860-1880* (Cambridge, 1992), p. 369. In general, see Wilner,
Ann Ruth, *The Spellbinders: Charismatic Political Leadership* (New Haven & London,
1984), esp. pp. 193-197; and also Mosse, George L., *The Nationalization of the
Masses: Political Symbolism and Mass Movements in Germany from the Napoleonic Wars
through the Third Reich* (New York, 1975).
[8] Schorske, Carl E., *Fin-de-siècle Vienna: Politics and Culture* (New York, 1979). In
this work, Lueger figures as an example of this new style of politics.
[9] Geehr, Richard S., *Karl Lueger: Mayor of fin de siècle Vienna* (Detroit, 1990) p. 16.
[10] Te Velde: *Stijlen van leiderschap*, p. 82.
[11] Biagini, Eugenio F., 'Gladstone e l' invenzione della "leadership" in une
democrazia imperfetta', *Ricerche di Storia Politica* (2002), pp. 341-350, and esp. p.
343.
[12] Beatrice Potter (1884 and 1887) cited by Marsh, Peter T., *Joseph Chamberlain:
Entrepreneur in Politics* (New Haven & London, 1994), pp. 167, 279.
[13] Regarding Lassalle, see Mosse, *Nationalization of the Masses*, pp. 161-165, and
Na'aman, Shlomo, *Lassalle* (Hannover, 1970).
[14] Gemkow, Heinrich and Miller, Angelika (eds), *August Bebel – "... ein prächtiger
alter Adler": Nachrufe – Gedichte – Erinnerungen* (Berlin, 1990), p. 203. This is a
reprint of obituaries and reminiscences.
[15] For Hardie's bohemian rather than common working class appearance see
Morgan, Kenneth O., *Keir Hardie: Radical and Socialist,* (1975; London, 1997), p.
55.
[16] Welskopp, Thomas: *Das Banner der Brüderlichkeit: Die deutsche Sozialdemokratie vom
Vormärz bis zum Sozialistengesetz* (Bonn, 2000), Chapter 5, differentiates between
these types of popular leaders within the socialist party (and there was also the
type of the professional propagandist).
[17] Gemkow and Miller: *Bebel*, pp. 180, 212.
[18] Reminiscences in *De Standaard*, 29 October 1937, a memorial issue of Kuyper's
former party daily.
[19] Gemkow and Miller: *Bebel*, p. 251.
[20] Ibid, pp. 274 and 299; Cartsen, Francis L., *August Bebel und die Organisation der
Massen* (Berlin, 1991), p. 247; Maehl, William Harvey, *August Bebel: Shadow
Emperor of the German Workers* (Philadelphia, 1980).
[21] For example, Seebacher-Brandt, Brigitte, *Bebel: Künder und Kärner im Kaiserreich*
(Bonn, 1988), pp. 307, 321, 380.
[22] Gemkow and Miller: Bebel, p. 143.
[23] Ibid, pp. 299-300.
[24] Weber: *Economy and Society*, pp. 216, 1112, cites the church historian Rudolf
Sohm as the main source for the concept.
[25] Weber: *Politics*, p. 32.
[26] Morley, John, *The Life of William Ewart Gladstone* 3 vols. (London & New York,
1903) II, p. 610; Biagini, *Liberty*, p. 417; Matthew, H.C.G., *Gladstone 1875-1898*
(Oxford, 1995) p. 54.
[27] Johnston, Thomas, 'James Keir Hardie: The Founder of the Labour Party', in
Herbert Tracey (ed), *The Book of the Labour Party. Its History, Growth, Policy, and
Leaders* III (London, c. 1925), p. 105.

[28] Benn, Caroline, *Keir Hardie* (1992; London, 1997), p. 180.

[29] Troelstra, P.J., *Gedenkschriften* IV (Amsterdam, 1931), p. 300.

[30] Gladstone, W.E., *Studies on Homer and the Homeric Age* 3 vols. (Oxford, 1858) III, p. 107.

[31] Benn: *Keir Hardie*, p. 180; Kossmann, E.H., *De Lage Landen 1780-1980: Twee eeuwen Nederland en België* 2 vols. (Amsterdam & Brussels, 1986) II, p. 39. The English version of this book uses a more lenient expression.

[32] Jenkins, Roy, *Gladstone* (London & Basingstoke, 1995), p. 156; Shannon, Richard, *Gladstone: Peel's Inheritor 1809-1865* (1982; London, 1999), p. 523.

[33] Stewart, William, J. *Keir Hardie. A Biography* (1921; London, 1925), pp. 342, 352; Troelstra: *Gedenkschriften* III, p. 223; Troelstra, Jelle, *Mijn vader Pieter Jelles* (Amsterdam, 1952) p. 150.

[34] Morgan: *Keir Hardie*, pp. 124, 276 (Moses), p. 266 (Gethsemane); cf. James Ramsay MacDonald in Stewart: *Keir Hardie*, p. xxi: 'He will stand out for ever as the Moses who led the children of labour out of bondage'.

[35] Burns, Michael, *Rural Society and French Politics. Boulangism and the Dreyfus Affair 1886-1900* (Princeton, 1984), p. 78; d'Almeida, Fabrice, *Images et Propagande* (1995; Paris, 1998), p. 12.

[36] Butler, Josephine E., *Personal Reminiscences of a Great Crusade* (London, 1896); cf. van Drenth, Annemieke and de Haan, Francisca, *The Rise of Caring Power. Elizabeth Fry and Josephine Butler in Britain and the Netherlands* (Amsterdam, 1999), p. 98; Wakowitz, Judith R., *City of Dreadful Delight. Narratives of Sexual Danger in Late-Victorian London* (London, 1992), p. 90: 'prophet and suffering magdalen', 'charismatic leader and gifted speaker'. I would like to thank Dr Hanneke Hoekstra, University of Groningen, who suggested Butler as an example.

[37] Jordan, Jane, *Josephine Butler* (London, 2001), pp. 3, 111 (Benjamin Scott).

[38] Purvis, June, *Emmeline Pankhurst. A Biography* (2002; London & New York 2003) pp. 99-100, 157, 340, and passim.

[39] Gemkow and Miller: *Bebel*, p. 274.

[40] Maehl: *Bebel*, p.7.

[41] Alvarez Junco: *Lerroux*, pp. 465-466, even though considering Lerroux as a transitional figure to a period of mass political parties, notes his criticism of parliament and parties; on p. 10, footnote 3, he incorporates charismatic leadership in his definition of populism.

[42] For example, Morgan: *Hardie*, pp. 106, 135, 216, 258, 285.

[43] Taggart, Paul, *Populism* (Buckingham & Philadelphia, 2000) pp. 2-3, 69-71, 81.

[44] Shannon, Richard, *Gladstone: Heroic Minister 1865-1898* (London, 1999), pp. 172, 429.

[45] Marsh: *Chamberlain*, p. 119.

[46] Morgan: *Keir Hardie*, p. 88.

[47] Winkler, Johan, *Pieter Jelles Troelstra* (Amsterdam, 1933), pp. 74-75.

[48] Hamann, Brigitte, *Hitlers Wien: Lehrjahre eines Diktators* (Munich & Zurich, 1996), p. 409.

[49] Shannon: *Peel's Inheritor*, pp. 169, 523.

[50] Shannon: *Heroic Minister*, p. 222.

[51] Biagini: *Gladstone*, p. 69, who is citing a comparison from 1885.

[52] Wehler, Hans-Ulrich, *Deutsche Gesellschaftsgeschichte* III (München, 1995), p. 375 and passim.

[53] Weber: *Politics*, p. 31.

[54] Weber: *Economy and Society*, p. 1452.
[55] See also Breuer, Stefan, *Bürokratie und Charisma. Zur politischen Soziologie Max Webers* (Darmstadt, 1994), esp. the chapter about 'Das Charisma des Führers'.
[56] Matthew: *Gladstone 1875-1898*, p. 30.
[57] Te Velde: *Stijlen van leiderschap*, p. 94.
[58] Matthew: *Gladstone 1875-1898*, esp. chapter II; Matthew, H.C.G., 'Gladstone, rhetoric and politics' in Peter J. Jagger (ed), *Gladstone* (London & Rio Grande, 1998), pp. 213-234; cf. Jenkins: *Gladstone*, p. 425. See also Biagini: *Liberty*, Chapter 7.
[59] Cf. Welskopp, *Banner*, and Loreck, Jürgen, *Wie man früher Sozialdemokrat wurde: Das Kommunikationsverhalten in der deutschen Arbeiterbewegung und die Konzeption der sozialistischen Parteipublizistik durch August Bebel* (Bonn & Bad Godesberg, 1977).
[60] One example among many is Kershaw, Ian, *The 'Hitler Myth'. Image and Reality in the Third Reich* (1987; Oxford, 2001), pp. 8-10.
[61] Manin, Bernard, *The Principles of Representative Government* (Cambridge, 1997).
[62] Wallas, Graham, *Human Nature in Politics* (1908; London, 1948), p. 55.
[63] See Kari Palonen, 'Die Verzeitlichung der Begriffe bei Max Weber', in: Jussi Kurunmäki and Kari Palonen (eds.), *Zeit, Geschichte und Politik.Time, history and politics. Zum achtzigsten Geburtstag von Reinhart Koselleck* (Jyväskylä 2003) p. 97.
[64] Pedersen, Susan, 'What is political history now?', in David Cannadine (ed), *What is history now?* (Houndmills, 2002) p. 42. Pedersen wrongly assumes that the new approach is not suitable for international comparison.

Chapter 5. Harry Pollitt's Memoirs

[1] This chapter draws upon research on communist biography funded by ESRC award number R000 237924.
[2] For a discussion see Morgan, Kevin, 'Parts of people and communist lives' in John McIlroy, Kevin Morgan and Alan Campbell (eds), *Party People, Communist Lives: Explorations in Biography* (London, 2001).
[3] Gotovitch, José, and Morelli, Anne (eds), *Militantisme et militants* (Brussels, 2000); Claude Pennetier and Benard Pudal (eds), *Autobiographies, autocritiques, aveux dans le monde communiste* (Paris, 2002).
[4] Studer, Brigitte and Unfried, Berthold, 'At the beginning of a history: Visions of the Comintern after the opening of the archives', *International review of Social History* 42 (1997), pp. 428, 439; Studer, 'La femme nouvelle' in Michel Dreyfus et al, *Le siècle des communismes* (Paris, 2000), pp. 381-2.
[5] Pollitt, Harry, *Serving My Time: An apprenticeship to politics* (London, 1941 edition) (henceforth SMT); Thorez, Maurice, *Fils du peuple* (Paris, 1949 edition); Foster, William Z., *From Bryan to Stalin* (London, 1937).
[6] See Morgan, Kevin, *Harry Pollitt* (Manchester, 1993).
[7] Sirot, Stéphane, *Maurice Thorez* (Paris, 2000), pp. 23-4.
[8] Pennetier and Pudal, 'Les autobiographies des "fils du peuple". De l'autobiographie édifiante à l'autobiographie auto-analytique' in Pennetier and Pudal, *Autobiographies*, pp. 223-9; Pudal, Bernard, *Prendre parti Pour une sociologie historique du PCF* (Paris, 1989), pp. 183, 222-7.
[9] Berger, Stefan, 'In the fangs of social patriotism. The construction of nation and class in autobiographies of British and German Social Democrats in the inter-war period', *Archiv für Sozialgeschichte*, 40 (2000), pp.1-29.

[10] *SMT*, p. 285.

[11] Sirot: *Maurice Thorez*, p. 28; Pennetier, Claude, and Pudal, Bernard, 'Stalinisme, culte ouvrier et culte des dirigeants' in Dreyfus: *Le siècle*, p. 372.

[12] Borkenau, Franz, *European Communism* (London, 1953); Pelling, Henry, *The British Communist Party: A historical profile* (London, 1975 edition), p.89.

[13] Sirot: *Maurice Thorez*, pp. 242-3.

[14] Pennetier and Pudal: 'Stalinisme, culte ouvrier et culte des dirigeants', pp. 369-76.

[15] Epstein, Catherine, 'The production of "official memory" in East Germany: old communists and the dilemmas of memoir-writing', *Central European History*, 32/2, p. 191; Pennetier and Pudal: 'Les autobiographies', pp. 240-6.

[16] Cited in Cullerne Bown, Matthew, *Socialist Realist Painting* (New Haven, Conn., 1998), p. 159.

[17] See for example Wrigley, Chris, *Arthur Henderson* (Cardiff, 1990), pp. 1-2.

[18] Pennetier and Pudal: 'Stalinisme', p. 373, citing Marie-Françoise Chantrault-Duchet.

[19] Sirot: *Maurice Thorez*, p. 28.

[20] Pennetier and Pudal, 'Du parti bolchevik au parti stalinien' in Dreyfus: *Le siècle*, pp. 338-9; Pennetier and Pudal: 'Les autobiographies', p. 218.

[21] Bellassai, Sandro, 'The party as schools and the schools of party: The partito comunista italiano 1947-1956', *Paedagogica Historica*, 35/1 (1999), pp. 93-4.

[22] Foster, William Z., *Pages From a Worker's Life* (New York, 1943 edition), p. 11 and passim.

[23] Johanningsmeier, Edward P., *Forging American Communism. The life of William Z. Foster* (Princeton, NJ, 1994), pp. 269-71.

[24] Foster: *Pages*, pp. 294-316.

[25] Pudal, *Prendre parti*, pp. 218-19, 225.

[26] Cited Sirot: *Maurice Thorez*, pp. 23-4.

[27] Pennetier, Claude and Pudal, Bernard, 'La "verification": L'encradrement biographique communiste dans l'entre-deux-guerres', paper kindly supplied by authors .

[28] Thorez: *Son*, pp. 58-9.

[29] Morgan, Kevin, 'The archives of the British Communist Party: A historical overview', *Twentieth Century British History*, 7 (1996), pp. 404 ff.

[30] See e.g. Russian State Archive for Socio-Political History (RGASPI) 495/14/216, 'The publishing activities in Britain', 16 July 1936.

[31] See Morgan, Kevin, 'The communist party and the *Daily Worker* 1930-56' in Geoff Andrews et al, *Opening the Books: Essays in the social and cultural history of British communism* (London, 1995), pp. 148-9.

[32] *SMT*, p. 188.

[33] Murphy, J.T., *New Horizons* (London, 1941), pp. 196-7.

[34] *SMT*, pp. 267-79; Labour History Archive and Study Centre (LHASC) Pollitt papers, *SMT* draft chapters.

[35] See for example Lawrence, Jon, 'Labour – the myths it has lived by' in Duncan Tanner, Pat Thane and Nick Tiratsoo (eds), *Labour's First Century* (Cambridge, 2000), pp. 344-7.

[36] Koestler, Arthur, *The Invisible Writing* (London, 1954), pp. 382-4.

[37] Chesterton cited in Haw, George, *From Workhouse to Westminster: The life story of Will Crooks MP* (London, 1909), p. 149.

[38] Lawrence: 'Labour myths', pp. 344-7.

[39] *SMT*, pp. 49-50. Pollitt then adds the caveat that he fully appreciates their 'class significance', which sounds like another editorial interpolation.

[40] *SMT*, pp. 43-4.

[41] Andreucci Franco, and Sylvers, Malcolm, 'The Italian communists write their history', *Science & Society*, 51/1 (1976), pp. 35-6; Berthold Unfried, 'L'autocritique dans les milieux kominterniens des années 1930' in Pennetier and Pudal: *Autobiographies*, p. 48 and n.

[42] Pennetier and Pudal: 'Les autobiographies', p. 346 n. 17.

[43] *SMT*, pp. 109-12.

[44] See RGASPI 495/100/1041, report on Bell's *History of the British Communist Party* by Max Raylock, 1937.

[45] LHASC, Pollitt papers, *SMT* draft chapters; *SMT*, p. 126.

[46] Cited Kenneth O. Morgan, *Keir Hardie: Radical and Socialist* (London, 1975), p. 225.

[47] *SMT*, pp. 109, 274-5.

[48] *SMT*, p. 134.

[49] LHASC, CP/Ind/Hann/10/11, W.T. Towler to Wal Hannington, 23 June 1958.

[50] Morgan: *Harry Pollitt*, p. 127.

[51] Thorez: *Son*, p. 1.

[52] *SMT*, p. 17.

[53] Ibid, p. 208, also pp. 65-6.

[54] Ibid, pp. 13, 248-53.

[55] Johnstone, Monty, 'The CPGB, the Comintern and the war, 1939-1941: filling in the blank spots', *Science& Society*, 61/1 (1997), p. 33.

[56] British National Archives, Kew, London (henceforth NA), KV2/1038/406, Kell to Wood, 7 January 1940.

[57] Originally established as Martin Lawrence, a fictitious name meant to mimic the conventions of the British publishing scene, Lawrence & Wishart was the product of an amalgamation in 1935 with a commercial publishing house owned by a communist sympathiser. Its French and American equivalents were Editions Sociales and International Publishers.

[58] Pennetier and Pudal: 'Les autobiographies', p. 231.

[59] See LHASC, CP/Ind/Hann/9/11, Hannington to E.G. Pryor, 25 September 1944.

[60] For example Mann, Tom, *Tom Mann's Memoirs* (London, 1923).

[61] *SMT*, 284.

[62] *Daily Worker*, 29 March 1940.

[63] Labour Party Thirty-Ninth Annual Conference <u>Report</u>, 1940, p. 136.

[64] Morgan, Kevin, and Cohen, Gidon, 'Rose Cohen (1894-1937), communist' in Keith Gildart, David Howell and Neville Kirk (eds), *Dictionary of Labour Biography* vol. 11 (Basingstoke, 2003), 31-9.

[65] See NA, KV2/1038/368, report on CPGB 23 November 1937.

[66] RGASPI 495/100/1040, Pollitt to Campbell 20 March 1939.

[67] Francis King and George Matthews (eds), *About Turn: The British Communist Party and the outbreak of the Second World War. The verbatim record of the Central Committee meetings, 1939* (London, 1990), pp. 202, 204.

[68] *SMT*, pp. 284-92.

[69] RGASPI 495/74/49, report on CPGB, 9 May 1940.

Chapter 6. A Mosleyite Life

[1] Hawks, Olive, *What Hope for Green Street?* (London, 1945); Hawks, Olive, *Time is My Debtor* (London, 1947); Hawks, Olive, *These Frail Vessels* (London, 1948); Hawks, Olive, *A Sparrow for a Farthing* (London, 1950). The frontispiece of her last novel also attributes a play to her, *The Devil's In It*, and mentions that another work of fiction, *Romayne*, is in preparation: See also my entry for Hawks in Lorna Sage (ed), *The Cambridge Guide to Women's Writing in English* (Cambridge, 1999).
[2] Chesser, Eustace and Hawks, Olive, *Life Lies Ahead: A Practical Guide to Home-Making and the Development of Personality* (London, 1951).
[3] See J. Christian (ed), *Mosley's Blackshirts: The Inside Story of the British Union of Fascists* (London, 1989); Charnley, J., *Blackshirts and Roses: An Autobiography* (London, 1990); Driver, N., *From the Shadows of Exile* (unpublished), J.B. Priestley Library, University of Bradford; Bellamy, R.R., *Memoirs of a Fascist Beast* (unpublished), British Union Collection, University of Sheffield Library. See also interviews conducted for Rawnsley, S.J., 'Fascism and Fascists in Britain in the 1930s: A case study of Fascism in the North of England in a period of economic and political change' (unpublished PhD dissertation, University of Bradford (1981).
[4] Jeffrey Wallder to the author, 11 December, 1997.
[5] See Gottlieb, Julie. V., *Feminine Fascism: Women in Britain's Fascist Movement, 1923-1945* (London, 2000).
[6] See Gottlieb, Julie V., 'Suffragette Experience Through the Filter of Fascism' in C. Eustance et al (eds), *A Suffrage Reader* (London, 2000), pp.105-125.
[7] See Gottlieb: *Feminine Fascism*.
[8] Dr Vivian to Oswald Mosley, 13 December, 1945, Mosley Papers, Nicholas Mosley Deposit, Box 7, University of Birmingham.
[9] 'Youth and Womanhood Turn to Fascism,' *Blackshirt*, No.70, 24 August 1933.
[10] Hawks, Olive, 'Ideals of Womanhood,' *Blackshirt*, No.76, 5 October 1934.
[11] Hawks, Olive, 'We Live,' *British Union Quarterly*, Vol. III, No. 3 (July-September, 1939), pp. 76-77
[12] Hawks, Olive, 'Chant for the People,' *British Union Quarterly*, Vol. IV, No.1, (Spring 1940), pp. 64-65.
[13] Ibid.
[14] 'Jewish MP Prevented from Opening New Cinema in Peckham,' <u>Blackshirt</u>, No. 251, June 1938. See also Gottlieb, Julie V. '"Motherly Hate": Gendering Anti-Semitism in the British Union of Fascists,' *Gender and History*, 14/2 (August 2002), pp. 294-320.
[15] Under Secretary of State, Home Office, 7 August 1940, HO45/25703.
[16] The Special Collections, University of Sheffield, hold his collection of newspaper clippings and other miscellaneous material.
[17] Edwards, Frederick, 'British Youth Refuse to Fight for the League of Nations,' *Saturday Review*, 14 March 1936.
[18] HO45/25703
[19] Advisory Committee to Hear Appeals Against Orders of Internment. Witness: - Sir Oswald Mosley, 2 July, 1940, HO283/14/2-125.

[20] In his appeal, Mosley was also questioned at length about Hawks' Women's Peace Campaign pamphlet. See HO283/14/2-117.

[21] Driver: *From the Shadows of Exile*, p. 60.

[22] Private and Confidential, November 1940 (HO45/25703). Helga wrote another letter to the Home Secretary on 27 December 1940, and it seems as though partial measures were taken to resolve the situation. F.E. Burdett was moved from Brixton to the York internment camp where he was more comfortable, but he still suffered from the fear of losing his wife. Helga still described her mother as 'ill with grief,' and Olive and Alexander's correspondence had not been prohibited.

[23] HO45/25703

[24] 26 July 1942. Home Office, HO45/25703.

[25] F.E. Burdett to Mr O. Peake, 13 December, 1943, Mosley Papers, Nicholas Mosley Deposit, Box 3, University of Birmingham Special Collections Department.

[26] See Hall, Lesley, *Sex, Gender and Social Change in Britain since 1880* (Houndsmill, 2000), pp.136-137.

[27] Hawks: *A Sparrow for a Farthing*.

[28] Joannou, M., *'Ladies Please Don't Smash These Windows': Women's writing, feminist consciousness and social change 1918-38* (Oxford, 1995) p. 170.

[29] Ethel Mannin, *Women and Revolution* (London, 1938) p. 31.

[30] Ethel Mannin to Allen Lane, 18 August, 1938, Box 26 DM1819, files 1-4, Penguin Archive, Special Collections, University of Bristol.

[31] Mannin to Lane, 3 April, 1940, 00.01778, Penguin Archive.

[32] Mannin to Lane, 28 June, 1940, 00.01778, Penguin Archive.

[33] Quoted in Huxley, Robert, *Reg and Ethel: Reginald Reynolds: His Life and Work and His Marriage to Ethel Mannin* (York, 1992), p. 148.

[34] Quoted in Huxley: *Reg and Ethel*, p. 148.

[35] Hawks: *What Hope for Green Street?*, p. 128.

[36] See Gottlieb, Julie, 'Women and Fascism in the East End,' *Jewish Culture and History*, 1/2 (1999), pp. 31-47.

[37] Hawks: *What Hope for Green Street?*, p. 15.

[38] Ibid, p. 28.

[39] Ibid, p. 62-63.

[40] Ibid, p.120.

[41] Driver, Nellie, 'The Mill: A Novel' (unpublished), J.B. Priestley Library, University of Bradford.

[42] Hawks: *These Frail Vessels*, p. 223

[43] The only exception to this is the character Owen Rayner, who becomes a Conservative MP in the course of the novel. However, the author's interest in him has nothing to do with political content, and his function is as the spurning lover (a villain) of the increasingly desperate and miserable Margery.

[44] Hawks: *These Frail Vessels*, p. 224.

[45] Ibid.

Chapter 7. Winston Churchill and War-Time Feature Films

[1] This research has been completed with assistance from the British Academy. I would also like to thank the following: The Trustees of the Mass Observation

Archives, University of Sussex; British Film Institute Special Collections; Winston S. Churchill Archives Centre, Churchill College, Cambridge; John Grierson Archive, University of Stirling; Laurence Olivier Archive, British Library Manuscripts Collection. I would also like to thank Dr. Jonathan Pearson and Dr. Oliver Zimmer for their comments on the text.

2 Churchill Papers, Churchill College, Cambridge (hereafter CP), CHAR 20/194b, Winston Churchill to Major R. Baker (Film Renters Society), 19 June 1945. f. 141.

3 The work of D.J. Wenden and K.R.M. Short has been particularly influential in this area. See in particular Wenden, D.J. & Short, K.R.M., 'Winston S. Churchill: Film Fan', *Historical Journal of Film, Radio and Television*, 11/3 (1991), pp. 197-214 and Wenden, D.J., 'Churchill, Radio and Cinema', in Robert Blake & Wm. Roger Louis (eds), *Churchill* (Oxford, 1993)

4 British National Archives, Kew, London, (hereafter NA), PRO HO 199/434. E.T. Crutchley, Home Publicity Sub-Committee to Ministry of Information (MoI), 18 September 1939. Also quoted in McLain, I., *Ministry of Morale: Home Front Morale and the Ministry of Information in World War II* (London, 1979), 29.

5 NA PRO HO 199/4341, 'Yardstick for the Measurement of Propaganda and Publicity.

6 NA PRO RG 23/44, Wartime Social Survey, 'Report on Film Attendance', 1943. 68% of people visited the cinema on a regular basis.

7 See in particular, the excellent chapter on *The Young Mr. Pitt* in Aldgate, A. and Richards, J., *Britain can take it: The British Cinema in the Second World War* (Oxford and New York, 1986); and also Mace, N., 'British Historical Epics in the Second World War', in Philip M. Taylor (ed), *Britain and the Cinema in the Second World War* (New York, 1988), Harper, S., *Picturing the Past: Rise and Fall of the British Costume Film* (London, 1994) and Chapman, J., *Britain at War: Cinema, State and Propaganda, 1939-1945* (London, 2000) amongst others.

8 Wenden and Short: 'Winston S. Churchill: Film Fan'.

9 For example see editorial of *The Cinema*, 18 March 1942, p. 5, and 15 May 1940, p. 3.

10 Wenden and Short: 'Winston S. Churchill: Film Fan', p. 197.

11 Indeed the only British request he refused, to the best of my knowledge, was a request by Walter Greenwood to contribute an introductory preface to the film *Love on the Dole*. For details, see CP, CHAR 21B, Churchill to J. S. Middleton, 11 March 1941.

12 Imperial War Museum Sound Archive, interview with Roy Boulting.

13 *Today's Cinema*, 17 September 1943, which suggests that 'the title and theme [of the film] ... were suggested by the Prime Minister' (p. 9). It is also interesting to note that the film was produced and edited by Korda, with whom Churchill had an established relationship.

14 CP CHAR 20/ 67, f. 7. M 357/2, Churchill to Bracken and MoI, 10 September 1942. See also NA PRO PREM 4/14/15. Also documented in Christie, I (ed), *The Life and Death of Colonel Blimp* (London, 1994).

15 US Pressbook, *The Life and Death of Colonel Blimp* (Powell & Pressburger, 1942). Held in British Film Institute Library, London (hereafter, Bfi).

16 CP CHAR 20/36, Prime Minister's Minutes, 1941. f.25/ M 922/1. Churchill to Ministry of Information, 23 September 1941.

[17] CP CHAR 20/92, Telegram from Churchill to Roosevelt, accompanying a copy of *Desert Victory*, 5 March 1943.

[18] CP CHAR 20/109. f. 35. T 428/3, Telegram from Stalin to Churchill, thanking him for his copy of *Desert Victory*, 29 March 1943.

[19] CP CHAR 20/107, Prime Minister's Personal Telegrams. F. 108. T 288/3. Telegram from Churchill to Frazer, 11 March 1943.

[20] CP CHAR 20/107, Prime Minister's Personal Telegrams. F. 111. 373   T 291/3. Telegram from Churchill to Smuts, 11 March 1943.

[21] CP CHAR 20/109, f. 35. T 428/3. Stalin to Churchill, 29 March 1943.

[22] CP CHAR 20/93A, f. 12. Churchill to Maisky, 29 March 1943.

[23] *The Cinema*, 13 November 1940. 'This Week's Studio News', 5. This was also reported in *Kinematograph Weekly* in 1942.

[24] James Roosevelt worked as a producer for Samuel Goldwyn Productions in the US from 1938-1939. He served as the Goldwyn representative on the board of United Artists. He eventually left Goldwyn productions to form his own production company, Globe Productions, which produced the United Artists feature *Pot o' Gold*, with Jimmy Stewart. Roosevelt remained interested in British production, particularly after the outbreak of war in 1939, presenting the Boulting Brothers' 1940 film *Pastor Hall* in the United States. He persuaded his mother, Eleanor Roosevelt, to introduce the film to US audiences. His film interest did not end with his career in the industry. In 1942, he joined the US Marine Corps and appeared briefly in John Ford's 1942 production *The Battle of Midway*. This information derives from *Variety,* 19 August 1991, p. 54.

[25] Gilbert, M., *Finest Hour: Winston S. Churchill, 1939-1941* (London, 1989, 1991), p. 52.

[26] CP CHAR 20/ 29A, f. 31. Cypher from Halifax (Washington D.C.) to Churchill, 8 April 1941.

[27] NA PRO INF1/990, Bracken to Churchill, following Halifax's request.

[28] Wenden: 'Churchill, radio and cinema', p. 227

[29] For a review of the film and plot summary see *Monthly Film Bulletin*, 10 (1943), p. 91.

[30] US Pressbook, *Mission To Moscow* (Michael Curtiz, 1943) US Production. Held in Bfi Library, London.

[31] Ibid.

[32] Ibid. *Today's Cinema* reported on 23 July 1943 that Malone bore 'some physical resemblance', but he was 'chiefly successful in hitting off Mr. Churchill's characteristic diction' (p. 8).

[33] Culbert, D., 'The Feature Film as Official Propaganda' in D. Culbert (ed) *Mission to Moscow* (Madison, Wisconsin, 1980), 26. This collection includes the full script and a number of documents relating to the film. For Stalin's reaction to the film, see pp. 37-38.

[34] Ibid, p. 197. For the entire scene, see pp. 195-201.

[35] Betts, E., 'Churchill Has Passed this Film', *Daily Express,* 22 July 1943, in CP CHAR 20/149.

[36] CP CHAR 20/104. Churchill to Bracken, MoI. M 505/3. 22 July 1943.

[37] British Board of Film Censors (hereafter BBFC) Scenarios. Bfi Special Collections. Scenarios Box 1941-1943. f. 57. *Warn that Man* (Associated British Picture Corp). 7 January 1943. John C. Hanna.

[38] British Pressbook *Warn that Man* 1943. Held in Bfi Library, London.

[39] CP CHAR 20/104, M. 491/3. Churchill to Brendan Bracken, 19 July 1943.

[40] *The Times*, 27 August 1943.

[41] Mass Observation Archive, University of Sussex (Hereafter M-O A), File Report (hereafter F-R) 446. Social Research and the Film: MoI Films, November 1940. Also reproduced in Sheridan, D. and Richards, J. (eds), *Mass Observation at the Movies* (London and New York, 1987). In particular see pp. 213-215.

[42] CP CHAR 20/143, f. 46. Churchill to Harold Laski, 21 September 1944.

[43] Short, K.R.M.,'"That Hamilton Woman" (1941): propaganda, feminism and the production code', *Historical Journal of Film, Radio and Television* 11/1 (1991), pp. 3-19. Further evidence on the impact of the film on Churchill can be found on pp. 14-15.

[44] H.V. Morton quoted in Wenden and Short, 'Winston Churchill: Film Fan', pp. 204-5.

[45] Churchill, W.S., *History of the Second World War: Volume Six: Triumph and Tragedy* (London, 1954, 1956), p. 218.

[46] M-O A: F-R 394. 'Mass Observation Film Work', 10 September 1940. L.E. M-O A: F-R 491. 'Battle for Britain'. Script for film that was not produced (Nolbandov), 13 November 1940.

[47] M-O A: F-R 485, 'Victorianism in Films and Music Halls', 7 November 1940. L.E.

[48] M-O A: F-R 257, 'Should Leaders Lead?: Critique of broadcast by Professor Gilbert Murray who accuses the public of ignorance and apathy', 6 July 1940

[49] M-O A: F-R 496, 'Popular Attitudes to Wartime Politics', 20 November 1940, p. 2

[50] Ibid, p. 16

[51] Ibid, p. 4.

[52] Ibid, p. 3.

[53] Ibid, pp. 5-6.

[54] Ibid, p. 15.

[55] John Grierson papers, John Grierson Archive, University of Stirling (Hereafter GP), G4.21:12. Untitled article on Films and the War, n.d., p. 2. Although Grierson was at this time working in Canada for the National Film Board, an analysis of his correspondence with influential film makers within the Films Division of the MoI and elsewhere, notably Arthur Elton, Basil Wright, Thomas Baird, Paul Rotha, Cavalcanti, John Taylor and Stephen Tallents, demonstrates that Grierson was fully briefed on developments in British film, and offered his opinion of key issues which were forwarded to the MoI and other agencies for film production. It is clear from an analysis that filmmakers working within the MoI respected Grierson's comments, as the 'Father of the documentary movement' and particularly valued his opinions on British film, propaganda and public opinion in the Dominions and the United States.

[56] Ibid.

[57] GP G4. 12.20, 6.

[58] GP G4. N13, John Grierson 'A letter from England'. 1941, p. 1.

[59] M-O A: F-R 202, 'Churchill: Replies to Question about whether Churchill should continue to be Prime Minister after the war', 8 February 1944, p. 1.

[60] M-O A: FR 654, 'Churchill: Public Opinion', April 1941.

[61] For a discussion of *This England*, see Richards, J., *Films and British national identity: From Dickens to Dad's Army* (Manchester, 1997), pp. 97-100.

[62] British Pressbook *The Prime Minister.* 1941. 'Film has parallel between Disraeli's time and our own'. Held in Bfi Library, London.

[63] For a textual analysis see Mace, N. 'British Historical Epics', pp. 114-5.

[64] *The Prime Minister*, US Press Book. Held at Bfi Library, London.

[65] *The Cinema*, 12 March 1941. Quoted in Aldgate and Richards: 'Britain can take it', p. 143.

[66] *Today's Cinema*, LVI/4540, 7 March 1941.

[67] *The Prime Minister*, British Press book. Held in Bfi Library, London.

[68] Ibid.

[69] M-O A: Topic Collection [hereafter T-C] 17/5, 'Letters to *Picture Goer Weekly*', DJM, Kenton, 10 November 1940.

[70] Bfi Special Collections. Dickinson Collection. Box 48. Item 1. Full unedited transcript of 'Interview with Thorold Dickinson', later published in *Film Dope*, no. 11, January 1977.

[71] Gielgud quoted in *Kinematograph Weekly*, in Richards and Aldgate: Britain can take it, p. 144.

[72] *The Cinema*, 1 January 1941, p. 5. It is claimed by Nicholas Wapshott that MGM Studios refused to release Donat from his studio contract. Mayer gave in after Donat reportedly told him that he was 'depriving hundreds of people … in the most difficult period in Britain's history'. Reported in Wapshott, N., *The Man Between: A Biography of Carol Reed* (London, 1990), p. 153.

[73] Full story synopsis released by the studio (Gaumont British) can be found in the British Pressbook, *The Young Mr. Pitt*, 1942. In Bfi, Library London.

[74] B. Davies, (ed), *Carol Reed* (London, 1978), pp. 5-6. Also confirmed in *Kinematograph Weekly*, 23 October 1941, p. 37.

[75] Ibid, p. 6. The studio, Gaumont British, was reported to have spent much energy ensuring historical accuracy within the film in terms of the set and the characters. *Today's Cinema*, 'This Week's Studio News', 1 October, 1941, p. 5. See also see the British Pressbook, *The Young Mr. Pitt*, 1942. In Bfi Library, London. The historian Cyril Hughes Hartman was hired to advise the production team throughout filming. *Kinematograph Weekly*, 7 August 1941, p. 25. 'Research Expert at Lime Grove: Progression on "The Young Mr. Pitt"'.

[76] *Today's Cinema*, 22 May 1942, p. 3.

[77] Interview with Frank Launder and Sidney Gilliat in G. Brown (ed), *Launder and Gilliat* (London, 1977), p. 104.

[78] Ibid.

[79] Ibid, p. 105.

[80] Ibid, p. 104.

[81] *The Cinema*, 17 June 1942, p. 4.

[82] *The Young Mr. Pitt*, British Press Book.

[83] Ibid.

[84] *Kinematograph Weekly*, 28 May 1942. Quoted in Aldgate and Richards: 'Britain can take it', p. 152.

[85] *Kinematograph Weekly*, 23 October 1941, p. 37.

[86] Ibid, 2 October 1941, p. 39.

[87] Wapshott, N., 'The Man Between', p. 154.

[88] Harper, S.: *Picturing the Past*, p. 89.

[89] *Truth*, July 1942. Quoted in Wapshott, N., 'The Man Between', p. 155.

[90] *The Young Mr. Pitt*, British Press Book.

91 Ibid.
92 All information here from ibid.
93 Ibid.
94 Interestingly, similar depictions of Hitler in German film fell within this same timescale. In particular, *Bismarck* (W. Liebeneiner, 1940), *Die Entlassung* (W. Liebeneiner, 1942) and *Der große König* (V. Harlan, 1942).
95 Laurence Olivier Archive, British Library Manuscripts Collection (hereafter L-O), Box 93, Laurence Olivier to Filippo del Giudice (Managing Director of Two Cities Films, the producer of *Henry V*), 6 December 1944.
96 British Pressbook, *Henry V* (Olivier, 1945). Held in Bfi Library, London.
97 L-O, Box 93, Stafford A Brooke, notes by Alan Dent during the production of *Henry V*, 1943.
98 L-O, Box 93. Alan Dent, notes for publicity matter, July 1944.
99 L-O, Box 93, Stafford A Brooke, notes by Alan Dent during the production of *Henry V*, 1943.
100 L-O, Box 93, Sir Edmund Chambers, writing in 1925. Notes by Alan Dent during the production of *Henry V*, 1943.
101 L-O, Box 93, Synopsis of *Henry V*, Alan Dent, 1943.
102 Ibid.
103 Harper: *Picturing the Past*, p. 91.
104 L-O , Box 93, Filippo del Giudice to Jack Beddington, 11 January 1943.
105 *Boston Post*, 7 April 1946. Quoted in Harper: *Picturing the Past*, p. 87.
106 GP G3 P7 Leslie, S.C., 'The Formation of Public Opinion', *The Citizen*, No. 10, July 1939, pp. 3-7.

Chapter 8. Clementine Churchill

1 Henry Moore's shelter drawings have been photographed and reproduced; see for example, Andrews, Julian, *London's War: The shelter drawings of Henry Moore* (Aldershot, 2002). There are numerous photographic collections, for example, Briggs, Asa, *Go To It! Working for Victory on the Home Front 1939-1945* (London, 2000); and Rodger, George, *The Blitz: The Photography of George Rodger* (London, 1990).
2 *The Gathering Storm*, first screened on BBC 2, 12 July 2002; The National Trust's pamphlet that is sold at Chartwell, *A Short Guide to Chartwell* (2003), explains that after Churchill bought Chartwell in 1922 'Clementine soon set her stamp on the place filling the brightly painted interior with comfortable furniture, and floral chintz curtains'.
3 Hough, Richard, *Winston and Clementine: The Triumph of the Churchills* (London, 1990).
4 Soames, Mary, *Clementine Churchill* (Harmondsworth, 1979); Soames, Mary (ed) *Speaking for Themselves: The Personal Letters of Winston and Clementine Churchill* (London, 1999).
5 Soames: *Speaking for Themselves*, pp. 453-531.
6 Ibid, p. xvi.
7 Soames: *Clementine Churchill*, pp. 296-298 and passim.
8 Clarke, Peter, *The Cripps Version. The Life of Sir Stafford Cripps 1889-1952* (London, 2002), pp. 20, 378; *The Times*, 12 June 1945.
9 Grigg, John, *Lloyd George: From Peace to War 1912-1916* (London, 1985), p. 402.

[10] Roberts, Andrew, *The Holy Fox: A Biography of Lord Halifax* (London, 1991), p. 11.

[11] Middlemas, Keith, and Barnes, John, *Baldwin: A Biography* (London, 1969), pp. 66, 28.

[12] Dutton, David, *Simon: A Political Biography of Sir John Simon* (London, 1992), p. 325.

[13] Dilks, David, *Neville Chamberlain vol. One: Pioneering and Reform 1869-1929* (Cambridge, 1984), p. 267.

[14] James, Robert Rhodes, *Anthony Eden* (London, 1986), pp. 131, 132, 322.

[15] Weiler, Peter, *Ernest Bevin* (Manchester, 1993), p. 4.

[16] Harris, Kenneth, *Attlee* (London, 1982).

[17] Pimlott, Ben, *Hugh Dalton* (London, 1985), pp. 380-381, 173-5.

[18] Robbins, Keith, *Churchill* (London, 1992), p. 67.

[19] Soames: *Clementine Churchill*, pp. 198, 247, 254-5, 276, 308, 342-343.

[20] *Picture Post*, 23 November 1940. Unfortunately it has not proved possible to secure permission to reproduce this image here.

[21] Soames: *Clementine Churchill*, p. 428.

[22] Gilbert, Martin, *Finest Hour Winston S Churchill 1939-1941* (London, 1983), p. 939.

[23] Churchill College, Cambridge, CSCT 3/37/1, Aid to Russia.

[24] Imperial War Museum Photographic collection. File Personalities. Churchill family. Mrs Churchill consults a chart of contributions to Aid to Russia Fund before her broadcast 23 May 1944.

[25] Churchill, Winston S., *The Second World War vol. iii The Grand Alliance* (London, 1950), p.421.

[26] Soames: *Clementine Churchill*, p.432.

[27] Women's Institute, Annual Report (1943).

[28] Imperial War Museum photographic collection file Personalities. Churchill Family. No date. Mrs Winston Churchill spends a day with shop girls now working in munitions factories. The cheque, which is for Mrs Churchill's Aid for Russia Fund, is being presented by Irene Harper, one of the munitions workers.

[29] Bodleian Library Oxford. Conservative Party archives, CCO 170/1/1/2. NUCUA Central Women's Advisory Committee 25 March 1942.

[30] Women were more attracted to the Auxiliary Forces than factory work, and this was the reason behind the film, *Millions Like Us* (1943), which emphasised the importance of factory work for the war effort, and its attractions.

[31] Soames: *Clementine Churchill*, pp. 437-537; Gilbert, Martin, *Winston S Churchill vol. VII 1941-1945* (London, 1986), pp. 101, 122, 382, 1254-5, 1267; Churchill, Clementine, *My Visit to Russia* (London, 1945), pp 9-28; Beaumont, Joan, *Comrades in Arms: British Aid to Russia, 1941-45* (London, 1980); The British Red Cross, *Quarterly Review* (July 1944).

[32] British National Archives (henceforward NA) PRO FO 371/32872, FO 18 October, 29 October 1942.

[33] Gilbert: *Winston S. Churchill vol. VII*, p. 382.

[34] Ibid, p. 1267.

[35] NA PRO HW1/3688, German propaganda directives. From: Ministry of Foreign Affairs, Berlin, 3 April 1945.

[36] This paragraph has drawn on the work of social psychologists in analysing the key elements in persuasion. See Weber, Ann L., *Social Psychology* (New York, 1992), p. 137.

[37] For a more detailed discussion see Jones, Helen, *Women in British Public Life, 1914-1950* (London, 2000), Chapter 8.

[38] For example, Soames: *Speaking for Themselves* and the television film *The Gathering Storm*.

Chapter 9. Harrod's *Life of Keynes*

[1] I am grateful to Philip Williamson, Daniele Besomi and Warren Young for comments, information and suggestions. Errors that remain are, of course, my own responsibility.

[2] Michael Holroyd's *Lytton Strachey: A Critical Biography*, (London, 2 Vols, 1967-8) was a key landmark in the move to greater biographical frankness. It was this book that revealed Keynes's homosexuality to the public. It is interesting to note Harrod's reaction: 'I knew most details of his [i.e. Keynes's] homo-sexual interests. I did not write blatantly about sex in my book, because at that time it would have been unsuitable; but anyone then, who was alive to the existence of homo-sexual proclivities, would have been able to learn the important facts "between the lines" of my book. I have been repeatedly questioned on American platforms about Michael Holroyd's references to Keynes in his Life of Strachey; I have replied "it is all in my book".' Roy Harrod to Harold Macmillan, 7 July 1969, Harrod Papers, British Library, Add 72742, f. 2.

[3] For details of his life, see Phelps Brown, Henry, 'Sir Roy Harrod: A Biographical Memoir', *Economic Journal* 90 (1980), pp. 1-33, Besomi, Daniele, 'Harrod, Sir Roy', in Thomas Cate (ed), *Encyclopedia of Keynesian Economics* (Aldershot, 1997), pp. 230-233; Blake, Robert, 'A Personal Memoir', in W.A. Eltis, M. FG. Scott, J.N. Wolfe, *Induction, Growth and Trade: Essays in Honour of Sir Roy Harrod* (Oxford, 1970,) pp. 1-19, and Harrod, Roy, *The Prof: A Personal Memoir of Lord Cherwell* (London, 1959) (which contains much autobiography).

[4] Skidelsky, Robert, *John Maynard Keynes: Hopes Betrayed 1883-1920* (London, 1983) pp. xxi-xxviii (quotation at p. xxiv); Skidelsky, Robert, *John Maynard Keynes: Fighting for Britain 1937-1946* (London, 2000) pp. 491-8.

[5] Doubtless Harrod's interpretation on these points was not perfect. But Keynes's attitude to the Labour party was far more complicated than Newton himself makes out. Thus, for example, whilst it is true that Keynes supported Sir Stafford Cripps's Popular Front campaign – as indeed did Harrod - this campaign was itself in clear opposition to the established policy of the official Labour leadership. The relationship remained troubled after the outbreak of war. Similarly, Newton is right to say that Keynes only supported British participation in a multilateral trade and payments regime 'on condition that domestic expansion was protected from the deflationary pressures of an external deficit.' But this was Harrod's position too. As he recalled in 1964, 'Over a long period one of Keynes's most insistent themes was that we must not allow a full employment policy (*alias* growth policy) to be impeded by balance-of-payments considerations. ... In his last phase he became convinced that we should move towards a less protectionist system – *on certain conditions*' (emphasis in original). This is the precise picture of Keynes's policy that Newton alleges Harrod was

trying to cover up in his biography. Newton, Scott, 'Deconstructing Harrod: Some Critical Observations on *The Life of John Maynard Keynes'*, *Contemporary British History* 15 (2001), pp. 15-27. Quotations at pp. 15, 18, 25. See also Newton, Scott, 'A "Visionary Hope" Frustrated: J.M. Keynes and the Origins of the Postwar International Monetary Order', *Diplomacy and Statecraft*, 11/1 (2000), pp. 189-210; Harrod, Roy, 'Are We Really All Keynesians Now?', *Encounter*, Jan. 1964; Harrod: *The Prof*, p. 245; Moggridge, Donald (ed), *The collected writings of John Maynard Keynes. Vol.21, Activities 1931-1939, world crises and policies in Britain and America* (London, 1982), p. 495; Toye, Richard, *The Labour Party and the Planned Economy, 1931-1951* (London, 2003), Chapter 4.

6 Strachey, John, *Contemporary Capitalism* (London, 1956) pp. 214, 248; Heilperin, Michael, *Studies in Economic Nationalism* (Geneva, 1960) pp. 97-128.

7 National Archives, Kew, London (henceforward NA), PRO T 199/209. Newton failed to locate this file: see Newton: 'Visionary Hope', n. 64. Daniele Besomi has written an extremely useful guide to Harrod's voluminous and widely dispersed papers: 'The papers of Roy Harrod', www.datacomm.ch/dbesomi/papers/Papers.pdf (16 July 2004). (See also Besomi, Daniele (ed), *The Collected Interwar Papers and Correspondence of Roy Harrod*, Cheltenham, 2003, and Riley-Smith, H., *The Papers of Sir Roy Harrod*, Swanton Abbott, Norfolk, n.d. but 1982). Besomi, however, does not mention the National Archives' holdings on Harrod. There is also a small quantity of material relating to Harrod's biography in the archive of Macmillan & Co. at the University of Reading.

8 Skidelsky has written that 'For writing the book Harrod relied on the Keynes Papers (which then included much fuller wartime files), many interviews, and personal knowledge.' It seems clear that the 'much fuller wartime files' were in fact not in the Keynes Papers at all but in the Treasury. Skidelsky: *Fighting For Britain* p. 493.

9 See Naylor, John F., *A Man and an Institution: Sir Maurice Hankey, The Cabinet Secretariat and the custody of Cabinet secrecy* (Cambridge, 1984) pp. 210-38

10 NA PRO T 199/209, Richard Kahn to Edward Bridges, 29 May 1946.

11 NA PRO T 199/209, Kahn to P.D. Proctor 30 March 1948. See also Proctor to Heads of Divisions, 'Lord Keynes' Personal Files', 9 December 1947.

12 NA PRO T 199/209, Proctor to Bridges, 'Lord Keynes' Papers', 15 April 1948.

13 NA PRO T 199/209, Proctor to Kahn, 21 April 1948.

14 NA PRO T 199/209, Roy Harrod to Bridges, 1 November 1948.

15 NA PRO T 199/209, Bridges to Thomas Padmore and H. Wilson Smith, 5 November 1948.

16 NA PRO T 199/209, Padmore to Mr. Griffiths, 22 November 1948.

17 NA PRO T 199/209, Laurence Helsby to B.F. St.J Trend, 21 January 1949.

18 NA PRO T 199/209, Bridges to Harrod, 25 January 1949.

19 NA PRO T 199/209, Harrod to Bridges, 31 January 1949.

20 NA PRO T 199/209, Bridges to J.A.C. Robertson, 2 February 1949.

21 'Trials of a Biographer', *Manchester Guardian*, 7 March 1951.

22 Ibid.

23 See Partridge, Frances, *Everything to Lose: Diaries 1945-1960* (London, 1985) pp. 81-2 (entry for 14 Jan. 1949).

24 Blake: 'A Personal Memoir', p. 14.

[25] Skidelsky: *Fighting For Britain*, p. 493.

[26] NA PRO T 199/209, Harrod to Bridges, 1 August 1949 (two letters of the same date).

[27] NA PRO T 199/209, Ernest Rowe-Dutton to Bridges, 'Harrod on Keynes', 22 Aug. 1949; Moggridge, D.E., *Maynard Keynes: An Economist's Biography* (London, 1992) pp. 667-8.

[28] NA PRO T 199/209, Rowe-Dutton to Harrod, 24 August 1949.

[29] NA PRO T 199/209, Harrod to Bridges, 30 August 1949.

[30] Harrod to Kahn, 19 September 1949, Kahn Papers, King's College, Cambridge, RFK 13/39/1; Newton, 'Deconstructing Harrod', p. 21.

[31] NA PRO T 199/209, Bridges to Harrod, 26 October 1949.

[32] NA PRO T 199/209, Bridges to Rowe-Dutton, 3 November 1949.

[33] Lee was a civil servant who had served on the Treasury delegation in Washington DC from 1944-6,. Brand had been head of the delegation in the same years. NA PRO T 199/209, Rowe-Dutton to Bridges, 'Harrod on Keynes', 22 August 1949.

[34] NA PRO T 199/209, Harrod to Bridges, 20 December 1949.

[35] NA PRO T 199/209, Rowe-Dutton to Bridges, 'Harrod on Keynes', January 1950.

[36] NA PRO T 199/209, Bridges to Stafford Cripps, 4 Jan. 1950, with marginalia by Cripps dated 6 January 1950.

[37] Harrod to David Garnett, 17 Feb. 1950, cited in Skidelsky: *Hopes Betrayed* p. xxvi.

[38] Kahn to Harrod 5 Apr 1950, Harrod Papers, Add. 72740, f.168.

[39] Skidelsky: *Fighting For Britain* p. 493.

[40] NA PRO T 199/209, Rowe-Dutton to Harrod, 24 Aug. 1949.

[41] NA PRO T 199/209, Harrod to Bridges, 30 Aug. 1949. It is not possible recover the original text of the passage in question, but the substitute passage, as eventually adopted, can be found in Harrod, Roy, *The Life of John Maynard Keynes* (London, 1951) pp. 614-6, beginning at 'The verdict of history...' and ending at '...consequent upon the Loan settlement'.

[42] NA PRO T 199/209, Harrod to Bridges, 30 August 1949. For the passages in question, see Harrod, *Life*, pp. 591, 596, 610-11. Initially, Harrod wanted to retain a further passage on Bevin, relating the latter's doubts about Bretton Woods to his long-standing opposition the gold standard, thus defending him against charges of 'philistinism'. But, without prompting, he subsequently decided to make his reference to this question far more muted. See Harrod to Bridges, 5 October 1949; Harrod, *Life*, p. 420.

[43] NA PRO T 199/209, Harrod to Bridges, 30 August 1949.

[44] Which is not to say that his own attitudes on the question were free from peculiarities. See Harrod: *The Prof*, pp. 107-111.

[45] For the full text of the letter, see Moggridge, Donald (ed), *The collected writings of John Maynard Keynes Vol.24, Activities 1944-1946: the transition to peace* (London 1979), pp. 625-8.

[46] NA PRO T 199/209, Harrod to Bridges, 30 August 1949.

[47] Harrod: Life, pp. 618-9.

[48] Harrod to Kahn, 19 September 1949, Kahn Papers, RFK 13/39/1; Newton: 'Deconstructing Harrod', p. 20.

[49] NA PRO T 199/209, Harrod to Bridges, 30 August 1949.

[50] 'Trials of a Biographer', *Manchester Guardian*, 7 March 1951.

[51] NA PRO T 199/209, Harrod to Bridges, 30 August 1949. See also Eugene Reynal (of Harcourt Brace, the book's US publisher) to Harrod 6 December 1949, Harrod Papers, Add 72747.

[52] NA PRO T 199/209, Bridges to Rowe-Dutton, 3 November 1949.

[53] NA PRO T 199/209, Rowe-Dutton to Bridges, 'Harrod on Keynes', January 1950.

[54] Harrod: *Life*, pp. 638-9. Newton: 'Deconstructing Harrod', p. 20, attacks Harrod for not publishing the following comment made by Keynes in a letter to Richard Kahn: 'I am pretty pessimistic. The Americans at the top seem to have absolutely no conception of international co-operation.' When Kahn sent him this letter, however, Harrod responded: 'This point of view is emphatically already in' – a comment which the inclusion of the description of the United States as 'a tyrant' surely justified. Kahn to Harrod, 15 September 1949, enclosing Keynes to Kahn 13 Mar. 1946, and Harrod to Kahn, 19 September 1949, Kahn Papers, RFK/13/39/1-5.

[55] Harrod: *Life*, p. 642.

[56] Harrod also came under pressure from sources independent of the Treasury and for different reasons. He was asked by Winston Churchill and Bernard Baruch, the US financier, to drop from his manuscript the suggestion that the latter had, at the former's behest, agreed not to testify to Congress against the 1945 US loan. The story, contained in a memorandum by Keynes, was true in its essentials; but, faced with the men's denials of it, Harrod had little choice other than to agree. See Winston Churchill to Harrod, 15 August 1949, and Bernard Baruch to Churchill, 28 July 1949, Winston Churchill Papers, Churchill College, Cambridge, CHUR 2/210-446-7; and Toye, Richard, 'Churchill and Britain's "Financial Dunkirk"', *Twentieth Century British History*, 15/4 (2004), pp. 329-360.

[57] Cairncross, Alec (ed), *The Robert Hall Diaries 1947-53* (London, 1989) p. 255 (entry for 11 November 1952); see also p. 147 (entry for 5 February 1951).

Chapter 10. Edith Summerskill

[1] I should like to thank the editors for their suggestions and also the following friends and colleagues who read and commented on this paper: Oliver Fulton, Peter Gatrell, Alison Oram, Susan Pedersen. The final outcome is of course my own responsibility.

[2] 'Lady in a Mask', *New Statesman And Nation*, 25 September 1954.

[3] Margaret Bondfield, Minister of Labour 1929-31; Ellen Wilkinson, Minister of Education 1945-47; Florence Horsburgh, Minister of Education 1951-54.

[4] Vernon, Betty D., *Ellen Wilkinson 1891–1947* (London, 1982); Hollis, Patricia, *Jennie Lee: a life* (Oxford, 1997); Perkins, Anne, *Red Queen: the authorized biography of Barbara Castle* (London, 2003); Alberti, Johanna, *Eleanor Rathbone* (London, 1996); Stocks, Mary, *Eleanor Rathbone: a biography* (London, 1949); Pedersen, Susan, *Eleanor Rathbone and the Politics of Conscience*, (New Haven, 2004).

[5] 'Obituary. Baroness Summerskill. Former Labour Minister and parliamentary campaigner', *The Times*, 5 February 1980.

[6] Jones, Helen, *Women in British Public Life 1914-1950: Gender, Power and Social Policy* (Harlow, 2000), p. 118.

7 Pugh, Martin, *Women and the Women's Movement in Britain* (London, 1992), pp. 281, 284.

8 Thus she does not feature in the accounts of the Labour Governments of 1945-51 offered in: Hennessy, Peter, *Never Again, Britain 1945-51* (London, 1993); Jefferys, Kevin, *Retreat from the New Jerusalem: British Politics 1951-1964* (Basingstoke, 1997); Pelling, Henry, *A Short History of the Labour Party* (Basingstoke, 1991); Sked, Alan and Cook, Chris, *Post-War Britain, a political history* (Harmondsworth, 1979). She is referred to extremely briefly in Morgan, Kenneth O., *Labour in Power 1945-51* (Oxford, 1985), pp. 121, 447 and dismissively in Annan, Noel, *Our Age, The Generation That Made Post-War Britain* (London, 1991), pp. 185, 295. As far as memoirs and autobiographies are concerned, there is no mention of her in Williams, Francis (ed) *A Prime Minister Remembers: the War and Post-War Memoirs of the Rt. Hon Earl Attlee* (London, 1961) or in Lee, Jennie, *My Life with Nye* (London, 1980). There are brief references to her in Dalton, Hugh, *High Tide and After: Memoirs 1945-1960* (London, 1962), pp. 365, 417, 419, 423. Hostile references are made to her in several autobiographies and diaries, including Castle, Barbara, *Fighting All the Way* (London, 1993), p. 161; Williams, Philip M. (ed), *The Diary of Hugh Gaitskell 1945-1956* (London, 1983), pp. 463-4, 534, 564, 569; Morgan, Janet (ed), *The Backbench Diaries of Richard Crossman* (London, 1981), particularly pp. 196-7, 224, 266, 329, 481, 613, 624, 714, 723; Mikardo, Ian, *Back-Bencher* (London, 1988), pp. 129, 133. We shall return to these hostile references later.

9 Vernon: *Ellen Wilkinson*, pp. 126-9.

10 Pedersen, Susan, 'The Future of Feminist History', a talk to the Committee of Women Historians of the American Historical Association, 8 January 2000, published under the same title in *AHA Perspectives*, October, 2000.

11 British National Archives, Kew, London (henceforward NA), PRO WO32/9423, Grigg to Morrison marked 'Secret' 22 December 1942; Mikardo: *Back-Bencher*, pp. 129, 133; Morgan: *Backbench Diaries of Richard Crossman*, entry for 14 November 1958, p. 723.

12 Stanley, Liz, *The autobiographical I: the theory and practice of feminist auto/biography* (Manchester 1992), p. 14.

13 Summerskill, Edith, *A Woman's World* (London, 1967).

14 Harrison, Brian, 'Women in a Men's House: the Women MPs, 1919-1945' *The Historical Journal*, 29/3 (1986), pp. 641-2. Harrison calculates that Summerskill came second (after Eleanor Rathbone) in terms of 'debating contribution on women's rights and status per sessional day in parliament' in the period he covers.

15 She explained in her autobiography that her father was a Gladstonian Liberal who once stood for election (unsuccessfully) as a town councillor. Summerskill: *Woman's World*, pp. 12-13.

16 'Obituary', *The Times*, 5 February 1980.

17 Summerskill: *Woman's World*, p. 37.

18 She reduced the majority from 21,146 to 2,663. Summerskill: *Woman's World*, pp. 47, 49.

19 Ibid, p. 50.

20 Graves, Pamela, *Labour Women. Women in British Working-Class Politics 1918-1939* (Cambridge, 1994), pp. 81- 98.

21 Summerskill: *Woman's World*, p. 53.

[22] Graves: *Labour Women*, pp. 195-199. See also Summerskill: *Woman's World*, p. 229.

[23] Summerskill: *Woman's World*, pp. 20-21.

[24] Ibid, pp. 41, 49, 54.

[25] Graves: *Labour Women*, pp. 90-97, 98.

[26] Summerskill was the first woman to be included such a parliamentary delegation. Brookes, Pamela, *Women at Westminster: an account of women in the British Parliament 1918-1966*, p. 142.

[27] Imperial War Museum Film Archive, COI [Central Office of Information] 668, 'British and Canadian MPs visit New Zealand'.

[28] Brookes: *Women at Westminster*, p. 128

[29] Parliamentary Debates, House of Commons, Fifth Series, vol. 376, 18 December 1941, col. 2158.

[30] Summerskill, Edith, 'Conscription and Women', *The Fortnightly*, vol. CLI, New Series, March 1942, p. 211.

[31] Ibid, p. 213. She put over the same view in an interview with the editor of 'Everywoman' in a Pathe News film, 'Mrs, Dr, M.P.' 23 January 1945, saying that, as a result of the war, women would expect more recognition for their services in the home and that, with the help of day nurseries and co-operative husbands, more of them would work outside the home: http://www.britishpathe.com/index.cfm (August 2003).

[32] Riley, Denise, *Am I that Name? Feminism and the Category of 'Women' in History* (Basingstoke, 1988); Cott, Nancy, 'Feminist Theory and Feminist Movements: the past before us' in J. Mitchell and A. Oakley (eds), *What is Feminism?* (Oxford, 1986).

[33] See for example Summerskill, Edith, *Letters to my Daughter* (London, 1957), p. 187.

[34] Pugh: *Women and the Women's Movement*, pp. 278; Jones: *Women in British Public Life*, p. 198.

[35] Pugh: *Women and the Women's Movement*, p. 299.

[36] Oram, Alison, '"Bombs Don't Discriminate!" Women's Political Activism in the Second World War' in C. Gledhill and G. Swanson (eds), *Nationalising Femininity: culture, sexuality and British cinema in the Second World War* (Manchester, 1996), p. 64.

[37] Pugh: *Women and the Women's Movement*, p. 309.

[38] 'Obituary', *The Times*, 5 February 1980.

[39] Summerfield, Penny, 'She wants a gun not a dishcloth! Gender, Service and Citizenship in Britain in the Second World War', in G. J. DeGroot and C. Peniston-Bird (eds), *A Soldier and a Woman, Sexual Integration in the Military* (Harlow, 2000), pp. 119-134; Summerfield, Penny and Peniston-Bird, C. M., 'Women in the Firing Line: the Home Guard and the Defence of Gender Boundaries in Britain in the Second World War', *Women's History Review* 9/2, 2000, pp. 231-255.

[40] DeGroot, G. J., 'Whose finger on the trigger? Mixed anti-aircraft batteries and the female combat taboo' *War in History* 4/4 (1997), pp. 434-53.

[41] Rhodes James, Robert (ed), *Winston S. Churchill. His Complete Speeches 1897-1963*, vol. VI (London, 1974), p. 6231 ('Wars are not won by evacuations' 4 June 1940).

[42] Parliamentary Debates, House of Commons, Fifth Series, vol. 362, col. 646, 2 July 1940.

[43] NA PRO/WO32/9423, Minute of meeting between Dr Summerskill and Sir James Grigg, 27 February 1942.

[44] Birkenhead Central Library, Wirral Archives, YPX/75, 1359/1, Wallasey Women's Home Guard Unit. Sheet of undated news cuttings concerning acceptance of women into Home Guard, April 1943. The figure of 20,000 comes from 'Women can join H.G.' by *Daily Sketch* correspondent Walter Hayes.

[45] For a full account of the campaign see Summerfield, Penny and Peniston-Bird, Corinna, *Contesting Home Defence: Men, Women and the Home Guard in Britain in the Second World War* (Manchester, forthcoming).

[46] 'Obituary', *The Times*, 5 February 1980.

[47] For example, 'Lady in a Mask', *New Statesman And Nation*, 25 September 1954.

[48] Summerskill: *Woman's World*, pp 73-75. She states that 'With the appointment of Captain H.D. Margesson, later Lord Margesson, I was accorded an entirely different reception' from that which Grigg had given her. Margesson 'thought that it was a practical proposition and he promised to give it his blessing'. In fact Margesson preceded Grigg as Secretary of State for War (December 1940 to February 1942), and it was James Grigg (Secretary of State from 22 February 1942 until Churchill's July 1945 election defeat) who reluctantly introduced the compromise.

[49] Mackenzie, S.P., *The Home Guard: A Military and Political History* (Oxford, 1995), Chapter 9; Kenneth Allsop, 'Do We need a Home Guard?', *Picture Post*, 2 October 1954.

[50] McCann, Graham, *Dad's Army: the story of a classic television show* (London, 2001).

[51] Summerskill: *Woman's World*, p. 74.

[52] One of many examples of male attempts to use sexist humour to deflate Summerskill, occurred when she challenged Ernest Bevin in the House on the use of womanpower in the war effort. Summerskill: '...he will admit that my figures are right'. Bevin: 'I think the hon. Lady's figures perfect'. Parliamentary Debates, House of Commons, Fifth Series, vol. 370, 20 March 1941, col. 377.

[53] Birkenhead Central Library, Wirral Archives, YPX/75, 1359/1, Wallasey Women's Home Guard Unit. Edith Summerskill's stand-down speech, no date, but December 1944.

[54] Brookes: *Women at Westminster*, p. 161. For the benefit of twenty-first century readers, 'mousetrap' refers to 'any cheese of indifferent quality' that might be used as bait in a mousetrap.

[55] Parliamentary Debates, House of Commons, Fifth Series, vol. 433, 25 February 1947, col. 2018.

[56] Brookes: *Women at Westminster*, p. 161; Summerskill: *Woman's World*, p. 92.

[57] This was the 1949 Milk (Special Designations) Act. Brookes: *Women at Westminster*, p. 162; Summerskill: *Woman's World*, pp. 93-94.

[58] Brookes: *Women at Westminster*, pp. 160-2. Jean Mann, Labour MP for Coatbridge and Airdrie from 1945-59, admitted to joining in the attack, particularly on snoek: Mann, Jean, *Woman in Parliament* (London, 1962), p. 16.

[59] Hinton, James, 'Militant Housewives: the British Housewives' League and the Attlee Government', *History Workshop Journal* 38 (1994); Zweiniger-Bargielowska, Ina, *Austerity in Britain: Rationing, Controls and Consumption 1939-1955* (Oxford, 2000), pp. 214-215.

[60] Annan: *Our Age*, pp.185, 295. Annan refers specifically to Summerskill's rebuke concerning French cheese.

[61] Summerskill: *Woman's World*, p.126

[62] Ibid, p. 44; see also Morgan: *Backbench Diaries of Richard Crossman*, entry for 10 April 1958, p. 683.

[63] See Oates, Joyce Carol, 'On Boxing' and Chandler, David, 'Introduction' in D. Chandler (ed) *Boxer: An Anthology of Writings on Boxing and Visual Culture* (London, 1996).

[64] Brookes: *Women at Westminster*, p. 186

[65] The other women were Alice Horan, Jean Mann and Alice Bacon.

[66] Mikardo: *Back-Bencher*, pp. 129, 133.

[67] Ibid, p. 133. He claimed that ever after he wore a brown suit to any meeting that she chaired. Castle: *Fighting All the Way*, p.161, refers to Summerskill as 'one of our bitterest critics' and by juxtaposition of the 'brown suit' story with a statement about Mikardo's Jewishness suggests that Summerskill's intention might have been anti-semitic. Summerskill does not mention Mikardo in her autobiography. In contrast she devotes a short chapter to Bevan whom she treats kindly but regretfully as a 'brilliant, unstable personality'. Summerskill: *Woman's World*, p. 210.

[68] Williams: *The Diary of Hugh Gaitskell*, entry for 2-3 August 1956, p. 564.

[69] Morgan: *Backbench Diaries of Richard Crossman*, entries for 6 November 1957, and 27 November 1958, pp. 624, 723.

[70] Jean Mann refers to her 'grande dame manner' when crossed: *Woman in Parliament*, p. 16. Another woman Labour MP, Leah Manning, wrote 'She had a sharp tongue and could often make an impertinent Tory look like a small boy whose mother has just given him a smart one across his backside'. Leah Manning, *A Life for Education* (London, 1970), p. 166. It is likely that Summerskill sometimes made her male colleagues in the Labour Party feel the same, and that she was not liked for it.

[71] Summerskill supported Gaitskell against Bevan, against the Conservative Government's policy towards Suez in 1956 and in favour of nuclear restraint.

[72] See Mann: *Woman in Parliament*, p. 40 for an anecdote relating to this difference.

[73] Of Castle, who was famously photographed by the press paddling at Scarborough during the 1958 Party Conference, Crossman wrote admiringly, 'what a girl she is!' Morgan: *Backbench Diaries of Richard Crossman*, entry for 8 October 1958, p. 713.

[74] Summerskill: *Woman's World*, p. 100

[75] On companionate marriage, see Summerfield, P (with Finch, J.), 'Social reconstruction and the emergence of companionate marriage, 1945-59', in D. Clark (ed), *Marriage, Domestic Life and Social Change, Essays for Jacqueline Burgoyne* (London, 1991), pp. 7-32.

[76] The relationship between Edith and Shirley as not only mother and daughter but as fellow doctors and as political colleagues a generation apart, merits future research. A starting point is Edith's 1957 volume, *Letters to my Daughter*, published when Shirley was 26 and had just completed her medical training.

[77] Summerskill: *Woman's World*, p. 65.

[78] 'Mrs, Dr, M.P.', Pathe Close-up of Dr Edith Summerskill, 23 January 1945, http://www.britishpathe.com/index.cfm. (August 2003).

[79] 'Obituary', *The Times*, 5 February 1980.

[80] 'Lady in a Mask', *New Statesman and Nation*, September 25, 1954, p. 350. The same article implied that under her apparently confident exterior she was really nervous, that she deserved all she got by way of criticism as a woman because 'she has made of herself the vanguard of the militant feminists', and that as a junior minister 'she was very very efficient, but no one could be quite as efficient as she managed to look'.

[81] 'Lady in a Mask', *New Statesman and Nation*, September 25, 1954, p. 350.

[82] Castle describes the parties in her 'Highgate Village flat' in *Fighting All The Way*, immediately after her damning description of Summerskill (p. 161). Summerskill also lived in Highgate, on the edge of Kenwood, a publicly accessible landscaped garden adjoining Hampstead Heath. She chose to call herself Baroness Summerskill of Kenwood when she became a life peer, because of her sentimental attachment to the area. Summerskill: *Woman's World*, p. 219.

[83] Ball, Stuart (ed), *Parliament and Politics in the Age of Churchill and Attlee: The Headlam Diaries 1935-1951*, (Cambridge, 1999), p. 492.

Chapter 11. Foot as Labour Leader

[1] Butler, D. and Kavanagh, D., *The British General Election of 1983* (London, 1984), p. 14.

[2] As Butler and Kavanagh put it: 'Looking back at the election of 1983 and the events preceding it, one figure stands dominant. Margaret Thatcher, to an increasing degree, towered over the political scene': ibid, p. 1.

[3] Ibid, pp. 14-15.

[4] Ibid, p. 59.

[5] Ibid, p. 60.

[6] Ibid., p. 133.

[7] Ibid, pp. 110, 161. On this decision see Foot, M., *Another Heart and Other Pulses* (London, 1984), pp. 99-104.

[8] This was certainly how it struck Barbara Castle: Castle, B., *Fighting All the Way* (London, 1993), p. 535.

[9] Butler and Kavanagh: *General Election of 1983*, p. 207.

[10] Ibid, p. 90. On this occasion ITN reported how Foot claimed that Hailsham had 'licked Hitler's jackboots': quoted in ibid, p. 157.

[11] See, for instance, Jenkins, Peter, 'The Final Collapse of Consensus Politics', *The Guardian*, 26 November 1980, which describes Foot as 'the political child of the thirties' who 'formed his attitudes in the world of the slump and the dictators': Foot press archive, Labour History and Archive Study Centre (LHASC), Manchester.

[12] *The Sun*, 14 November 1980, Foot press archive.

[13] Johnson, Frank, 'A Spin on Michael's time machine', *Now!*, 21 November 1980, Foot press archive.

[14] Healey, D., *The Time of My Life* (London, 1989), p. 496. Healey claimed that, if he had not been on holiday at the time, he 'would have tried to moderate some of Michael's rhetoric': ibid.

[15] Jones, M., *Michael Foot* (London, 1994), pp. 485.

[16] Mervyn Jones aptly comments that so far as the Falklands were concerned 'what he saw was a clear case of unprovoked aggression, and he was vividly reminded of aggressions by Hitler and Mussolini in the 1930s which were among

the most emotionally powerful memories of his youth': ibid, pp. 484-5. Indeed, Foot told the Labour party conference in September 1982 that for him the decision to reclaim the Falklands was a question not of 'imperialism' but of 'upholding international authority and international rights ... which we, as socialists, have always said have got to be substituted for international anarchy'. Foot himself argued he had responded to the Falklands in the same way that George Orwell had responded to the Second World War: *Labour Party Annual Conference Report* (hereafter *LPACR*) (London, 1982), p. 85.

[17] Butler and Kavanagh: *General Election of 1983*, p. 279.

[18] Mitchell, A., *Four Years in the Death of the Labour Party* (London, 1983), p. 53.

[19] Sampson, A., *The Changing Anatomy of Britain* (London, 1981), p. 92, states that Foot 'presided over the most agonising period in the party's history'; Austin Mitchell was even more critical arguing that a leader has 'to perform certain inevitable functions. Michael Foot did not and never could': Mitchell, *Labour Party*, p. 54.

[20] Morgan, K. O., *Labour People: Leaders and Lieutenants, Hardie to Kinnock* (Oxford, 1987), p. 283, argues in a short essay that 'it is hard to see how any leader bent on preserving unity and mass appeal of a disintegrating coalition could have done much better'. Shaw, E., 'Michael Foot 1980-83', in K. Jefferys (ed), *Leading Labour: from Keir Hardie to Tony Blair* (London, 1999), pp. 151-170, argues that Foot was operating under enormous constraints, not least his lack of a power base in the party.

[21] Jones, *Foot*, p. 450.

[22] For more information on Foot's early life and career see Jones, *Foot*.

[23] Foot, M., *Aneurin Bevan: a biography: volume one, 1897 to 1945* (London, 1962), p. 155.

[24] On the early relationship between Foot and Castle see Castle: *Fighting All the Way*, p. 78.

[25] See, for instance, the abundant references to Bevan in Foot, M., *Loyalists and Loners* (London, 1986).

[26] Jones, *Foot*, pp. 433-5.

[27] Foot, M., *Debts of Honour* (London, 1980). Foot's essay on Brailsford is Chapter 7.

[28] See Addison, P., *The Road to 1945* (London, 1975), for the emergence of consensus.

[29] Of course, some historians dispute the existence of a political consensus: see in particular Pimlott, B., 'Is the "post-war consensus" a myth?', *Contemporary Record*, 2/6 (1989), pp. 12-14.

[30] Williamson, P., 'Baldwin's Reputation: Politics and History, 1937-1967', *Historical Journal*, 47/1 (2004), pp. 127-168, quotation at p. 127.

[31] Ibid, esp. pp. 137-8, 145, quotation at p. 145; See also Williamson, P., *Stanley Baldwin* (Cambridge, 1999), introduction.

[32] For instance, in autumn 1981 a great deal of attention was given to a march to commemorate the anniversary of the Jarrow crusade. In October and November 1936 out-of-work men from the North East shipbuilding town had marched to London in order to highlight their plight. With unemployment edging towards three million, the 45th anniversary seemed to have particular contemporary relevance.

[33] *Daily Telegraph*, 30 November 1980, Foot press archive.

[34] Foot: *Another Heart*, p. 48.

[35] Foot, M., 'An Outrage Against Human Decency', *Sunday Mirror*, 23 November 1980, Foot press archive.

[36] Comparing the actions of the National and Thatcher governments, he said: 'I hear the same accents and the same policies' claiming that there was 'no alternative': *Sunday Telegraph*, 23 November 1980, Foot press archive.

[37] For instance, Foot stressed that he did not want to see a return to the 1930s 'with all that means in terms of human misery and collapse': Message from Michael Foot, *Ogmore Forward: the official newspaper of the Ogmore Constituency Labour Party*, Issue no. 1, April 1981, Michael Foot papers, LHASC, MF/L14.

[38] *LPACR*, 1982, p. 80.

[39] He argued that 'the whole wider experience of the Western World since 1945 proves what can be done when governments set before them full employment as a target': 'Foreword to the New Hope for Britain, Labour's 1983 Manifesto', in Foot: *Another Heart*, pp. 175-9 at p. 177.

[40] Foot: *Another Heart*, p. 48. In the book Foot repeated (almost to the word) the arguments he had made in the *Sunday Mirror* on 23 November 1980 – see pp. 46-7.

[41] Verbatim extract from speech at Ebbw Vale, June 1983, quoted in Foot: *Another Heart*, pp. 134-5.

[42] 'The Curse of Monetarism', 15 November 1980, Foot papers, MF/L15.

[43] 'A Contract for the 1980s', Lecture delivered at the Royal Institute of Public Administration in Cardiff in November 1982, Appendix C in Foot: *Another Heart*, pp. 184-196, at p. 184.

[44] *Trades Union Congress Annual Report* (hereafter *TUCAR*) (London, 1981), p. 473.

[45] Foot, 'An Outrage Against Human Decency'.

[46] Parliamentary Debates, House of Commons, 6th series, vol. 10, 28 October 1981, col. 880. See also ibid., vol. 12, 4 November 1981, col. 16.

[47] *The Times*, 5 March 1982. See also Williamson: 'Baldwin's Reputation', p. 168.

[48] *The Times*, 5 March 1982.

[49] See Morgan, K. O., *Britain since 1945: the people's peace* (Oxford, 2001), p. 442, for illuminating discussion of Thatcher's selective 'Victorian values'.

[50] Speech at Ebbw Vale, June 1983, quoted verbatim in Foot: *Another Heart*, p. 141.

[51] 'Rt. Hon. Michael Foot MP (leader of the Opposition), speaking at the Annual Conference of the Welsh Labour Party in Llandrindod Wells on Saturday 23 July 1983 at mid-day', Foot papers, MF/L14.

[52] Shore, P., *Leading the Left* (London, 1993), p. 137; also quoted in Shaw: 'Michael Foot', p. 167.

[53] *The Independent*, 20 November 1998, quoted in Shaw: 'Michael Foot', p. 168.

[54] Shaw: 'Michael Foot, p. 155.

[55] For an excellent overview see Thorpe, A., *A History of the British Labour Party* (London, 1997), pp. 202-206.

[56] Heffer, E., *Never a Yes Man: the life and politics of an adopted Liverpudlian* (London, 1991), p. 182.

[57] Benn diary, 21 March 1981 in Benn, T., *The End of an Era: diaries 1980-90* (London, 1992), p. 110.

[58] Foot: *Another Heart*, p. 161.

[59] See Jones: *Foot*, pp. 476-7.

[60] Foot: *Loyalists and Loners*, p. 119. Foot memorably described how - in his view - Cripps in the 1930s had 'declared the class war without ever having studied the contours of the battlefield': Foot: *Bevan* vol. I, p. 156.

[61] Foot draft for *The Guardian*, 10 September 1981, Foot papers, MF/L14; *The Guardian*, 10 September 1981.

[62] *TUCAR*, 1981, p. 474.

[63] Morgan: *Labour People*, p. 286.

[64] *LPACR*, 1981, p. 118.

[65] Jones: *Foot*, pp. 476-7; Benn diary, 10 November 1981 in Benn: *End of an Era*, p. 166.

[66] For Foot's criticism of the show trials in the late 1950s (and his regret at not speaking out in the 1930s) see Foot, M., 'The road to ruin' in Thomas, E. (ed), *Tribune 21* (London, 1958), pp. 7-8. His stance is analysed more fully in Corthorn, P., 'Labour, the Left, and the Stalinist Purges of the late 1930s', *Historical Journal*, forthcoming.

[67] Foot, M., 'My Kind of Party', *The Observer*, 17 January 1982, Foot papers, MF/L14.

[68] Thorpe: *British Labour Party*, pp. 208-9.

[69] Ibid, p. 210; Shaw, 'Foot', p. 163-4.

[70] See, for instance, Shaw, 'Foot', pp. 162-4.

[71] Transcript of Foot interview with Brian Walden, 'Weekend World, 3 October 1982', 'After the Conference ... on the road to power', 2/18, Foot papers, MF/L14.

[72] *LPACR*, 1982, p. 52.

[73] Foot, *Another Heart*, p. 168.

[74] For the early influence of Bevan on Kinnock see Westlake, M., *Kinnock: the biography* (London, 2001), pp. 25-7, 40.

[75] Ibid, pp. 62-3. See also Kinnock's approving references to Bevan: Kinnock, N., *Making Our Way* (Oxford, 1986), pp. 7, 95, 195.

[76] *LPACR*, 1983, p. 116.

[77] The broader point this raises relates to Cripps's problematic reputation in general. Clarke, P., *The Cripps Version: the life of Sir Stafford Cripps* (London, 2002), pp. xiii-xiv, comments that while 'subsequent advocates of moderation' have found 'Cripps's well-publicised posturings [in the 1930s] ... silly', on the other hand 'socialists sympathetic to the pre-war Cripps, the founder of *Tribune*, have tended to deplore his later apostasy. The *Tribune* group were to be identified as Bevanites, but there were no Crippsites in the post-war Labour party'.

[78] Lawrence, J., 'Labour – the myths it has lived by', in D. Tanner, P. Thane and N. Tiratsoo (eds), *Labour's First Century* (Cambridge, 2000), pp. 341-366, esp. p. 357.

[79] Foot: *Another Heart*, pp. 115-16.

Chapter 12. Thatcher and Gender.

[1] I am most grateful to the editors of this volume and especially to Dr. Julie Gottlieb: my chapter has profited a great deal from her comments and assistance. Furthermore I would like to thank my American colleague at the Free University Dr. Markha Valenta, who gave me good advice on the use of several English expressions.

2 'Groene-eregalerij van sterke vrouwen', *De Groene Amsterdammer* (15 December 1999), pp. 36-37.

3 Ibid.

4 Genovese, Michael, 'Women as national leaders. What do we know?', in Michael Genovese (ed), *Women as National Leaders: Political Performance of Women as Heads of Government* (London, 1993), pp. 211-218.

5 Ibid, pp. 211-218, q.v. p. 212.

6 Thatcher, Margaret, *The Downing Street Years* (2nd edition, London, 1995), p. 860. See also Evans, Eric, *Thatcher and Thatcherism* (London, 1997), p. 1.

7 Clarke, Peter, 'The Rise and Fall of Thatcherism', *London Review of Books*, 10 December 1998.

8 Ibid.

9 Thatcher: *Downing Street Years*; Thatcher, Margaret, *The Path to Power* (London, 1995). Thatcher, Carol, *Below the Parapet. The biography of Denis Thatcher* (London, 1996), p. 290.

10 Campbell, John, *Margaret Thatcher, vol. 1: the Grocer's daughter* (London, 2000), and *vol. 2: Iron Lady* (London, 2003). Young, Hugo, *One of us. A biography of Margaret Thatcher* (3rd edition, London, 1993).

11 See for example Campbell, Beatrix, *The Iron Ladies: Why do women vote Tory?* (London, 1987); Pilcher, Jane, 'The Gender Significance of Women in Power: British Women Talking about Margaret Thatcher', *The European Journal of Women's Studies* (November 1995), pp. 493-508; and Lewis, Jane *Women in Britain since 1945: Women, Family, Work and the State in the Post-War Years* (3rd edition, Oxford, 1994).

12 Campbell: *Margaret Thatcher*, vol. 1, p. 402 ff. London, Nick, *Prime Minister Maggie*, television broadcast, Dutch Television, 23 September 2003.

13 Campbell, *Margaret Thatcher*, vol. 1, p.1.

14 Margaret Thatcher in 1980, quoted in London: *Prime Minister Maggie.*

15 Campbell: *Margaret Thatcher*, vol. 1, Chapter 1; London: *Prime Minister Maggie.*

16 Knapen, Ben, 'Het land van de kwaaddoeners: Karel van Wolferens aanklacht tegen George Bush en de neo-conservatieven', *NRC Handelsblad*,12 September 2003.

17 Campbell: *The Iron Ladies*, q.v. p. 251. Between the introduction of women's suffrage in 1918 and the end of the 1970s the proportion of female MPs never exceeded 5 per cent. For a comparison with other Western countries see Leijenaar, Monique, *De geschade heerlijkheid. Politiek gedrag van vrouwen en mannen in Nederland, 1918-1988* (The Hague, 1989), p. 244.

18 This was a limited women's suffrage. General women's suffrage was not achieved in Great Britain until 1928.

19 Thatcher: *Below the Parapet, passim*, but especially pp. 112, 113, 153, 162, 289.

20 Lewis: *Women in Britain since 1945*, pp. 10-26.

21 Campbell, *The Iron Ladies*, p. 238; Pilcher, 'The Gender Significance', p. 495.

22 Thatcher: *Path to Power*, pp. 81, 82.

23 Thatcher: *Below the Parapet*, p. 71.

24 Campbell: *Margaret Thatcher*, vol. 1, p. 105 ff.

25 Vallence, Elisabeth, *Women in the House: A study of Women members of Parliament* (London, 1979); Leijenaar, Monique and Saharso, Sawriti, *Vrouwen en politieke macht. Trendrapport over vrouwenstudies en emancipatie-onderzoek op het gebied van vrouwen en politieke macht* (The Hague, 1983), pp. 60-62; Linders, Anneke, *'Frappez, frappez*

toujours!', N.S. Corry Tendeloo (1897-1956) en het feminisme in haar tijd (Hilversum, 2003), p.145; Ribberink, Anneke, *'Leidsvrouwen en zaakwaarneemsters.' Een geschiedenis van de Aktiegroep Man Vrouw Maatschappij (MVM) 1968-1973* ('Leading ladies and cause minders'. A history of the Pressure group Man Woman Society (MWS) 1968-1973) (Hilversum, 1998).

[26] Thatcher: *Below the Parapet*, p. 71.

[27] Hennessy, Peter, *The Prime Minister. The Office and its Holders since 1945* (London, 2000) pp. 379-436, q.v. pp. 435,436.

[28] Ibid, p. 435.

[29] Evans, *Thatcher and Thatcherism*, p. 39.

[30] Martin, Bernice, 'Postwar Austerity to Postmodern Carnival: Culture in Britain from 1945', in Anneke Ribberink and Hans Righart (eds), *The Great, the New and the British. Essays on Postwar Britain* (Hilversum, 2000), pp. 39-66.

[31] Good overviews of Margaret Thatcher's period in office are provided in Evans, *Thatcher and Thatcherism*, and Morgan, Kenneth, *The People's Peace. British History since 1945* (2nd edition, Oxford, 1999).

[32] See for instance Genovese, Michael, 'Margaret Thatcher and the Politics of Conviction Leadership', in Genovese, *Women as National Leaders*, pp. 177-210, q.v. p. 203.

[33] Righart, Hans, 'Great Britain and the Netherlands from a Comparative View. Postwar History and Postwar Histories, 1945-2000', in Ribberink and Righart, *The Great, the New and the British*, pp. 177-210, q.v. p. 98.

[34] Morgan: *The People's Peace*, p. 470.

[35] Hennessy: *The Prime Minister*, p. 425.

[36] Laybourn, Keith, *Fifty Key Figures in Twentieth Century British Politics* (London & New York, 2002), pp. 42-50.

[37] See for example Campbell: *The Iron Ladies*, Chapter 7.

[38] Pugh, Martin, *Women and the Women's Movement in Britain, 1914-1999* (2nd edition, Houndmills, Basingstoke, 2000), p. 335.

, p. 341; Lewis, *Women in Britain*, Introduction and Chapter 1.

[39] Campbell: *The Iron Ladies*, p.173. See also Pilcher: 'The Gender Significance', p. 494.

[40] Pilcher: 'The Gender Significance', p. 495; Pugh: *Women and the Women's Movement*, p. 335.

[41]Vallence: *Women in the House*, pp. 80 ff; Leijenaar and Saharso: *Vrouwen en politieke macht*, pp. 60-64.

[42] Henig, Ruth and Henig, Simon, *Women and political power. Europe since 1945* (London & New York, 2001), p. 19.

[43] See for instance London: *Prime Minister Maggie*.

[44] As quoted in Pilcher: 'The Gender Significance, p. 495.

[45] Pugh: *Women and the Women's Movement*, pp. 336, 337.

[46] Genovese: 'Margaret Thatcher', p. 200.

[47] Hennessy: *The Prime Minister*, pp. 422, 428.

[48] Ibid, pp. 430, 431.

[49] Campbell: *Margaret Thatcher*, vol. 1, p. 408. See also Hennessy: *The Prime Minister*, p. 398.

[50] Young: *One of Us*, pp. 37,118,136-139; Morgan: *The People's Peace*, pp. 442, 443.

[51] As quoted in Evans: *Thatcher and Thatcherism*, p. 43.

[52] Evans: *Thatcher and Thatcherism*, p. 42.

53 Thatcher: *The Downing Street Years*, pp. 865-882.
54 Evans: *Thatcher and Thatcherism*, p. 44.
55 Campbell: *Margaret Thatcher*, vol. 1, p. 409.
56 Pilcher: 'The Gender Significance', p. 494; Campbell: *The Iron Ladies*, pp. 234, 235.
57 Campbell: *The Iron Ladies*, pp. 234, 235.
58 Morgan, Kenneth, 'British political culture since 1945: Consensus, Protest and Change', in Ribberink and Righart, *The Great, the New and the British*, pp. 4-22, q.v. p. 16.
59 Campbell: *The Iron Ladies*, pp. 113-122.
60 Hennessy: *The Prime Minister*, pp. 426, 427.

Chapter 13. New Labour and *The Sun*

1 Author's interview with George Pascoe-Watson, 6 November 2002.
2 Oakley, Robin, 'The Today Programme', BBC Radio 4, 18 March 1997.
3 Butler, David and Kavanagh, Dennis, *The British General Election of 1997* (London, 1997), p. 244.
4 *The Daily Herald*, a traditionally working-class, Labour-supporting newspaper was relaunched in 1964 as *The Sun*. It retained its party allegiance until 1974 when it supported the Conservative Party in the election of February that year. It did not revert back to supporting Labour at an election until that of May 1997.
5 Jones, Nicholas, *Campaign 1997: how the general election was won and lost* (London, 1997), *Control Freaks: How New Labour gets its own way* (London, 2001), *Soundbites and Spindoctors: how politicians manipulate the media and vice versa* (London, 1998), and *Sultans of Spin: Media and the New Labour Government* (London, 1999).
6 Butler, David and Kavanagh, Dennis, *The British General Election of 1992* (London 1992), p. 164.
7 MacArthur, Brian, 'Perhaps it was The Sun "wot won it" for John Major, *Sunday Times*, 12 April 1992; Linton, Martin, *The Guardian*, 30 October 1995.
8 Butler and Kavanagh: *The British General Election of 1992*, p. 209.
9 Author's interview with Trevor Kavanagh, 6 November 2002.
10 Greenslade, Roy, *The Guardian*, 24 June, 2002.
11 Butler and Kavanagh: *The British General Election of 1997*, p. 47.
12 MacIntyre, Donald, *Mandelson: The biography* (London, 1999), p. 374.
13 Greenslade, Roy, *The Guardian*, 24 June 2002.
14 Oborne, Peter, *Alastair Campbell: New Labour and the art of media management* (London, 1999), p. 140.
15 Ibid.
16 Ibid, p. 141.
17 MacIntyre: *Mandelson*, p. 373.
18 Routledge, Paul, *Mandy: The Unauthorised Biography* (London, 1999), pp. xiv-xvi.
19 MacIntyre: *Mandelson*, p. 375.
20 Author's interview with Trevor Kavanagh, 6 November 2002.
21 Piers Morgan, *The Insider* (London, 2005), pp. 93-4
22 Ibid.
23 Kemp, David, *The Sun*, 23 September 1995.
24 *The Sun*, 25 September 1995.
25 Author's interview with Trevor Kavanagh, 6 November 2002.

[26] *The Sun*, 17 August 1996.

[27] Author's interview with Fergus Shanahan, 13 November 2002

[28] Ibid.

[29] Author's interview with Trevor Kavanagh, 6 November 2002.

[30] Author's interview with Fergus Shanahan, 13 November 2002.

[31] *The Sun*, 18 March 1997.

[32] Higgins, Stuart, 'Nice one Sun, says Tony', *Guardian Media*, 19 May 1997.

[33] Author's interview with George Pascoe-Watson, 6 November 2002.

[34] Ibid.

[35] 'Family side of the man set to be our next PM', *The Sun*, 28 April 1997.

[36] *The Sun*, 1 May 1997.

[37] Author's interview with George Pascoe-Watson, 6 November 2002.

[38] Colin Seymour-Ure in P. Norris and N.T. Gavin (eds), *Britain Votes 1997* (Oxford 1997), p. 92.

[39] Author's interview with George Pascoe-Watson, 6 November 2002.

[40] Ibid.

[41] Ibid.

[42] Bartle, John and Crewe, Ivor, 'The Impact of Party Leaders in Britain: Strong Assumptions, Weak Evidence', in Anthony King (ed), *Leaders' Personalities and the Outcomes of Democratic Elections* (Oxford, 2002), pp. 70-95, at p. 90.

[43] Ibid, p. 95.

[44] Ibid, p. 72.

[45] Butler and Kavanagh: *The British General Election of 1997*, p. 165

[46] Ibid, p. 166

[47] Butler and Kavanagh: *The British General Election of 1992*, p. 191

[48] *The Sun*, 4 April 1997.

[49] Dave Gaskill's cartoon of a muscular Tony Blair dressed in a red New Labour weightlifting suit while pushing up a Union Jack barbell.

[50] Butler and Kavanagh: *The British General Election of 1997*, p. 164.

[51] Author's interview with Trevor Kavanagh, 6 November 2002

[52] Ibid.

[53] Ibid.

[54] MacIntyre: *Mandelson*, p. 377.

[55] Jones: *Sultans of Spin*, p. 179.

[56] Ibid, p. 174.

[57] Author's interview with Trevor Kavanagh, 6 November 2002.

[58] Jones: *Sultans of Spin*, p. 179

[59] Author's interview with Trevor Kavanagh, 6 November 2002

[60] Author's interview with Fergus Shanahan, 13 January 2003

[61] Jones: *Sultans of Spin*, p. 179.

[62] 'Is this the most dangerous man in Britain', *The Sun*, 24 June 1998.

[63] Author's interview with Fergus Shanahan, 13 November 2002.

[64] MacIntyre: *Mandelson*, p. 374

[65] Ibid.

[66] 'Kinnock senses Murdoch influence', *BBC Online*, 20 April 2004. Similarly, see Neil, Andrew, 'Murdoch's Sun still shines on the PM ... for now', *The Scotsman*, 22 April 2004.

[67] Author's interview with George Pascoe-Watson, 6 November 2002: 'all parties will, by definition, favour the newspapers or the people that support them. That's

patronage and that will always be about. We make no secret of that and we have no shame in it'.

[68] Author's interview with Trevor Kavanagh, 6 November 2002: 'I think that the relationship between the two governments has not changed it has been a seamless process in the same way it has between other media organisations and other governments'.

[69] Oborne: *Alastair Campbell*, pp.143-144.

[70] Ibid, p. 181.

[71] Author's interview with George Pascoe-Watson, 6 November 2002.

[72] Oborne: *Alastair Campbell*, p. 181.

[73] Indeed, *The Mirror* was one of the staunchest critics of Blair's policy on Iraq. Errors in the way in which this opposition was pursued led to the departure of its editor Piers Morgan in May 2004. Morgan's growing disenchantment with New Labour can be traced in his book *The Insider.*

[74] Marr, Andrew, *The Independent*, 23 April 1997.

[75] Although Blair's post-election memo to Stuart Higgins would suggest the contrary.

[76] One can only speculate as to whether or not this was a conscious aim of Blair's.

Index

Index